OUTWEIGHED BY OUTCASTS

SARAN S. & PRERNA JATAV

Contents

Contents

Foreword

Dr. Preeti Oza
Assistant Professor
Department of English
St. Andrew's College
University of Mumbai

"Freedom cannot be achieved unless the women have been emancipated from all forms of oppression" –**Nelson Mandela.**

"We make her paint her face and dance
If she won't be a slave, we say that she don't love us
If she's real, we say she's trying to be a man
While putting her down we pretend that she is above us" — **John Lennon**

Various factors have been cited as contributing to the oppression of women, the most significant of which is cultural conditioning. With its roots in patriarchal rules, attitudes, and behaviours, the assumption that men are superior to women still has an impact on women in the modern world. The cultural practices that are enforced by those who believe they are important and superior still marginalise women. Indian Hindu groups have been divided into castes from the reign of King Manu, who created the caste system by dividing the Hindu people into groups based on their occupations and skills. As a result, it became a way of life and a career for them. Because they are viewed as being of a lower social status than men, women of all castes have been subjected to discrimination. Women from Dalit (untouchable) communities are subjected to horrific abuse because they are seen as second-class citizens by upper castes. Due to the triangular amalgamation, Dalit women have had the worst and slowest growth (being women, lower caste, and Dalit).

Despite several social programmes and caste-based reservation regimes, we have left Dalit women without both a voice and a route out, and it is killing them. They're trapped in a patriarchal system from the past, with no way to speak up for themselves or get help to improve their lot in life. The oppressive social framework that denies them any other identity than that of an untouchable woman has chained them and they have no escape route. The upshot is that they are economically disadvantaged, with women experiencing numerous levels of discrimination because of their gender, including caste-based, gender-based, economic and political discrimination. Women from Dalit communities were the last to receive equal treatment.

Some women have rejected patriarchal norms and created literature that has influenced and mobilised other women to do the same. Dalit women have been sexually abused for as long as anybody can remember in broad areas of rural India. Many of these areas‘ land, wealth, and social power are still controlled by the upper or middle castes. Violence against Dalit women continued despite a law implemented in 1989 to reduce crimes against the Dalit people. Stalked, molested and murdered, they still face no consequences.

As a result of their caste, Dalit women face three forms of discrimination: being viewed as untouchables and outcasted; being subjected to sexism and being economically disadvantaged as a result of low wages and undervalued labour. According to Hindu tradition, there are four distinct castes in society: Brahmins (the priest caste), Kshatriyas (the warrior caste), Vaishya (the tradesman caste), and Shudras (the non-priest caste) (menial task workers). A fifth caste, referred to as the untouchables, sits on top of the previously mentioned four (Panchamas). Further undermining and strengthening the connection between women's untouchable status and the idea of purity. To maintain the caste system and Brahminical ideas, conservative Hindus advocate for the continuation of the caste system. No matter how many social welfare programmes come and go, a Dalit woman will always be a Dalit since her caste is passed down only through her mother's lineage. However, she will never be Prime Minister or a member of the upper caste because of this. Due to their low social status, Dalit women have traditionally been particularly vulnerable.

"प्रभु भल कीन्ह मोहि सिख दीन्हीं। मरजादा पुनि तुम्हरी कीन्हीं॥
ढोल गवाँर सूद्र पसु नारी। सकल ताड़ना के अधिकारी"

(Spoken by Samudra Dev in Shri Ramcharit Manas)

To live a virtuous life, Manusmriti is considered to be the ultimate guide, and any divergence from it will have serious consequences. People from various walks of life are well-represented in the material, which is exhaustive in scope. In the opinion of many scholars, the work was not written by a single author but rather by several.

On the other side, The Bhagwad Gita says,

अधर्माभिभवात्कृष्ण प्रदुष्यन्ति कुलस्त्रियः |
स्त्रीषु दुष्टासु वार्ष्णेय जायते वर्णसङ्करः || 41||

(With the preponderance of vice, O Krishna, the women of the family become immoral; and from the immorality of women, O descendent of Vrishni, unwanted progeny are born.)

'The Rise and Fall of Hindu Woman", an article by Dr. B.R. Ambedkar, makes it clear that these so-called sacred Hindu scriptures

are the primary cause of women's suffering in India (books like the Manusmriti divide people into a stratified caste system and encourage inequity between men and women). According to the Manusmriti, women are not entitled to education, freedom, or wealth. Sexist and violent crimes against women are not the only things it excuses when it comes to Dalit women and the encouragement of underage marriage.

According to a UN assessment on India's impoverished and Dalit women, 'living uneducated, dying young' is what they face. Patriarchal discourse hurts Dalit women by limiting their access to society's productive resources and restricting their sexuality. A patriarchal weapon, Disciplinary Power, determines appropriate gestures and behaviour and normalises a dominant male order via constant surveillance. A phallocentric system sees Dalit women as amorphous property that may be mutilated and sculptured following its desires. A "new woman" was born, one who came from urban middle-class families and was exposed to the social changes brought about by reforms in the educational system. While she was educated, this "new woman" was neither Westernized nor repressed by patriarchy, which denied her educational opportunities and a position in society. For example, by releasing "Amar Jibon (1876)," Rassundari Devi became one of the first women in Bengali history to publish an autobiography that questioned the institution of patriarchy. At the time, educated women were considered a detriment to society, and she was not one of them.

Writers and thinkers from the women's movement created new kinds of action and self-governed organisations. It was wealthy, urban, upper-caste, middle-class women who were in control of selecting the direction of their revolution against oppression, even though leadership was passed down to them. It did not adequately convey the oppression that Dalit women, rural women, and Muslim women were subjected to at the time. The analogy goes like this: Let's say you're in a bad spot. A bone has been broken or you have been injured in some other way. As soon as you feel pain, your initial instinct is to say, "I'm hurt and I need help." Actively coping with hardship is asking for and accepting help. Resistance began with a single word, "Help!" This impulse to share one's thoughts and feelings emerge when a problem impacts someone to the point that they are in pain. For this, poetry is the ideal medium since it uses words, ideas, and emotion promptly. To put it another way, poetry can be a rallying cry that helps us see ourselves in others, helping us to let go of our narrow sense of self. Poetry may have been one of the earliest #metoo movements.

"Feminism has never been about getting a job for one woman. It's about making life fairer for women everywhere. It's not about a piece of the existing pie; there are too many of us for that. It's about baking a new pie."

— Gloria Steinem

Writing has always been a way for the oppressed to express themselves, especially during upheavals. It's possible that reading this book, which acknowledges the ongoing struggles taking place around the world, will provide some solace and inspiration to individuals who are struggling. It is for this reason that this book explores the numerous ways in which women have been oppressed, as well as the ways in which cultural practices have supported or hindered this oppression. An outsider's view on society and politics is presented in the book's chapters, which often take a radical and unconventional approach to these topics. Fiction and poetry written in opposition to the status quo by people in marginalised socioeconomic groups are referred to as protest literature. This research will address a wide range of topics, including global protest narratives as well as film, media and literary criticisms of totalitarianism.

Editor

Saran S.
Assistant Professor & Head
Department of English
University Institute of Technology-Pathiyoor
University of Kerala

Saran S. (MA, Ph. D.) is a writer, Poet, Nature Activist, Teacher, and Research Scholar. He has completed his Doctoral Research from the Department of English, M. S. University in 2020. Currently, he is working as an Assistant Professor and Head in the Department of English, University Institute of Technology Pathiyoor, University of Kerala. His areas are Comparative

Literature, Cultural Studies, Film Studies, Psychoanalytical Studies and Eco Studies. He is the author of several articles published in various national and international journals as well as six academic books on topics of current interest like English Language, Film Studies, Partition Studies and Cultural Studies. He also authored a collection of poems and short stories. He also edited twenty-two international books. He is the chief editor of Edit Academic, an advisory board member and Associate Editor in *The Creative Launcher*, international, open access, peer-reviewed refereed, e-journal in English and also Editorial Board Member in *Shodhkosh: Journal of Visual and Performing Arts* (UGC-Care Listed Journal).

Editor

Prerna Jatav
Assistant Professor & Head
Department of English
RD & SH National College
University of Mumbai

Prerna Jatav heads the Department of English of RD & SH National College which also has a Masters in English Course under its aegis. She is an Assistant Professor and has teaching experience of over 22 years. Her area of specialization is Indian English Literature. A gold medalist from the University of Mumbai, she has several research articles to her credit and is currently pursuing her Ph. D. from the University of Mumbai in the area of Food and its impact on Indian English Fiction. She has been awarded The Jyotu Kundnani Award for her research publication. She is also a member of the Centre for Memory Studies, IIT Madras.

Contributors

1. “The Other Side of Multiculturalism: Violence in Gloria Naylor’s the Women of Brewster Place”. - **Aashlesha V. Lele**
2. “The Plight of Women in the Contemporary Indian Society in Meena Kandasami’s Selected Works”. - **Bhima Bansode**
3. “Sharing Similarities, Celebrating Differences: A Search for the Self in Baby Kamble’s *The Prisons We Broke* and Lakshmibai Tilak’s *I Follow After*”. - **Mrs. Deepti Mujumdar**
4. "Bapsi Sidhwa’s *The Pakistani Bride*: A Feminist Study”. – **Devika,** Ph. D. Research Scholar, Central University of Haryana.
5. “A Deconstructive Reading of Masculinity in the Korean Drama It’s Okay To Not Be Okay” - **Elsa Sebastian.**
6. “Stereotypical Portal of Muslim as a Terrorist and My Name Is Khan as a Counter-Narrative” - **Iram Abdul Qadar.**
7. “Voice of Untouchable Mortals Born From the Feet of the Creator: Thrice Marginalized Dalit Women in India in Selected Novels of Urmila Pawar” - **Jennifer Dias.**
8. “Not Straight Out of the Closet” - **Miss. Madhura Sudhir Walavalkar.**
9. “The Dramatic Monologue and Its Universal Nature: A Case Study of Robert Browning and Frank Bidart’s Poems” - **Manjari Nagori.**
10. “Cultural Bonding, Women Empowerment, and Ecofeminism in Sudha Murthy’s Novels House of Cards and Gently Falls the Bakula” - **Pallavi Kadam.**
11. “A History of Food: Exploring Dalit Poetry” - **Priyanka Corda.**
12. “Search for Identity, Immigrant Psychosis and Subaltern Voices in Sathnam Sanghera’s Diasporic Memoir The Boy With The Top Knot” - **Manmit Kaur Chadha.**
13. ‘Hybridization of Culture and Identity in Jhumpa Lahiri’s The Namesake” - **Umang Jangid.**
14. “Marxist Reading of the Doll’s House by Katherine Mansfield

and the Stolen Party by Liliana Heker" – **Shaik Anam Abdul Qadar.**

15. "City Life, A Progressive Change for Survival – A Narrow Study on the Character of Hari in Anita Desai's Novel, The Village By The Sea" - **Heena Ansari.**
16. "Toxic Behaviour such as Stalking, Physical Abuse, Mental Torture Being Glorified as True Love in Bollywood Movies" - **Sara Pawaskar.**
17. "The Gothic, Grotesque and Ghosts in Ghost Stories from the Raj" - **Sara Mahimi.**
18. "Exploring Masculinities in Millennial Bollywood Movies" - **Ms. Priyal Jairaj Master.**
19. "Psychic Peregrination Of Anita Desai's Bye Bye Blackbird" - **Ms. Naazish Baig**

Introduction

Outweighed by Outcaste

"All politics is a struggle for power and the ultimate kind of power is violence" - **C. Wright Mills**

A deep study of human existence brings to the fore a sharp realization of the fact that the flip side of western education and advancement is the covert attempt at colonization. From food to our software, dependence upon the capitalists of the world is complete. This kind of dependence is a resultant of empowerment for the colonizers who then command absolute power. The story of human society is no different, as the struggle for power remains the same and all aspects of human life viz gender, race, religion, money and even nationality become agents of power and thereby core centres of tyranny. This tyranny then radiates onto the demographics of the weak and creates several groups of outcastes that do not or cannot conform to the power centres.

The unequal distribution of power tilts the tables and while the treacherous ones contest for power, the meek, deluded by prayers, move to the corners. The process keeps getting intensified leaving no place for the less aggressive but the margins. This compilation researches several such avenues that have subtly created such outcast pockets and is an attempt to bring to light all such struggles. A handful comprises the hegemonic centre of power while each day, newer forms of discrimination are devised to keep the inner coterie limited. This has resulted in margins bleeding into the centre! If most of the people are marginalized, then we are talking about a very large margin! Protest writings are registering their wrath on new hoardings for attention, throwing the gauntlet at the hegemony now, warning them that they shall be," Outweighed by Outcasts"!

"In a world where language and naming is power, silence is oppression is violence." - **Adrienne Riche.**

To overcome this suppression about twenty critical thinking minds have contributed their ideas of protests and explored different situations of marginalization. The outcasts in the literary works chosen by these research scholars are out to protest loud enough to shake the stronghold of the power centres. Meena Kandasamy the renowned Dalit poet is an epitome of protest when she exclaims," My Kali kills . My Draupadi strips. My Sita climbs on a stranger's lap. All my women militate. They brave bombs, belittle kings, take on the sun, take after me ." questioning all preset notions, unjust norms and serving a potential possibility of rebellion.

The challenges registered in this edition are not only need not only be the more prevalent sorts. The outcasts are everywhere, the village folk are outcasts in the urban scenario, the reluctantly settling Indian in America, a Muslim in post 9/11 New York, a believer in the midst of powerful exploitative capitalists, the Dalit amongst the brahmins, the poor amidst the rich, the woman in the clutches of patriarchy. Women display a rising graph of exploitation from childhood roles played by a little girl to old age and even widowhood, her life is chased by second-hand treatment at every stage. The editor's intent in compiling a book like this is to change the dynamics of the equation with the range of outcasts that outnumber the authorities that provide it with the nomenclature. The outcasts are sweeping into the centre and perhaps it is time now that the centre moves to the fringes!

CHAPTER I

THE OTHER SIDE OF MULTICULTURALISM: VIOLENCE IN GLORIA NAYLOR'S THE WOMEN OF BREWSTER PLACE

Aashlesha V. Lele

ABSTRACT

Multiculturalism can be defined based on its dual reception on the social front. The ideal utopian expectation remains a far-fetched dream in reality. The African American writer Gloria Naylor highlights this negative discourse of multiculturalism and sets her novel 'The Women of Brewster Place' in the typical multicultural background, presenting a diverse socio-cultural society. Along with highlighting the plight of the Women implicitly, the paper also thrives on bringing out the lopsided view of multiculturalism, issues of the multicultural society, the existential struggle and troubled experiences of 'the coloured folks', particularly black women. The paper essentially delves into the territory that presents the other side of multiculturalism, especially in the African American context, with predominant issues related to identity, sexuality, racism and psychological degeneration.

Keywords: Multiculturalism, Social Violence, Racism and Discourses of Multiculturalism.

• • •

INTRODUCTION

Multiculturalism as a concept is predominantly concerned with the diversity of perspectives. Like every moment and idea, multiculturalism too has various aspects and facets. Some advocating the positive stance view multiculturalism as a compatible seamless intermingling of different cultures while others consider it a utopian delusion - a potential threat to a coherent national identity and secularism, thereby fostering discrimination based on race, culture, ethnicity and colour. The present paper rejects the former ideas to solely focus on the negative aspects of multiculturalism in a particular socio-cultural community and in the desired coherent multicultural nation in general. Countries like Canada witnessed the success of multiculturalism, whereas the visible adverse effects of the same were experienced in Germany and United Kingdom. The impact of multiculturalism, both direct and indirect, can be seen in writers from various parts of the world, especially those living in multicultural societies. Focussing more on the undesirable aspects, this paper plans to study multiculturalism in an unfavourable setting, presenting it as a significant barrier to the coherent national identity, thereby leading to its fragmentation. This discussion will focus on how multiculturalism leads to violence, trauma and destruction.

The United States of America, a multicultural nation, is often referred to and interpreted as a "Salad Bowl", which has had a very traumatic past. Its traumatic history of slavery, racism and implementation of racial discrimination has hindered the nation's 'true assimilation'. In The Women of Brewster Place (1982), the African American novelist Gloria Naylor, focusing on the dominant feminist themes of the life and experiences of black women also deals with the issues of violence that seem to pose its roots on adversities of multiculturalism. Various episodes in the novel highlight the issue of violence which is seen manifesting itself through the complexities of multiculturalism, viewing its adverse effects that led to psychological distortions, identity crisis and physical abuse among the people of a particular ethnic group.

Through this fictional setting of Brewster place, the author is capable of successfully dealing with the real-life issues, retelling how the stings of racism and wounds of segregation have divided the human race, leading to destruction and degeneration.

"Prejudice" according to Maya Angelou 'is a burden that confuses the past, threatens the future and renders the present inaccessible.' It won't be wrong to say that every writer from a multicultural background of 'the coloured' race expresses this burden of the past accompanied by confusion, chaos and unrest in his / her works. Speaking to Angels Carabi in one of the interviews, Gloria Naylor talked of her personal experience of racism and segregation which was felt in a direct manner in the South while in the North it was disguised in the air of subtlety, as she says "Racism here was more subtle" (1991, p. 24). In another interview with Ashford, speaking on the racial segregation of her nation the author says "I think we're still struggling under the scars of slavery, and I think that the Civil Rights Movement did not work. The country is almost as divided as before" (2005, 74-75).

The Trauma of Psychological Abuse

The novel witnesses one of intense psychological damage caused in the character of Kiswana Browne, a mixed-race offspring born of a white father and a black mother, a condition that pulled her still closer to experience a continuous clash of culture, both within and around her. Though she is an outcome of the union of black and white parents, she is always drawn towards the black. She celebrates and asserts her negritude and her being black. She knew that Black is something to do with negativity, yet she overlooks the fact and takes pride in everything that would contribute to her identity as a black. Regarding such obsessions with one's own identity, Amartya Sen in his book Identity and Violence: The Illusion of Destiny proclaims, "A sense of identity can be a source not merely of pride and joy, but also of strength and confidence" (Sen, 1).

The way in which Naylor presents the character of Kiswana is very interesting. Kiswana is of a light complexion with straight hair. Dissatisfied with her physical attributes, she is often seen complaining to her mother for her physical dissimilarity with her race that does not project her as a black. She actively participates in all sorts of revolutions for the emergence of black republicans in college. In order to resemble a 'negro' and achieve a sort of assimilation with her roots, she tries to curl her hair and even changes her original name Melanie to adopt a name that sounds more African– 'Kiswana'. Kiswana's conversations with her black mother, bring out her psychological rage and the emotional turmoil when she says, "Oh, God, I can't take this anymore. Trying to be something I'm not–trying to be something I'm not mama! Trying to be proud of my heritage and the fact that I was of African descent. If that's being what I'm not, then I say fine. But I'd rather be dead than be like you–a white man's nigger who's ashamed of being black!" (TWBP, 1983, 85)

Amartya Sen, also while discussing the negative aspects of such identical obsessions writes, "And yet identity can also kill and kill with abandon. A strong–and exclusive–sense belonging to one group can in many cases carry with it the perception of distance and divergence from other groups" (Sen, 1-2). This proves to be true in the case of Kiswana. Her obsessions about her identity and her strong sense of belonging with the 'blacks' strengthen her rage and incompatibility towards the whites or any other racial or cultural groups. On the contrary, her physique prevents her from identifying herself with the blacks, eventually, her psyche refrains her from relating herself to the whites as well. It manifested itself into a state of "identity disregard" according to which an individual is seen continuously "ignoring" or "neglecting" any sense of identity with others (Sen, 20).

Gloria Naylor, through her male characters like Fuller and Woods, tries to portray the ever-persisting intense psychological turbulences of what she calls it, to be a "scarred psychology" (Ashford, 86). These characters of colour in Naylor's The Women of Brewster Place seems to be deeply affected by the prevailing adverse notions of Colonialism and Eurocentrism. The notions, for ages, have developed a negative impact on the minds of a black, colonizing their psychology and accordingly streamlining their thoughts. Thus the thought of a man of colour regarding himself and his physical appearance is always shaped on negative grounds, generating a kind of shame for himself and his entire race. This is the result of the deep-rooted psychological upheaval taking place among the blacks as a result of racism.

Apart from the "scarred psychology" of Kiswana, this implicit form of long-condensed and genetically-transmitted psychological abuse is seen in the daily conversations and dialogues of these male characters like Butch Fuller and also in the prayers of Reverend Woods. For instance, in a conversation between Mattie Michael and Butch Fuller (in the 1st section of the novel entitled 'Mattie Michael'), while they were walking under the scorching sun of April and Fuller was trying to protect his skin from getting dark in the sun, he asserts, "Too much sun on the main road and since black means poor in these parts–Lord knows, I couldn't stand to get no poorer" (12). A similar outcome of the deep-seated psychological violence is cited in the speech of Reverend Woods when he, while in the process of preaching delivers these lines, "Yes, Lord–grind out the unheated tenements! Merciful Jesus– shove aside the low-paying boss man. Perfect Father fill me, fill me till there's no room, no room for nothing else, not even that great big world out there that exacts such a strange penalty for my being born black" (65).

This way, Naylor extends the Euro-centric notions of blackness through the dialogues and thoughts of her characters that are so much burdened with a load of such notions in the form of psychological violence that they are bound to reflect through their daily conversations and psychologies. Here violence resulting from racism in the form of psychological destruction is seen as a driving force for the generation of dialogues in the novel.

The "Unstrung Puppet": Sexual Violation and Racism

In the novel, the problem of multiculturalism is subtly dealt with a biangular discourse in the section entitled "The Two". While the first angle is grounded in the context of the differences in skin colour of 'the two, the second is fueled by the uncanny sexuality shared between 'the two women. Here, "The Two", stands both as a suitable title for a particular section in the novel as well as for the lesbian couple– Lorraine and Theresa. Naylor is very particular in her description of the external features of these two characters.

She describes Lorraine as "the lighter, skinny one" who was "readily accepted" (129) by the women of Brewster Place. Theresa on the other hand is described as "the short dark one-–too pretty, and too much behind", for whom "breaths were held a little longer" (129). The phrases apparently tend to be describing the physical attributes of the two ladies. Though at a deeper level, it is a more racist approach abusing the doctrine of multiculturalism. The bodies of these women, therefore become a reflection of one's own (racist) perception, the stereotypes governing human existence, as it is truly said that, "women's bodies [the black women in particular], in patriarchal societies, are fashioned into conventional notions of femininity, and if the body resists the disciplining process, "subtle coercion" is exercised" (Ghosh et al., 2017, 219).

Lorrain's "lighter" skin colour and "skinny" body type associate her more to a white occidental woman than to a black woman of colour. On the other hand, there's a "dark" complexion and "short" body type with "too much behind" associates her with a woman of colour, thereby projecting her as the typical oriental woman of the East. A more realist approach of the portrayal reflected racism when the author describes Theresa pertaining to the stereotypical norms of a black female body objectifying and presenting it as something that the black feminist critics like Hooks term to be "transgressive", "promiscuous" or "sexually deviant" (Hooks, 1982; Young, 2007), when Naylor further writes, "And she insisted on wearing those thin Qiana dresses that the summer breeze moulded against the maddening rhythm of the twenty pounds of rounded flesh that swung steadily down the street" (129-130).

Apart from their opposing physical appearance both Lorraine and Theresa participate equally in the bond of homosexuality that exists between the two. Lorraine, because of her skin colour and body type that resembles the occidental woman is viewed as an 'other's-other' in the conservative black society of Brewster Place. In relation to the multicultural context, Lorraine is viewed under two lights, one as an 'occidental' and the other as a 'lesbian', where both sets her culturally out of the mainstream. Even though

Theresa's black body is stereotypically viewed as something that Hooks calls "expendable" with its "accessibility" and "availability" (Young, 2007, 13) the trauma of rape befalls solely upon the shoulders of Lorraine, assuming her to be the most suitable victim. By violating Lorrain's "tall" and "yellow" body, C. C. Baker and his friends consider that they have culturally overpowered the "others". This ironic ideology of cultural overpowering is reflected through the dialogues of Baker when he persistently abuses Lorraine while raping her, "I am gonna show you somethin' I bet you have never seen before." C. C. Baker takes the back of her head, presses it into the crotch of his jeans, and jerkily rubs it back and forth while his friends laugh, "Yeah, now don't that feel good? See, that's what you need. But after we get through you, you are never gonna wanna kiss no more pussy" (TWBP, 170).

Such abusive lingual addressing reflects a faulty cultural overpowering of patriarchy over heterosexuality (lesbianism) where the former tries to restore his lost hegemony over the latter through sexual violence. This idea of violence against gay and lesbians is dealt with in one of the sections (entitled 'Violence against Gay and Lesbian People') in Beckett and Macey's essay Race, Gender and Sexuality: The Oppression of Multiculturalism". According to this analysis, the society and its people (in particular those adhering to the Qu'ran and the Bible) "see it as their duty to physically harm people who are not heterosexual" (313). While regarding the physical (ie., the racial and colour) context, the rape of Lorraine reminds us of the episode of the rape of Lynne in Alice Walker's Meridian. Like the rape of Lynne, Lorrain's rape too, can be read as a black man's fallacious act for his "need to liberate himself from white oppression by taking revenge upon white women" (Lauretqtd. in Tanritanir and Aydemir, 2012). The other female characters in the novel, like Ben's daughter Etta, and Mattie too, endure sexual violations in the garb of either slavery or marriage or maybe through the expression of momentary love. While Ben's daughter embraces sexual harassment by a white master as a compromise at the hands of her poverty, Etta is used for physical gratification by Woods suggesting false intentions of marriage. Also, Mattie is made to offer her virginity to Butch just to fetch his thirst that always lusted for her "full round breasts" (17) and "high round behind" (9).

In all the cases of rape and sexual assault of these women of Brewster Place, the root cause of violence is seen to be arrested in the issue of multiculturalism that attacks the harmonious cultural hybridity of a society nurturing racism and intolerance. While Lorraine's rape was a result of racial intolerance, the sexual use of Ben's daughter, Etta and Mattie depict the racial segregation of black women projecting them as what Hooks calls the most "undesirable" yet the most "accessible" beings as per the established Euro-centric norms (Hooks, 1982). Black men tend to rape their own women in their own frustrations as a result of their "scarred psychologies" that generates from these cultural differences. While dealing with the atrocities inflicted on the black women, the writer intends to "touch(es) upon the larger black feminine sensibilities. She narrates the lives of these women with a purpose– to legitimize their female self, its history and culture. In the process of unravelling the hidden histories of the characters, she invents a new poetics" (Sonal and Singh, 209).

CONCLUSIONS

According to critics like Markus, Plaut, Wolsko et al., the notion of multiculturalism was established to stress the importance of cultural diversities, the recognition of diverse ethnic, racial and cultural groups and the explicit valuing of this diversity in the mainstream settings. This traditional ideology, though many times seemed to fail in achieving its proposed goals. According to Plaut's unfavourable concept of multiculturalism, it is defined as something that stands in contrast to the so assumed concept of 'colour-blindness' that overlooks any existing differentiation in terms of one's skin colour. Multiculturalism thus celebrates differences, intolerance and violence. A report on multiculturalism under the study of the American Nationalist Party, read by the heading, 'Multiculturalism, Racism, Violence and Balkanization', attacks its ideology of racial differences claiming multiculturalism to have been at its strongest when racism is at its best. It also proclaims that multiculturalism is the highest form of racism.

Writers have taken this issue as a nexus for their discussion to portray one's historical, social and personal predicaments. In the case of some of the black female writers and black women in general, it goes "indisputable that their own victimization has led these women towards social activism" (Das and Singh, 2016, 219). Though multiculturalism projects its diverse discourses both good and bad, Gloria Naylor still finds herself and her entire race struggling under the scars of racism and slavery (Carabi, 1991). Her novel The Women of Brewster Place thus projects the problem of multiculturalism that degrades the larger human race necessarily leading to violence, thereby portraying violence as an embedded discourse of Multiculturalism.

Works Cited

Ashford, Tomeiko R. (2005). "Gloria Naylor on Black Spirituality: An Interview".

MELUS, 30(4),7387.Retrieved from http://www.jstor.org/stable/30029635

Beckett, Clare. and MarieMacey (2001)."Race, Gender and Sexuality: The Oppression of Multiculturalism". Women's Studies International Forum 24(3/4), 309319.

Carabi, Angels. (1991). "Interview with Gloria Naylor."Revista de Estudios Norte americanos.n., 23-35.

Das, Ankita. and Rajni Singh (2016)."Empowering Lives: The Journey of Jaycee Dugard, Elizabeth Smart, and Mukhtar Mai" .Journal of Dharma 41(1), 201-220

Ghosh, Soumya M. and Rajni Singh. (2017). "Violated Bodies and the Reclamation of Female UshaGanguli's Ham Mukhtārā and Maya Krishna Rao's Walk".Archiv Orientalni 85,219-252.

Hooks, Bell (1982). Ain't I A Woman: Black Woman and Feminism. Pluto Press: London.

Naylor, Gloria. (1983). The women of Brewster Place. U.S.A: Penguin books. Subjectivity in

Niru Sharan, Violence Against Women and the Laws in India, IMPACT: International Journal of Research in Humanities, Arts and Literature (IMPACT: IJRHAL), Volume 5, Issue 7, July 2017, pp. 197-202

Sen, Amartya. (2007). Identity and Violence: The Illusion of Destiny. U.S.A: Penguin Books.

Sonal, Smrity.and Rajni Singh (2017).“Black Female Bodies and Resistance in

Gayl Jones’ Corregidora and Eva’s Man”.Rupkatha: Journal on Interdisciplinary Studies in Humanities9(2),203-211.Retrieved from https://dx.doi.org/10.21659/rupkatha.v9n2.21

Tanritanir, Bulent C.and Y. Aydemir (2012). “The Suffers of Black Women in

Alice Walker’s Color Purple and Meridian and Toni Morrison’s Novels Beloved and The Novels the Bluest Eye”.The Journal of International Social Research 5(23).437-444.

Rajesh Kumar MD, Domestic Violence Against Women in Indian Context:

Causes and Impact on Family, IMPACT: International Journal of Research in Applied, Natural and Social Sciences (IMPACT: IJRANSS), Volume 5, Issue 8, August 2017, p. 27-34

Young, Tiffany Ann (2007). Rape in Contemporary American Literature: Writing

Women As Florida State University)Electronic Theses, Treatises and Dissertations. Paper 868.

Sonal, Smrity and Singh, Rajni, Violence, an Embedded Discourse of Multiculturalism in Gloria

Naylor’s *The Women of Brewster Place* (February 3, 2018). IMPACT: International Journal of Research in Humanities, Arts and Literature, Vol. 6, Issue 2, February 2018, 257-262 , Available at SSRN:https://ssrn.com/abstract=3133494

CHAPTER II

THE PLIGHT OF WOMEN IN THE CONTEMPORARY INDIAN SOCIETY IN MEENA KANDASAMI'S SELECTED WORKS

Bhima Bansode

ABSTRACT

Meena Kandasami, a Chennai based poet, novelist, a Dalit herself, is the first Dalit woman writer to write in the English Language, is a social reformer, activist, a translator, an artist and an angry woman who wants to uplift the living family and social conditions of the Dalit women and men also. She has explored the pathetic, agonising conditions of Dalit women and has given it a living life through her two poetry anthologies, 'Touch' and 'Ms. Militancy', and her debut novel 'The Gypsy Goddess'. It's almost more than 5000 years, right from Vedic and Pre Vedic times. Since the time of Manusmriti of Manu, women have been given second place, kept away from education tied to a kitchen fireplace expected to beget children. They had no right to expression, free will, choices and women had to follow the rules of the man of the house.

At home and outside the house's threshold, there prevailed patriarchal society. Men ruled the community. The social tradition placed the man at the peak of the organisation. Over the world, patriarchal society led and in India, property, movable and immovable, the legacy of heritage, leadership, decision making power belonged to men in the house and community. This was set in the Vedic times; the society was divided into the chaturvarnya as Brahmin, Kshatriya the Vaishya and the Shudras the fourth Dalit society which was untouchables for the rest of the society.

Manusmriti of Manu, our forefather, the prime man, set these social rules, and they have come down to us as they were gone to minus zero. Dalit women were denied water from the village well, bathing and washing clothes spot at the river at the available area in Gujarat, Rajasthan and Madhya Pradesh; women have been attacked for wearing white jewellery clothes, metal pots for water filling, which is the monopoly of Hindus. These women and men have been enslaved on farms, not allowed to leave the place. It is an open jail. The upper-caste Hindus, the zamindars, landlords raped the Dalit women. Dalit women could not scream against this and could not lodge complaints to the police station and lodge complaints. They'd be killed if they did this. Women would be killed if they refused to sleep with the upper caste Hindus.

Women in general Hindu homes also were given secondary treatment, denied freedom, were not supposed to go out of the threshold. Dalit women also had to bear the atrocious behaviour of the husband, and thus, Dalit and nomadic women were twice thrice low cast and subordinated. The whole Dalit samaj was marginalised, literally kept beyond the margin of the village, no proper means of living, but a significantly marginalised work of cleaning the town, dragging the dead animals from the village stables, skinning them, selling the animal skin to a cobbler and eating the dead animal's flesh at home.

In her two anthologies' Touch' and 'Ms. Militancy', Kandasami has composed how women are raped, how they are then discarded in the home and society, and how they are rejected in marriage. Then they turn to the life of Devadasis and get married to God, have to learn dance, in a musical group they move from village to village, entertain the people, lure them, and live in the temple. Then the village heads want to enjoy them at night. If they refused, they were raped. They bear children who do not know who their father is. Devadasis' daughters also have to follow the same path. Upon this, the Dalit women earn their bread and not butter. Knowing this, which is India's main national problem, I appreciate at the heart of my heart, the literature of Meena Kandasami and I have undertaken to do the basic study of her poetry and fiction and want to understand the plight of Dalit women and enrich my knowledge of literature.

INTRODUCTION

The subject of the sorrowful condition of the Dalit women and men has always called the attention of educated elites and ordinary people. As Ravindranath Tagore has said, "an ocean of people" and therefore it's an ocean of problems and difficulties. The Shudras or the Dalits were marginalised. All progress, joy, food animals and fertile land was occupied by the upper caste Hindus, and all leftover out of this, i.e. the left food, the barren land, the waste land, went to the Dalits. of all the things, Dalits were at the receiving end. They were untouchables to caste Hindus, the Brahmins. They were others. I always wondered as to how all men are equal, but some men are more equal.

Already in the past, Mahatma Gandhi, Ravindranath Tagore, Sant Kabir in later middle ages, Sant Tukaram, Ramdaas, Mahatma Jyotiba Fule, Vinoba Bhave and Dr. B.R. Ambedkar had thought on this social evil and did attempt to eradicate this Chaturvarnya but failed until it had to dawn 15th Aug. 1947. Dr. Ambedkar included into the Indian Constitution, in article 13, that practising untouchability is a punishable crime. But even after 70 years of Independence, untouchability different form is practised, Dalits are looked down upon, Dalit women, Adiwasi women are raped, and therefore, there is a need to work on this National problem the need to investigate.

The prior studies have already lain foundation, created a house, now we've to re-search the obstacles and do away with them. This study has left some gaps. No doubt, writers, poets, thinkers have contributed the solutions. The gaps are

1. The executive body is partial, Dalit complaints are not accepted. they need to be straitened and punished.
2. Dalit men and women should be provided protection.
3. Wrong doers to be immediately arrested and imprisoned. No bail for them.
4. judiciary should be prompt to expedite justice though justice hurried up is justice buried but Justice delayed is justice denied

also.

Literature has addressed the evils but the gaps have remained as they are.

The social system is an inverted triangle since ages and it's sooner the better. Hence it becomes very essential to study and understand what Meena Kandasami has borne, what atrocious events she has witnessed and how she is rejuvenating Dalit women, know their worth and become 'Durgashkati' and fight the patriarchal system. Dr. Ambedkar, himself a Dalit born like Meena Kandasami, underwent every aspect of untouchability, wept at the agony of his fellowmen but fought with pen in the hand and a book in the other. There is no parallel to his social contribution of annihilation of caste.

Methodology

The plight of Dalit women and the men too, in the society, now in the present contemporary society and in pre-independent India has been pathetic. Brahmins educated the society looked after the scriptures and rituals Kshatriya, the warriors protected the state, Vaishyas undertook trade, at home and abroad. Shudras had no profession at all. They had to clean the village, the toilets of the village, carry the dead animals off the village, un-skin them, eat the dead flesh and sell the skin to the cobbler of the village. Shudras were therefore untouchable, forlorn, forsaken, their habitation was out of the margin of the village and they were endowed with barren lands, Dalits had to work on the farms of the caste Hindus. they were truly marginalised. So, it was easy for upper-caste Hindus to catch Dalit women and rape them in the fields. If they refused, the woman and her husband, used to be killed. This unjust, inhuman treatment was going on from pre-Vedic times to Vedic times, carried up to Mahabharat times which dates 5000 years in the past.

As socratis has said "masses consist of asses". So masses – the caste Hindus continued this all the time. But there is always Natural Justice in Nature. At different times great, philanthropic, kind people rose in the society and tried to reform the society, white wash it and it is still being washed. Sant Kabir in later 17th century, Sant Dnyaneshwar in 15th century, Mahatma Phule, Gandhi, Dr. Ambedkar, Vinoba Bhave put forth their social methodology for annihilation of the caste. It was a difficult task, Herculean task to eradicate caste system and untouchbility. Sant Eknath and Dnyaneshwar were outcaste. Sant Tukaram's literature was thrown into river Indrayani.

To sum up, it was is a super difficult task. Gayatri spivac put forth subaltern theory in which she says a subaltern cannot speak. he has no voice. "Auto ethno theory" came up in Europe for black Martin Luther King asserted his methodology against 'Apartheid Policy'. Shri Vinoba Bhave moved all over India, requested all landlords, the zamindars to donate their excess farming land to him and he donated that land to the landless Dalits in the same village. In this theory, 'Sarvodaya' and 'Antyodaya' he preached caste Hindus, Brahmins to discard the prison caste system, untouchability love Dalits, treat them as their brothers. He also told them that they were also God's people and called them Harijans (nefjpeve), stop physical assaults on Dalit women and establish equality, liberty and fraternity in the society. He and Mahata Phule opened village wells to Dalit women, cohabited them and entreated sawarnas to open temples to Dalits. But Vinoba Bhave partly succeeded in this.

But a golden climax was put on this Himalayan task by Dr. B.R. Ambedkar. (14th April 1891 – 6th Dec. 1956) who himself was a Shudra, an untouchable, a Dalit. He and his family and all his society all over India bore all sorts of atrocities by Hindus. He was not touched in school, sat alone outside the class at Satara and was not allowed to drink school water. He took inspiration from Sant Kabir, Mahatma Jyotiba Phule and put affront his 'Annihilation of caste' theory. I am using Vinoba Bhave's Sarvodaya theory, his 'Antyodaya' theory which says all should develop and the last man at the bottom, the last Dalit also should develop.

What a noble thought ! But mere social reform doesn't bring a change over immediately. social mission is a time consuming matter. men don't change, minds don't change for 500 years also. It's more than 5000 years that caste system doesn't dwindle. Social mission has to be backed up by state, the Government. Unless it's entered into Law of the land, the constitution of India and unless Untouchability is/was declared a punishable crime, people would not be afraid.

Dr. B.R. Ambedkar, having spotted this, declared untouchability a crime, opened common water places, wells for Dalits. education, common habitation became priority. He recommended inter-dining and inter-marriages in the society. His second wife was a Brahmin. His theory and method is that unless caste is abolished, Chaturvarnya is removed, unless open caste transgression is there, inequality, untouchability will not be abolished. We're enjoying the fruits of his sky-high efforts and the nation is grateful to him.

'Research writing'

Meena Kandasami is a young Chennai-based creative writer, a Dalit poet-translator and a Social Activist. Has seen injustice, atrocities caused to her fellow women, men also and she has also undergone physical and mental torture, therefore who could write and write poetry better than her? Meena has been the first Dalit to write poetry in English and Dr. B.R. Ambedkar has been the first ...... Dalit to write in prose, the essays, pamphlets and number of books 0n Indian Social structure – the oppressive caste system, the four-walled caste system, namely Chaturvarnya. This was slavery, a bonded labour and Meena Kandasami and Dr. Ambedkar raised a social revolt against the high class Brahmins, the so-called Good's people, not by a sword, but by a pen, by literature.

Apart from Meena Kandasami, other writers poets, critics also gave way to censure Dalit atrocities through their poetry Kamal Das, Chakraborthy, Sangita Alwar, Jayodeep Sarangi, Sagar on Indian soil and abroad in Europe and America, Asia, poets & critics David Damrosch, Franz fanon, Amie cesaire, Langston Hughes, a jew poet Niemoller Pakistani poet Faiz Ahmad Faiz, a Russian poet szymborska, Spanish poet Neruda, Afghan poet farrokhjad, Goethe of Germany, Vajda, Dionyz Durisin, also put forth the inhuman, slave treatment given to African and Carribians and Jamaicans. All intellectual, elites and philanthropic think alike, of the betterment of the forlorn and forsaken, even though they live at the different corners of the mother earth.

Meena Kandasami's two poetry collections' Touch' and 'Ms. Militancy' and other writings have reached world boundaries and her writings have got honourable place in world literature. Meena's first collection of poems' Touch was published in 2006 and it revolves around the theme of love and the caste system in India. Her poems describe and depict the pathetic plight of Dalit and Adivasi women, raped for joy by the higher caste jamindars, assaulted if they refused to submit or killed or their husbands would be killed.

The higher caste people, the Brahmins, the Thakurs, Jamindars assume that Dalit women are meant for sexual enjoyment. For Dalit women, oppression often means sexual a subjugation. Meena's poems show a sense of gender inequality. She assaults the patriarchal society and suggests that being a woman in patriarchal society is another form of being lower caste. Indian society has been male-dominated and women in higher class were also treated secondarily. So it's clear that Dalit women have been still treated lowly, twice subjugated.

In the 'Touch' anthology, Touch is an outstanding poem, 'you don't know if you are yielding or Resisting', 'Dead woman walking', 'Lady Justice', 'Martyr', 'Why do heroes die?', 'one eyed', 'This poem will provoke you', 'Six Hours of chastity', and 'Passion. Becomes piety' are some other poems burning with social anger, and are .... thought-provoking. 'Touch', a collection of 84 poems, revolves around the subject of caste and love a mature work written in sharp language. Being a woman, she is more concerned about women's agony as she herself has gone through that and her poems are a sense of gender discrimination and being a woman in a patriarchal society is being another lower caste in Shudra.

Kamala Das, Another feminist writer, in her foreword to Meena's 'Touch' has highly praised her. she says, "Older by nearly half a century, I acknowledge the superiority of her poetic vision and wish her access to the magical brew of bliss and tears each true poet is forced to partake of, day after day, month after month, year after year." Meena dedicates the second part of 'Touch' to Dalit issues. The Touch is the first poem of the collection and representative of love, real physical love experienced by skin touch, is a heavenly pleasure. every Dalit wants to be loved, want to be accepted, want to be a part of things, they also want to be touched that way. Dalit women also want, solitude, space and to be limited. But in the poem Touch she says, Dalit women, nomadic women are caught in field areas and raped. this harsh reality pains them, it gives the opposite pleasant footings of skin touch.

In the poem 'we will Rebuild worlds' Meena cries that a Dalit woman could not love a higher caste or a Dalit man, if a Dalit tried to be a Brahmin or read 'Vedas' or heard 'Vedas'- poison and pesticide through his nose ears and mouth were poured in Meena further says that all men and women have passion and want to pacify them Dalit woman's passion is crime but 'Sawarna's passion is passion. If a Dalit woman dares to love a higher cast man, she is given poison and pesticide. The poem reads thus. 'But the crimes of passion'.

In the poem'Ekalavya', Kandasmi, criticises the injustice done to Ekalavya by Dronacharya. In the poem, she draws our attention to the discrimination meted to Ekalavya in the Mahabharat where Dronacharya refused to train 'archery' to Ekalavya since he belonged to the lower caste, a shudra. And when Ekalavya made a statue of Guru Dronacharya and worshipping him everyday, learnt archery on his own and to take Dronacharya's blessing offered him to pay Gurudakshina, Dronacharya asked for his right thumb, so that he should not excel the prince Arjuna, the Kshatriya, obedience to Gugu and to the Brahmin, Eklavya cut off his right thumb and offered to Dronacharya. Prince Arjuna had no rival.

Ekalavya
You can do a lat of things
with your left hand

Besides, faseist Drinacharyas warrant
Left handed treatment
Also
You don't need your right thumb
to pull a trigger or hurl a bomb

In the poem 'Narration', Meena ... comes out with bitter truth of age-old oppression in typical Tamil society

I will weep to you about
My landlord and with
My mature gestures
You will understand
The torn sari, disheveled hair
Stifled cries And meek submission
I was not an untouchable then. (12)

In what a mature, precise words, Kandasami has brought out the bitter truth, the hypocrisy of the landlord in particular and high class people in general that, even though the poetess refused and was meek, the landlord raped her, for a rape a Dalit woman is no more an untouchable and Dharma doesn't get corrupt.

In another poem 'Liquid tragedy Karamchedy 1985', Kandasmi narrates another event of injustice to a 'Madiga' woman, a lower caste woman, who ... protested against the Kammas, the higher caste people against bathing their buffallows in their drinking pond. Enraged by this audacity of a downtrodden, raising voice against the higher caste, the upper caste people, killed six Madiga men and raped three Madiga women.

This shows every upper caste man was a tyrant dictator in the Chatuvanya Society too. 'Ms. Militancy' is her second collection of the poems. This brave title is symbolic of the fighting mood of Meena Kandasami. Her verse is unapologetic, in this verse she has targeted two oppressors – the high class Brahmins' Hindu Society and the patriarchy – the male dominance in the society. 'A cunning Stunt' is the opening poem of the anthology In this poem she directly accuses the sinful men habituated to molest Dalit and Gypsy women.

In her preface, she is loud and says every woman is an heir of Goddess and sadly explores that, in all ages, woman was taken as a thing of consumption and joy and was looted of her chastity. She bitterly explores. “My Maarimma bays for blood, My Kali Kills, My Droupadi Strips, My Sita Climbs on to a stranger’s lap. All my women militate” (8).

In other words, she is lamenting for whatever has happened to her ancient predecessors. In her first poem ‘cunning Stunt’ she speaks of the family and community honour and how she has to keep quiet even though she is raped. A woman has to bear the sexuality come what may.

The Poem

The poem ends with woman’s cunningness and the woman says that, he who raped her, tore her apart, as if did this to contain the meaning of family and she had no go but to surrender and say ‘I did not want to displease him’ having spoiled with chastity, looted by high class men, Dalit women have to turn to prostitution and earn the livelihood, live with children who do not know who their father is. Her poem ‘Backstreet Girls’ speaks of girls turned to prostitution in the dark lane behind.

Meena Kandasami’s ‘Six Hours of chastity’ is the finest poem showing the masked face of the so-called sophisticated people in the society. The self-righteous men who make a show of piousness to maintain their status, visit a whorehouse after the sunset and enjoy the city-bride a Dalit, Adiwasi girl, corrupted by patriarchal men who took shelter in a brothel. Here she shows how up-caste people are and how they use and throw a Dalit woman, Discard first and then enjoy.

In six hours of the brothel, the poetess tells us, various people visit the house enjoy sex and go away, first is the gambler and the priest is the last who enters before dawn. A priest at a whorehouse is unbelievable but true. In the daylight everybody follows religion, treats Dalits untouchable but, at night, when the natural instinct arises, a Dalit woman is not an untouchable. Her another poem, ‘Princess In Exile’ is about Sita, the chaste Queen of Ramayana, who walked out of her place from her husband Rama who questioned her piety of character. She abandoned him and took shelter in the 'ashram' of Walmiki. Sita was a Princess of Ram, who also went in exile with Ram but Ram suspected her chastity and abandoned her. Sita was pregnant when abandoned.

In the poem 'Princess In Exile', Meena Kandasami's Sita is a chaste woman. She avenges her husband for his suspicious nature after having gone through 14 years exile, subjected to hunger thirst, sex, wind, rain, heat and a great sacrifice. Meena wants women not to follow the rules of a patriarchal society. Her Sita is brave, independent and she has perfected the art of vanishing from the day she was kidnapped. Her 'walkout is her way to take revenge on Ram who failed to protect her and could not release her from Rawan's open imprisonment as early as possible. Sita proved chastity by going through the fire, the Agni, but still, she abandoned Ram because she wanted to maintain Woman's self-respect

In this poem Meena has given modern identity and form to Sita and interprets Ramayan Sita in the free modern times and proves that it was not Sita's fault that she was kidnapped by mighty Rawan. A woman looses in physical power in fight and if at all she was enjoyed by Rawan, it was none of her faults. the woman is 'Deyeuee' a helpless creature in a patriarchal society. Ramayan period, which is 'Pre-Vedic' period at least 10 to 15 thousand years before (?), before 'ceneYeejle', Mahabharat which dates back to 5000 years, is not an exception to this.

thus, Meena shows that woman, at all times, Vedic, Pre-Vedic and Dwapar age times, was always subordinate to man, his property which was sold in 'ceneYeejle' Mahabharat times in the form of 'êewHeoer' Droupadi. woman was and is taken as a commodity of consumption at all times, if consumed by someone else, is abandoned. Modern times is the climax of it, where woman, old or young, child age girls are raped often in north India and elsewhere in India.

Meena's Sita is a transformed woman and through this poem, Meena wants to preach women to be brave, free-minded, revolting to slavery and kill the killer. During Victorian period, woman was given two types of images. an 'angel in the house' and 'A Devil in the flesh'. One obedient and adhering to patriarchal rule, keeping her desires compressed and the other who expressed her will freely and open-minded, abhorred social norms.

In Ramayan ' Shurpanaka' is a Devil in flesh who was Meenakshi, Rawana's sister, was married and divorced by husband and Sita is an Angel in the house. Under the garb of an Angel, woman's voice and freedom were suppressed. In this eminent poem, Meena Kandasami, has defined Sita as a person, who, even after scorn, preferred to lead a life of a recluse. The following lines of 'The Princess in Exile' are self-explanatory.

Scorned, she sought refuge in spirituality
and was carried away by a new age guru
with saffron clothes and caramel words
years later, her husband won her back
but by then, she was adept at walkouts
she had perfected the vanishing act. (13)

'A Dead woman Walking' is another poem, with another incident happing to various women at different times. This poem depicts the pathos and the pathetic plight of Dalit women, assaulted, raped and left to winds by the rapist and the society. Meena kandsami deplores and condemns to say she walks like a dead woman. She is a living death. Her pain is expressed in the following line:

'I wept in vain, I wailed
I walked on my head,
I went to god'

'The Gypsy Goddess' is a memoir of events, the record of atrocities thrown on Dalits, the nomadics, the gypsies, moving from village to village in search of gainful labour. Tamil Nadu faced a horrible famine in 1877. One Karuppaayi of Thiruchuli narrated the anecdote to the novelist that, during the famine, she lost her man and three sons. People died of starvation. Karuppaayi managed to survive by eating mud. Because of her pregnant condition, a worker took pity an her and fed her. In December 1877, Gundar river, in flood, swelled suddenly and engulfed people Karuppaayi took shelter at the same relief worker who saved her life.

Many were flown away in river spet. 'The Royal Gazetteer' of the British recorded over a thousand deaths in one week. In this pathetic social condition, a natural calamity, Chinnamma, old Karuppaayi's grand-daughter, later on 15th August 1925, died. Dalit women were dragged from houses and raped. In 1925 only, Tranguebar witnessed sixteen rapes on Dalit, gypsy women, living an the outskirts of Tringubar, in one week.

In Kariokkal, on 14 April 1965, the Dalits expressed to the cast-Hindus that they be allowed to participate the 'Shri Ram Chariot Procession' and be allowed to pull it. The sawarnas refused permission. Dalits, in the heat of insult, dismantled the chariot as a protest. Brahmins, taking the chariot as unchaste as the untouchables touched it, burnt it. Sansai, an untouchable, was suspected as mastermind and was abducted the next day. His body was found after two weeks in Kariokkal. Police closed the case as a mysterious death. All are equal before God, he loves all but only upper caste Hindus are equal before God. Even God, the father of all Human beings, is snatched away from the untouchables.

God never classified his sons as untouchables. 'Gypsy Goddess' is thus a memoir of various atrocious events to Dalits, one worse than the other. The book ends with a massacre of 44 Dalit untouchables, the labourers in paddy fields, working on daily wages. This incident took place in village kilvenmani an the Christmas eve of 1965. By this time, communist propaganda was very high in Tamil Nadu and Kerala. They used to instigate the poddy workers to go on strike for petty demands. This massacre took place because Dalit labourers asked for little more share of rice.

Upto and even after independence, Dalits suffered mental, physical torture at the hands of cruel landlords. As such they are sick, hungry, molested. they have been suffering through famine, hunger, injustice, who are made naked, beaten up, raped, molested, fortuned. God's people have no pity and compassion in their soul. Meena Kandasami, through her poetry and the novel, 'The Gypsy Goddess', has affirmed to the nation that, in this land of Gods, the Dalits, gypsies, nomadics are worse than animals.

But Dr. Bhimarao Ramji Ambedkar, a Dalit like Meena Kandasami, also underwent untouchability, poverty and like Kandasami, he took the pen in hand and wrote about the atrocities caused to Dalits, all Shudras, thrown out of the villages, whom the upper-caste Hindus, the sawarnas denied public well water, cohabitation, used them as bonded labourer their farm's underpaid hem, gave them barren farmlands, denied education and all sorts of progress. The plight of men and women in peshawa Rule was too inhuman to be thought of.

Dr. B. R. Ambedkar gave voice to 9 crore Dalits, untouchables. For that he educated himself, studied Law and History of India and humanities and thrashed the caste Hindus, their hypocrisy, wrote essays, papers, books, ran a news paper 'Dalit Mitra', established 'Samata Sainik Dal' and aroused his people. He taught them that they were not low to anybody, they had self-respect. No other leader, writer, poet worked as hard as Dr. Ambedkar did. Finally he accorded his fellowmen fundamental rights - Liberty Equality and Fraternity to them. He wrote the constitution of free India and abolished untouchability by law. It's now a punishable crime to practice untouchability. All are equal before the law and Constitution.

In his book 'Annihilation of Caste' he has affirmed that caste is the root cause of untouchability and castes should be abolished. In his 'Annihilation of Caste' Dr. Ambedkar has shown how women were degraded and men were beaten up in British India, Peshawa Rule and even in free India. Dr. Ambedkar says that the plight of women was pathetic in caste system. He quotes the incident of atrocity on the 'Balais' untouchable community which appeared in Times of India of 4th January 1928. The high caste Hindus the Kalotas, Rajputs, and Brahmins including patels, Patawaris of villages of Kanaria, Bicholi-Hafasi, Mardana and about 15 other villages of Indore District informed the Balals that, if they wished to live among them.

1. They must not wear gold-lace-bordered Pagadis.
2. They must not wear dhotis with coloured or fancy borders.
3. they must convey intimation of the death of any Hindu to relatives of the diseased – no matter how far their relatives lived.
4. In Hindu marriages, Balais must play music before the procession.
5. Balai women must not wear gold or silver ornaments, they must not wear fancy gowns or jackets.
6. Balais women must attend all cases of confinement of Hindu women.
7. Balais must render services without demanding remuneration.
8. If the Balais did not agree to abide by these terms, they had to clear out of village.

The Balais refused to this, the Hindu element proceeded against them. Balais women were not allowed to get water from village wells. The Balais submitted petitions to the Darbar against this persecutions. But timely help was not provided to them. Hundreds of Balais with their wives and children had to abandon their homes in which their ancestors lived. Dr. Ambedkar quotes another incident of Gujrat, of Yana in Ahmadabad District that, in Nov. 1935, some Dalit women of well-to-do families started fetching water in metal pots. The Hindus took that as their insult, they couldn't bear the growth of the untouchables and looked at it as an affront to their dignity and assaulted the untouchable women for their impudence.

In 1935 only, in Chakurara in Jaipur, an untouchable of Chakurara who returned from pilgrimage, offered a dinner to his fellow untouchable brothers, as an act of piety. The host offered a sumptuous meal and the items served, included ghee in it. As the untouchables were enjoying their meals, the Hindus in hundreds, armed with lathis, rushed to the scene, despoiled the food and lathi-charged the untouchables who left the food and ran away for their lives.

Thus all doors of progress, the Hindus closed for all Shudra castes. Thus, whichever direction, the Dalit turned, the monster of caste was available in front of him.

CONCLUSION

Much has been said and much progressive work has been done by Dalit writers and poets. May be Meena Kandasami took inspiration from Dr. Ambedkar along with Kamala Das and others. Kandasami has done best in realistic poetry Dr. Ambedkar uplifted the mountain of Chaturvarnya and overthrew it out of the planet. He has done best in prose and ideological essays and books.

So, I conclude that, even after 70 years of Independence, poverty, inequality untouchability, caste-system, sexual abuse to Dalit, women, dishonour to them prevail in different forms. In rural areas, dictatorship of caste Hindus, the zamindars continue in this direction. I also conclude that the poor are Dalits, hungry are Dalits, unemployed, uneducated are Dalits. Even now Dalit women are raped and killed. Caste Hindu women are untouchable for rapes. India is a poor country with these people. sick people are these. India is progressing in science and materialistically but socially, spiritually and Humanly it's dwarf and backward. evening prayer of Sant Dnyaneshwar sings, we've to make all happy.

What should be done for this? Laws should be observed and applied fully. All should be equal before Law but some are unequal. All crimes should be strictly dealt with. Not only Dalit but different caste women are raped every day in the country of Ahimsa. Dalit woman rape or any woman rape should be settled within a week and there should be instant Death Punishment to a rapist and his moral and physical supporters. Once under custody of police, a criminal, a rapist should straight way go to 'the guillotine'. Landless Dalits should be provided land and farms, equipment under Bhudan Yadnya Yetoeve ³e%e of Vinoba Bhave. Still, there are gaps in imparting justice to Dalit women. They'd be provided with some jobs, loans to erect cottage industry, boarding schools be opened area wise and a mobile school bus should pick them up and drop too. So far Dalit women are concerned, every village must have armed police force of male and female constables and political interference must not be there.

Every Dalit Adiwasi family should be provided with grains and more maintenance allowance be given. Every Dalit and Adiwasi child must go to school. A head of the village should keep record of everything in village. The atrocity act of Dalits should be revised and the loopholes in it should be found out. For atrocious act, death punishment should be there. Strict adherence to Law and complete execution of Law and punishment may appear dictatorial but what Law can do, nothing else can.

If we want to develop India, the Downtrodden, the Dalits should be economically raised. There'd be no slums. Saluting Meena Kandasami and Dr. Ambedkar, I maintain to say that they are handsome and noble as whatever they did for the upliftment of Dalits and giving voice to their agony, is handsome and noble.

Works Cited

Anthology of Poetry, "Touch". 2006 by Meena Kandasami: Poetry on Love Caste.

Anthology of Poetry, "Ms. Militancy", 2010, by Meena Kandasami: Poetry on the Atrocity and Cruelty inflicted on Dalit Women and Men.

The Hindu Code Bill by Dr. B. R. Ambedkar. 1951.

CHAPTER III

SHARING SIMILARITIES, CELEBRATING DIFFERENCES: A SEARCH FOR THE SELF IN BABY KAMBLE'S THE PRISONS WE BROKE AND LAKSHMIBAI TILAK'S I FOLLOW AFTER

Mrs. Deepti Mujumdar
Department Head of English
Chikitsak Samuha's Patkar-Varde College, Mumbai.

ABSTRACT

All of us know and understand that there exists an intimate and vital connection between literature and life and that literature is an expression of individual and social life and thought through language. Good literature is always appreciated for the length and breadth of life it paints, the ways in which it grasps and reflects the truths of life that emerge triumphant out of the ruins of the past, and the way it emancipates the human mind from its limitations. Since autobiography as a genre explores the nexus of life, language and literature in an interesting manner, this paper focuses on the search for the self in two autobiographies by women writers – one a Dalit woman and the other an upper-caste brahmin woman.

Keywords: autobiography, women and self.

• • •

"Sharing Similarities, Celebrating Differences" - A Search for the Self in Baby Kamble's *The Prisons We Broke* and Lakshmibai Tilak's *I follow After*

This paper is divided into four sections – the first section discusses Autobiography as a genre, the second focuses on Autobiography as a chosen medium of expression by women writers, the third section introduces the two texts selected and the last section compares and contrasts the texts to bring out the intended meaning of the title of the paper, "Sharing Similarities, Celebrating Differences". Though not very easy to define, autobiography in the broader sense of the word is used almost synonymously with "life writing" and denotes all modes and genres of telling one's own life. More specifically, autobiography as a literary genre signifies a retrospective narrative that undertakes to tell the author's own life, or a substantial part of it, seeking, to a certain extent, to reconstruct his/her personal development within a given historical, social and cultural framework.

The emergence of autobiography as a literary genre and critical term coincides with what has frequently been called the emergence of the modern subject around 1800. Since then, it has evolved as a genre of non-fictional, yet 'constructed' auto diegetic (narrator who is also the protagonist) narration wherein a self-reflective subject enquires into his/her identity and its developmental trajectory. While autobiography on the one hand claims to be non-fictional (factual) in that it proposes to tell the story of a 'real' person, it is inevitably constructive, or imaginative, in nature and as a form of textual 'self-fashioning' ultimately resists a clear distinction from its fictional relatives (autofiction, autobiographical novel), leaving the generic borderlines blurred.

Autobiography constructs an individual life course as a coherent, meaningful whole. Even if autobiography's aspect of re-living experience, of rendering incidents as they were experienced at the time, is considered, the superior 'interpreting' position of the narrative present remains paramount, turning past events into a meaningful plot, making sense of contingency. The field of life writing as narratives of self—or of various forms of self—has now become significantly broader, transcending the classic model of autobiographical identity qua coherent retrospective narrative. Yet whatever its theoretical remodelling and practical rewritings, even if frequently subverted in practice, maybe, the close nexus between narrative, self/identity, and the genre/practice of autobiography continues to be considered paramount. The underlying assumption concerning autobiography is that of a close, even inextricable connection between narrative and identity, with autobiography the prime generic site of enactment.

A lot of notions about autobiography as a narrative genre have been challenged with the emergence of new theories and perspectives – like gender studies and the postcolonial and subaltern theories. If gender studies exposed autobiography's individualist self as a phenomenon of male self-fashioning, a postcolonial theory further challenged its universal validity. While autobiography was long considered an exclusively Western genre, postcolonial approaches to autobiography/ life writing have significantly expanded the corpus of autobiographical writings and provided a perspective that is critical of both the eurocentrism of autobiography genre theory and the concepts of selfhood in operation (Lionett, 1991).

In this context, too, the question has arisen as to how autobiography is possible for those who have no voice of their own, who cannot speak for themselves (whom Spivak calls the 'subaltern'). Such 'Writing ordinary lives', usually aiming at collective identities, poses specific problems: sociological, ethical and even aesthetic (Pandian 2008). Whatever the markers of difference and semantic foci explored, the notion of autobiography has shifted from literary genre to a broad range of cultural practices that draw on and incorporate a multitude of textual modes and genres. By 2001, Smith and Watson (eds. 2001) were able to list fifty-two "Genres of Life Narrative" by combining formal and semantic features. Among them are narratives of migration, immigration or exile, narratives engaging with ethnic identity and community, prison narratives, illness, trauma and coming-out narratives as much as celebrity memoirs, graphic life writing and forms of Internet self-presentation. These multiple forms and practices produce, or allow critics to freshly address, new 'subject formations' within specific historical and cultural localities.

In *Writing a Woman's Life*, Carolyn G. Heilburn says that a woman's life can be described in four ways: "... the women herself may tell it, in what she chooses to call an autobiography; she may tell it in what she chooses to call fiction; a biographer, woman or man, may write a biography, or the woman may write her own life in advance of living it, unconsciously and without realising or naming the process". A woman's autobiography generally deals with the various relationships like those with her parents, siblings and with her spouse, children and other women of her family. Her identity is established only based on these relationships. A man's autobiography is mainly concerned with his success story, achievements, and the world of work. He rarely focuses on his familial relationships. Although each author may have significant, sometimes dazzling accomplishments to her credit, the theme of accomplishment rarely dominates the narrative.... Indeed to a striking degree, they fail directly to emphasize their own importance, though writing in a genre which implies self-assertion and self-display.

George Henry Lewes says that a woman's literature 'promises a woman's view of life, woman's experience: in other words, a new element'. But he further adds, "Masculine mind is characterized by the predominance of intellect and the feminine by the predominance of emotions... Woman, by her greater affectionateness, her greater range and depth of emotional experience, is well fitted to give expression to the emotional facts of life" (9). But is that all that a woman autobiography writer has to offer? Fortunately, no. When a woman chooses to write an autobiography, she is making a conscious choice. An autobiography enables women to correct the histories of their lives, enables them to introspect, think deeply about their lives and develop a positive self-identity. Writing an autobiography becomes a therapeutic process. It becomes a weapon of self-assertion, a political act, helpful in achieving a sense of identity and mobilizing resistance against different forms of oppression. It provides a rounded and complete picture of the Self, located in a community with which it is symbiotically linked and in the process the writer also becomes a Social Historian.

The first text being reviewed is an autobiography by Lakshmibai Tilak, published in the 1930s in Marathi and translated later in English by E. Josephine Inkster. In Marathi, the work is titled *Smriti Chitre* which can be loosely translated as 'Glimpses of my Memory' or 'As I remember. However, the title of the translated work *I Follow After* has resulted in a general interpretation that the narrative is a story of a self-effacing woman, following the path led by her husband, without questioning. Reading against the grain, the narrative tells the story of the triumph of an independent woman who wants to lead a life on her own terms. beneath the superficial chatty and humorous narrative, there is a narrative of pain and sufferings, there is a story of resistance to the social norms that govern life and a transformation to a newer and more satisfying world views, which is a personal choice quite contrary to the prevalent social norms.

Lakshmi begins her narrative with the description of her stifled childhood experiences under the persecution of her eccentric father. Her childhood description, if read carefully can be seen as the portrayal of pain and sufferings of her mother, her grandmother and of other children of the household but Lakshmi's chatty and racy tone gives it a different hue and the pain gets encrusted in humour. At the same time, she gives a detailed account of her mother's generous, amiable and rational disposition that was the source of solace for all.

I Follow After is characterised by the elaboration of every trifle issue of the banal life. It seems such elaboration of trivial helped her to give the description of many obnoxious realities quite naturally, which would otherwise be impossible to talk about if she had relied on precise and to the point depiction, without causing outrage. Lakshmibai Tilak belongs to a nineteenth-century orthodox society of Maharashtra, where religion was a sacrosanct affair and anyone challenging it was punished by ostracism from society. In such a milieu it was really a momentous task for a person, especially a woman from a peculiar Brahmanical background to cross the religion and caste boundaries and to adopt Christianity. Lakshmi's husband Narayan Waman Tilak, a famous poet of his time opted for Christianity and his conversion

Lakshmibai Tilak's autobiography manages to draw a comprehensive portrait of the husband. Rev.Tilak, as the book portrays him, is a multifaceted personality- a poet who can write poems in the act of speaking, an actor whose performance in a play can move the audience to tears, an eloquent orator who wins a number of prizes in elocution competitions, a great teacher whose teaching can turn even urchins into poets. Apart from that, he is also a man of vanity who seems to value respect and honour a lot and to fear that everyone is out to insult him, a man with a sense of humour, absent-minded, irascible, impractical, courageous, unconventional, spiritual, a loving but whimsical husband. Though she praises her husband at every stage and gives all credit to him for guiding her in her life, she does not hesitate to comment on his whimsical nature and criticize his behaviour. Though her husband wants her to convert to Christianity as he does, Lakshmi resists and is able to hold her fort against his wishes. His conversion creates a lot of clamour in Lakshmi's life. She faces all these with her indomitable spirit and logical disposition. Commenting about her restorative capacity, she writes, "Many and many a time I had been on the point of forsaking this earthly body, but I had never actually done it, and I believe it was never possible. It was characteristic of me to grope on through the darkness of despair, but still to keep to the road. It was not me to lie down and die halfway. In short, I rebounded like a rubber ball" (40).

Her choice of converting to Christianity is lighted by her understanding and consciousness. By adopting Christianity she tries to free herself from all bondages of caste and religion. Her conversion is the proof of her tenacity, independence of mind and the inherent spirit of rebellion, which according to Susie Tharu and K. Lalitha, "she had inherited from her grandfather, Vasudev Bhagwat Jogelkar, who was hanged in the aftermath of 1857 Sepoy

Rebellion." (Tharu and Lalitha, 309)

The autobiography can be seen as a tale of twofold transformation of a woman – one from a simple and docile housewife to a self-conscious and self-sufficient woman leading and managing her life on her own accord. The other transformation is in terms of her adoption of the broad world view of Christianity leaving the narrow and superstitious outlook of Hinduism, as experienced by her in her interaction with her family and society of that time. The main intent of her writing seems to enumerate both physical and mental struggles such transformations involved and also to subtly document her triumphant emergence, overcoming all these. Her conversion to Christianity widens her perspective and provides her insight into the empathetic stance of Christianity towards women. Such insights helped her in retrospective analysis through the lens of Christianity, the sufferings of her mother, her mother- in –law and also her own at the hands of the patriarchs of the household, and through her narrative, she has given voice to all these silent sufferings.

The second text being discussed is by a Dalit woman writer Babytai Kamble and its title is *The Prisons We Broke*. Originally written in Marathi and published in 1986 as *Jeena Amucha* , it was translated by Dr. Maya Pandit and published in English in 2008. Her words, firmly rooted in the Ambedkarite ideology, have continued to inspire Dalit activists to this day, urging them to look beyond the individual to the community in the struggle for freedom and equality. Her autobiography is path-breaking for being the first critique of twofold patriarchy – an experience of Dalit women's lives recognizing their dual oppression by caste and gender.

Like an auto-ethnographer, Baby gives a detailed descriptions of the houses, the locality of the houses in the village: the Maharwada, the restrictions faced by Mahars in the other parts of the village or even in their area in the presence of a higher caste man. She narrates all this not just from the experience of being a Mahar, but a Mahar woman.

She identifies the notions of double consciousness within the Mahar women. Although 'Hindu philosophy had discarded us as dirt and thrown us into their garbage pits, on the outskirts of the village' yet Mahar women desperately tried to preserve whatever bits of Hindu culture they could imitate so that they would be able to live like the upper caste, enjoy wealth like their wives and practice their rituals. She is aware that these rituals marked their difference from the upper caste and they were denied to them to keep them suppressed. At the same time, the Mahar women imitated the Hindu rituals as 'an outlet for their oppressed souls'.

Her narration is from the various angles of the self's experience, shared experience from women of her community and her own observations. This covers in it the temporal span of her childhood and adult life which also brilliantly captures the experience of her community and the women of her community at the height of Dr Ambedkar's revolutionary leadership and beyond. There is in her story a history of a great leader and the Dalit movement under his able and revered leadership, and later a lament for the way the movement had lost its aim in the political mayhem and personal agendas of the people of the community itself, but there is hope too for the re-emergence of the movement of pride and dignity.

Babytai is outspoken and does not dilute her narration in the self-glorification of the community. Rather she is critical of the community, its behaviour towards its women, towards its way of life. While she tells the story of her father who was educated and ready to sweat it out in his work as a contractor for buildings, she also brings out the helping nature of his which at times would leave the family with nothing to eat. She portrays the anguish of the women against the hardships and poverty in the sharp remarks of her mother for her father who would never save (he would always say that one does not need more than a bellyful). The helpless requests of the mothers of the poorer families (who would ask their husbands to get some cactus flowers to cook) at the same time shows the terrible side of the same women as mothers-in-law.

Babytai gives us a dark picture of the situation of a Mahar girl—married at a young age; devoid of education to stand for self; beaten and bruised by in-laws and husband; working long hours; getting whatever is left over after families consumption, and undergoing regular pregnancies where she has no choice. All this leaves her at the bottom of the ladder of development. Her movement curtailed and under surveillance very much the same as that of women from the upper caste, her sexuality controlled by her family and relatives through taunts and thrashings, her position as the last in the family from basic consumption to decision making, the Mahar women is under the dual burden of her caste and her sexuality.

Baby breaks the myth of a democratic Dalit family. She brings out the inhumane acts of the chopping off of the nose of women by the husband and his family; the regular burden of torture and taunts. She remarks that in the days prior to the 1940s that at least one woman in a hundred would have her nose chopped off by the husband under the provocation of his mother or father. The overall condition of women is pitiable not just because of the troubles they have with the other castes but also because of an existing disrespect for women at large. Women have to bear the burden of purity; they could be questioned if they do not veil themselves properly, called a 'slut' by the men and women for any shortcoming (the connotation of the word 'slut' itself is derogatory to women only; there is no mention of an equivalent term for the male). It has been an enigma how a community which is obsessed with the worship of the Goddess and celebrates the possession of the bodies of their women by Goddesses can butcher the same body as filthy and polluted.

In Baby's autobiography, there is a tension between tradition and modernity to which the Mahars respond with the determination to achieve modernity. This modernity is embodied by Ambedkar and is epitomised by him. Again there are traditional structures within the community such as the chawdi (30) which is very much a modern concept of public space available for debates and deliberation. The change in the space of action, dialogue and doing: here the schoolboys plan their temple entry; here the Mahar wada[31] celebrate their first Ambedkar's birth anniversary; here, Baby and her husband start the first shop of their wada as a protest against the shopkeepers of the village who practised untouchability. It is also the place of traditional get-togethers and celebrations.

The work mostly revolves around the day-to-day lives of the Mahar community; the perpetual shortage of food, battered, stitched together pieces of rags as dresses, the snot-nosed and dirty children, the trials and methods of bringing home food from collections of leftovers; in exchange of labour, collection of dead animals during epidemics, to poisoning someone's cattle in the most difficult situation. The autobiography speaks of the lives of the Mahar people, their traditions, celebrations, their Gods and Goddesses. A large part of the work consists of retelling myths and stories around evil forces, superstitions and the belief of the people in forces that write their destiny, difficult processes of treatment in case of ill health. According to Baby Kamble, Mahars opt for these beliefs, superstitions and treatments in the face of want and needs. They have no money or means for alternatives.

Baby never mentions her own life events—marriage, the birth of children—except for her own birth. However, she mentions her enrolment in school; her experience in a new school with caste-Hindu girls; the opening of their shop in the Maharwada—the first one. She writes of her decision to be equally involved in the shop; her decision to write about her experiences; the decision to send her children to school; their success in the academic and professional world; her involvement and service for the community in terms of running a government-supported orphanage for the backward caste. These are significant events in her life.

Baby Kamble breaks the boundary of given notions of womanhood and creates a self that dares to challenge the given. In her choice of significant life events, she mentions those events which she has imbibed as important from her close engagement with Ambedkar's thoughts. As she affirms, 'I made a firm resolve, at a young age to lead my life according the path sketched by Dr. Babasaheb Ambedkar, the light of my life. His principles have exercised a strong influence on me.' It was his principles of education, economic independence and political participation of Dalits and especially Dalit women, that worked as her framework for her life and hence life events. Baby Kamble narrates her and her community's shared experience of breaking prohibitions, internalised and imposed—' the prisons'—that excluded them. It is the prisons of hunger, illiteracy, untouchability, patriarchy, economic dependency, superstition, disease and social disability related to caste and gender that they broke. It is through the breaking of these prisons that the Dalit, including the Dalit women, assert their selfhood. Thus, both Lakshmibai Tilak and Babytai Kamble become social historians, giving the readers glimpses of the society and the milieu they belonged to – one does it subtly and almost unconsciously, while the other makes it her main intention of writing.

We see both Lakshmibai and Babytai resisting the norms of the society, at times even at the cost of pain and suffering at the hands of their immediate families. It is their strong, indomitable spirit that keeps them going. Both the autobiographies speak of conversion. People have criticised Lakshmibai's decision to convert to Christianity as being solely influenced by her husband. But what they fail to see is how she resisted her husband's attempt to convert her and prefers a life of separation from him, while enduring constant humiliation and pain from her family. It is only when she herself is convinced of the worldview upheld by Christianity does she decide to convert and this surprises even her husband. Thus, it is a very conscious and rational reason as is Baby Kamble's decision to convert to Buddhism based on her understanding of Ambedkarite ideology.

Lakshmibai's son wanted to write his father's biography and hence needed his mother to describe his father as she remembered her. So Lakshmibai starts writing about her husband, but the act soon becomes a way for her to talk about her life as well. Again, people have criticised her by saying that if she were to write about her life exclusively still she wouldn't have been able to write any differently for she had merged her identity with her husband. Sadly, these people only read superficially and are largely misled by the title *I Follow After*. Lakshmibai's autobiography, though paints a positive image of her husband, yet it largely talks of her independent decision making, her social work and her life after his death as well. Staying within the framework of her milieu, Lakshmibai chooses a language with humorous undertones and speaks what is there on her mind. Babytai, though very outspoken in her narrative, has to hide her writings from her husband because her husband is well. 'just like any other husband!'

Kamble's autobiography shows a greater awareness of the socio-political movements of her age than Tilak's and projects a self that is intrinsically linked with the community. Lakshmibai Tilak's work is more personal and projects a self that desires to change and does change due to her willingness and assertion. Both the works are remarkable in their projection of a strong self, and it will be wrong trying to judge who does a better job while forgetting the different social milieu these two women came from. Both are imperfect and boldly acknowledge this fact whiling commenting on the imperfections of others. But they inspire in their own unique way. Hence, we need to celebrate their differences and appreciate the lessons they give.

Works Cited

Bamberg, Michael (2011). "Who am I? Narration and its contribution to self and identity." Theory & Psychology 21.1, 3–24.

"The Autobiographical Process." R. Folkenflik (ed.). The Culture of Autobiography: Constructions of Self-Representations. Stanford: Stanford UP, 28–56.Burke, Peter (2011).

"Rethinking narrative identity." M. Klepper & C. Holler (eds.). Rethinking Narrative Identity. Persona and Perspective. Amsterdam: John Benjamins, 1–31.Kohli, Martin (1981).

On Autobiography. Minneapolis: U of Minnesota P.Lionett, Françoise (1991).

Sharmila Rege, Writing Caste/Writing Gender: Dalit Women's Testimonies, New Delhi: Zubaan, 2006.

S Punalekar, 'The sociology of Dalit autobiography', in Social Transformation in India: Essays in Honour of Professor I.P. Desai, edited by. G. Shah, Jaipur: Rawat Publishers, 1993, pp. 371–96.

Conditions and Limits of Autobiography, Autobiography: Essays Theoretical and critical Ed. James Olney, Princeton university press, 1980.

Susie Tharu and K. Lalita, eds., *Women Writing in India: 600 B.C to the Present. Volume 1: 600 B.C to the Early Twentieth Century.* New York: Feminist Press, 1991. *Volume 2: The Twentieth Century.* Feminist Press, 1993.

Bio-Note:

Mrs. Deepti Mujumdar is currently the Head of the Department of English at Chikitsak Samuha's Patkar-Varde College (Autonomous), Mumbai. She has teaching experience of 20 years at UG and 12 years at the PG level. She has published 17 research articles in various Peer-reviewed National and International journals and has co-authored a book titled "An anthology of Indian Poetry". Her core area of research is feminism and other areas of specialisation are post-colonialism and gender studies. Mrs. Deepti Mujumdar is a blogger and is currently focusing on "Revisiting Indian Mythology", wherein she takes a look at the stories through a feminist lens. These blogs have been appreciated internationally, with over 5000 views in four months. She is also a winner of four National Awards for education and social work.

CHAPTER IV

BAPSI SIDHWA'S THE PAKISTANI BRIDE: A FEMINIST STUDY

Devika

Ph. D. Research Scholar

Central University of Haryana.

ABSTRACT

The Pakistani Bride, written by Bapsi Sidhwa, a well-known Pakistani novelist, is a notable work in the field of feminism. Sidhwa's goal in the work is to show the silent parts of domestic abuse in marriage, in which women play a minor role. The protagonist, having firsthand knowledge of the challenges that women confront in patriarchal society, refutes the sacrosanct notion of marriage, in which women are ensnared by various social regulations created by male representatives of society. This study makes an attempt to present all of the social conventions and techniques that males use to subjugate women through the ostensibly sacred institution of marriage. Sidhwa emphasised that the marital system is designed to suit the needs of men, whether they are physical or sexual. Marriage is not pre-planned in heaven, but it is in a patriarchal society that restricts women's independence.

Mary Wollstonecraft initially addressed the feminist themes of gender disparity and inequality in her book *A Vindication of the Rights of Women* (1792). Virginia Woolf explored and posed comparable themes in her novel *A Room Of One's Own* (1929). With the publication of Simone de Beauvoir's *The Second Sex*, the feminist wave grew even stronger (1949). In her book *Sexual Politics* (1970), Kate Millet emphasised the biological nature of sex and the social construct of gender. Toril Moi's *Sexual/Textual Politics* (1985) and Sandra Gilbert and Susan Gubar's *The Madwoman in the Attic: The Woman Write*r and the Nineteenth-

Century Literary Imagination made significant contributions in this regard (1979).

Feminism developed into a specialised and systematic field of study. The lines between phallocentric and gynocriticism were drawn. Phallocentric principles predicated on 'woman' presented in literature from the perspective of male authors. The feminist era is thought to have ended in the 1970s, while the post-feminist era began in the 1980s. Since ancient times, women's connection to nature has been undeniable. Ecofeminism arose from the bond between women and the environment. *Surfacing* by Margaret Atwood is an example of this style of specialism. For feminine works, the French used the term "ecriture feminism."

Gynocriticism is "a French term that refers to criticism primarily obsessed with the inspiration, creation, and analysis of writing by women on women," according to N.Krishnaswami. In the paper, 'Feminist Criticism in the Wilderness' Showalter manifests that, "the first task of gynocritic criticism must be to plot the precise cultural locus of female literary identity and to describe the forces that intersect an individual woman writer's cultural field." Thus a gynocritical reading of *The Pakistani Bride* would be 'palimpsest'(1) in nature. Patrocinio P. Schweickart says, "today, the dominant mode of feminist criticism is 'gynocritics', the study of woman as writer, of the 'history, styles, themes, genres, and structures of writing by women ; the psychodynamics of female creativity...".

Women are prisoners and victims in Islamic society's sex-role paradigms, according to a gynocritical reading of *The Pakistani Bride*. Feelings of weakness and subjection in women set the path for insurrection. An isolated hill village inhabited by Pakistani Islamic tribes' is the setting at the beginning and end of the tale. Here, tribal laws and punishments are in effect. Cut off from modern culture, the style of life, conduct, and thought has become archaic. The patriarchal or phallogocentric culture.

The novel begins with a delicate depiction of women's subordination and epitomises the man (even as a toddler) as the master of sexual and physical strength. Resham Khan, unable to repay the loan, gives Qasim's father his daughter, Afshan. Afshan is considered like a commodity rather than a person. Qasim's father considers marrying Afshan because he only has one wife, but due to a "twinge of paternal conscience" he marries Afshan to Qasim, who is only ten years old. She finds out she was married to a boy on her wedding day and asks, ``Are you my husband?" She questioned incredulously, and Afshan couldn't decide whether to laugh or cry. She accepts her fate, and her relationship with Qasim is more like that of a mother than that of a spouse. Marriages are decided by the menfolk in this country, and women have no voice in the matter. As if everything were predestined, they simply accept and harmonise with the situation.

Female marginalisation is a common occurrence in Pakistani society, as men seek to keep their women hidden from men's gaze. Qasim dismisses Nikka ,``don't ask a hill-man anything about his womenfolk , understand? I would slit your throat ...."(Sidhwa,36).Strangely all vulgar and disgraceful terms are connected to one's mother and sister,``... incestuous lover of your mother , lover of your sister , son of a whore ..."(Sidhwa,42).

In the ambience of the city of Lahore watching Zaitoon Miriam says,"she'll (Zaitoon) be safe only at her mother-in-law's ....a girl is never too young to marry"(Sidhwa,53). Thus , the moment a girl reaches adolescence, marriage in the eyes of the society, is the *summum bonum* of a woman's life as Semone de Beauvoir writes in *The Second Sex* ,``marriage is the destiny traditionally offered to women by society"(Beauvoir,445). A woman is supposed to be the man's possession. The development of a woman's personality is discouraged. She is reminded that she is unique in comparison to men. After her menstruation, Miriam instructs Zaitoon after her menstruation , "you are now a woman.Don't play with boys and don't allow any man to touch you.This is why I wear a burkha..."(Sidhwa, 55). A woman is not even permitted to enter a mosque to offer prayers under Islamic practice, ``the men .... Gathered in mosques ... the women ... prayed silently for the duration of the call carrying on with whatever they were doing, stirring the pot in the kitchen or breast feeding the baby"(Sidhwa,58).

Qasim observes a horrific scene while visiting a brothel. A pimp forced a prostitute to perform contortions in order to perform dancing routines. Unfortunately, the fatigued and exhausted woman was unable to express her sexuality ,``the woman continued her monotonous , mechanical spasms ,one hip jerking higher , jaws dribbling spittle ....A man obscenely shaking his body called to her as to a monkey (Sidhwa , 65).In reality, this advice is intended to extort money from her rather than to protect her honour. Chapter 10 opens up with the statement ,``marriages were the high points in the life of the women``(Sidhwa , 88). The zenana, or special quarters for women, are found in Islamic residences and allow them to move freely without veils or burka. Qasim delivers his promise to Misri Khan, a companion from his native land, at a wedding. He arranges her wedding without even asking Zaitoon's opinion. Miriam was sensitive to realise it , she quips ,``how can a girl , brought up in Lahore , educated – how can she be happy in the mountains? Tribal ways are different, you don't know how changed you are ....They are savages . Brutish , uncouth , and ignorant ! She will be miserable among them"(Sidhwa, 93).

Despite constant warnings from Miriam about Zaitoon's unhappy future Qasim goes ahead with his decision . Even Zaitoon complies without putting up a question . Zaitoon respected her father's decision and ,``a blind excitement surged through her "(Sidhwa, 96).On Miriam's advice ,``tell your father you don't want to marry a tribal .We'll help you"(Sidhwa , 98). Zaitoon expresses her inability to cross her father . Carol , the American wife of Farukh wrote to her friend Pam,``I love Lahore.... I don't feel programmed ! The people are kind and hospitable. I'm having a ball" (Sidhwa, 108). But this was a veneer . Farukh often accused Carol of , ``displaying your honky-tonk pedigree ! You laugh too loudly. You touch men ....Don't you know if you only look a man in the eye it means he can have you?" Farukh's enmity bordered on insanity. He was always curious about her daily routine while he wasn't around. Farukh's replies reveal a woman's fragility in the absence of a male presence to shield or defend her. In his absence, he suspected other men of taking advantage of Carol's westernised lifestyle..A "... male is fortunate in having opportunities for releasing his impulse to domination and the fury of his frustrated ego , because he always has a wife whom he can treat as an inferior" (John Stuart, 40).

Another officer, Mushtaq, was drawn to Carol. The three tribesmen burst out laughing and making wicked catcalls as they saw them in a compromising situation. Carol is embarrassed by the male attention.``The obscene stare stripped her of her identity.She was , a female monkey , a gender opposed to that of the man – charmless , faceless , and exploitable "(Sidhwa , 120). Carol is upset by Farukh's brash behaviour. Carol is impressed by Zaitoon's hesitancy while probing him about marriage at the officer's mess. Farukh's unkind remark ,``our women , particularly the young girls , are modest , you know "(Sidhwa, 133). This remark not only offends her, but it also alienates her; the phrase "our women" clearly excludes non-Pakistanis, including Carol in this case. As Qasim reveals about Zaitoon's separation from her true parents during the division days, Zaitoon begins to cry. Carol forms a female bond with Zaitoon and expresses her sisterly compassion for her by offering her a shawl and food.

Mushtaq, who was acquainted with tribal culture, knew that a woman was a symbol of status, the symbol of a man's honour, and the focal point of his job as a provider for tribals. A woman is only viewed in the context of a male. As Gilbert and Gubar observe in The Madwoman in the Attic, she has no independent existence. To be selfless is not only admirable but also to be dead. Zaitoon notices the tribal people's 'savagery and harshness' instinctively. Her background and education in Lahore makes her revolt and she tells Qasim , ``that jawan at the camp , Abba , I think he likes me. I will die rather than live here"(Sidhwa, 157). Zaitoon becomes selfless' as a result of Qasim's harsh scolding. She is willing to marry Sakhi and live with him. After marriage a girl cannot maintain her individuality , ``their is a unanimous agreement that getting a husband – or in some cases a 'protector' is for her the most important of undertakings....She will free herself, from the parental home, from her mother's hold; she will open up her future not by active conquest but by delivering herself up, passive and docile into the hands of a new master"(Beauvoir, 352). Zaitoon's tantrums and reclusive behaviour are unwelcome in the family. Yunus Khan warns Sakhi, ``she requires a man to control her"(Sidhwa, 170). Wife battering is accepted , Sakhi not only beats Zaitoon ,``you are my woman! I'll teach you to obey me!"(Sidhwa , 172-173) but also Hamida, his mother . Following this occurrence, Zaitoon became sure that she would not live long.

The existence of a woman is determined by the service she can provide to a man.Marriage is the beginning of a pitiful period of women's marginalisation. A woman is portrayed as a tool for a man to have sexual delights..``Slowly Carol had begun to realise that even among her friends , where the wives did not wear burqas or live in special , women's quarters , the general separation of sexes bred an atmosphere of sensuality . The people seemed to absorb it from the air they breathed "(Sidhwa , 112). Though Carol came from a highly liberated background, she also understood that ,``men here expected subtlety from women" (Sidhwa, 112).

During Carol's affair with Mushtaq , she never realises that ,``he was having a fling , merely killing time"(Sidhwa ,179).But later she realised that his attraction towards her was due to,``long separation from his family , his need for a woman in the loneliness of his remote posting"(Sidhwa, 180). Mushtaq's attitude does not change even after Carol slaps him. For Mushtaq , Carol was only a sex object . He no longer found her sexually provocative .``... in every age , woman has been seen primarily as mother , wife, mistress and as sex object in their roles in relationship to man"(Ferguson 4-5).

In the hills Zaitoon did not have the freedom of moving around unwatched . Sakhi furiously beat her up abusing her as, ``you dirty , black little bitch , waving at those pigs ..."(Sidhwa , 185 ). Zaitoon had to beg for mercy and on that particular night Zaitoon resolves of running away as,`` she knew that in-flight lay her only hope of survival. She waited two days , giving herself a chance to heal"(Sidhwa, 186). There is a limit to how much pressure and sublimation can be applied to something. Zaitoon's life takes a U-turn at this point, as she bravely flees to a place that is hostile to her. Rather than showing care for the bereft lonely woman, society fuels the fire. In culture, a woman is revered only if she has a husband at her side, yet the runaway cartoon antagonises her spouse and is raped in another town while she is alone. She was cornered like a 'flustered hen' and a man whispers to her ,``you can't escape us , my dove "(Sidhwa , 214). Even at this point Zaitoon does not give up she continues her chase in search of her promised land. After her own rape at Lahore, "abandoned and helpless, she had been living on that charity of her rapists ...and on theft"(Sidhwa, 231).

Meanwhile Carol in her room with Farukh feels, "women the world over , through the ages , asked to be murdered , raped , exploited , enslaved , to get impregnated , beaten-up , bullied and disinherited . It was an immutable law of nature. What had the tribal girl done to deserve such grotesque retribution?"(Sidhwa, 226)Carol recalled her Pakistani female acquaintances who appeared to be westernised but appeared melancholy, probably due to Islamic countries' rigid narrow-mindedness regarding women. Zaitoon was miraculously saved, and the tribal men are overjoyed at the news of her death. ``Misri Khan's massive shoulders straightened . He thrust his chest forward and his head rose high . It was as if a breeze had cleared the poisonous air suffocating them and had wafted an intolerable burden from their shoulders."(Sidhwa , 244).

Sidhwa eloquently demonstrates that a guy in society is not only physically strong but also a skilled manipulator in the power game through the storey of Zaitoon. Despite the fact that a woman is neither physically stronger nor adept at manipulating the power game, Zaitoon's khudi (will strength) may be a sign of societal transformation.

I would like to quote a verse by Iqbal on Khudi

Khudi ko kar buland itna - Heighten your khudi touch majesty
Ke har takdeer say pahaylay- That before every turn of fate
Khuda benday say poochy - God himself asks the man
Buta teri raza kya hai? - Tell me what you wish?

Works Cited

1. Sidhwa, Bapsi. *The Pakistani Bride*. New Delhi: Penguin, 1990
2. Beauvoir, Simone de. *The Second Sex* .Harmondsworth:Penguin,1983.
3. Mill, John Stuart .``The Subjection of Women" .*Women's Liberation and Literature* ,ed. Elaine Showalter . New York:Harcourt Brace , 1971.
4. Fergusson, MaryAnn. *Images of Women in Literature* . Houghton Mifflin: Co-Boston, 1973.

CHAPTER V

A DECONSTRUCTIVE READING OF MASCULINITY IN THE KOREAN DRAMA IT'S OKAY TO NOT BE OKAY

Elsa Sebastian

ABSTRACT

Masculinity is socially constructed; although studies indicate that it is biologically influenced, the researcher believes that it is indeed a mixture of both. Among the different types of masculinity present, the researcher will be focusing on the hegemonic masculinity and soft masculinity also called Pan-East Asian soft masculinity with reference to the Korean Drama "It's okay to not be okay". In the Korean drama "It's okay to not be okay," we see that the male characters are portrayed as soft-hearted, sensitive, which contrasts the ideal type of masculinity, i.e., being solid and rigid. The researcher's approach will be to engage a deconstructive reading of hegemonic masculinity and to focus on soft masculinity in the drama "It's okay to not be okay." Based on the views of masculinity about the west by Michael S. Kimmel, the researcher will be discussing the Pan-East Asian masculinities and how they have taken the world aback.

Keywords: Masculinity, Pan-East Soft Masculinity, Michael S. Kimmel and Hegemonic Masculinity.

A deconstructive reading of masculinity in the Korean Drama "It's okay to not be okay"

Masculinity is a set of attributes and traits that are seen in men and boys, they are also a set of social practices and cultural representations that have been practised over the years. Researches show that they are genetically gained, but theories have it that it is socially influenced too. The involvement of both, i.e., genetic and social, is still a topic to debate. Studies on masculinities came into the limelight in the 1980s and early 1990s. Masculinity is defined as a configuration of organized practices about the structures of gender identities and relations (Connell, 1987). Studies on masculinity were done in the 1980s to understand a man's power over a woman. These studies were used to explain a man's health behaviours and the use of violence. Back in the fifties, men were displayed as someone who is supposed to be strong and that he is superior, there are several advertisements that proved this theory. One of them was by Alcoa Aluminum regarding a ketchup bottle. Their tagline read - "You mean a woman can open it? Easily – without a knife blade, a bottle opener, or even a husband!" Seriously?". A woman was expected to be weak and vulnerable, whereas a man to be strong, courageous and aggressive.

Society has always played a significant role in developing masculinity, and toxic masculinity is caused because of them. Chimamanda Ngozi Adichie, an award-winning author, has portrayed masculinity concerning society; she states that "By far the worst thing we do to males — by making them feel they have to be hard — is that we leave them with very fragile egos." Right from childhood, boys are expected to display certain behaviours such as being tough and hard, which pent up frustration and egos as they grow up, and they either vent it out on the opposite sex or the same sex. This behavior is then passed on genetically. There's an Indian short film named #StartWithTheBoys by Vinil Mathew, and that film is the epitome of our society. There's a line that a mother tells her son, "Are you a girl? Boys don't cry," (0.10 – 0.13) and that's exactly what society has been teaching men so far. The message that this film gives out is that "It's time we teach them not to make girls cry" instead of teaching the boys not to cry. Masculinity is also defined by one's job, identity, and personality as well. Jobs like being a nurse, caregiver, a nanny can question one's masculinity. In the series F.R.I.E.N.D.S., Ross is uncomfortable when Rachel hires a male nanny because he not comfortable with the idea of a man being a nanny, and Chandler goes ahead and makes a joke out of it "You've got a man whose is a nanny, you've got a manny?" (20.50 –

20.51, Season 9, Episode 6). Even though it was meant to be funny but that's rather a reality. A job that requires constant care and affection is seen as a job for a woman, in this episode as well, we can see that Ross's masculinity is being threatened. Men take up such jobs significantly less because of such criticism. Even colors are characterized into feminine and masculine. Masculinity is defined by everything except for being kind, humane and sensitive.

According to Connell, masculinities have a higher ranking than feminists in the gender hierarchy of modern western society. The hierarchy goes like this - hegemonic masculinity (which is the traditional practice of masculinity), complicit masculinity, and the last is subordinated masculinity. Hegemonic masculinity practices men's dominant position in society, and this type of masculinity explains why and how men hold more power than women in society. In this trait, men are considered the dominating gender, and every other group is deemed feminine. It's a traditional type of masculinity that is being practised over the years. This type of masculinity is often seen in old cowboy movies and novels as well. Hegemonic masculinity is a principal type of masculinity or the cultural ideal of manliness, chiefly reflective of a white heterosexual who is widely middle-class male (Kimmel 2006). E.g., In the west, macho men or machismo masculinity is mainly associated with men being stronger, muscular, independent. It must indulge in leadership and courageous skills. Complicit masculinity or marginalized masculinity is a process of becoming a hegemonic man and not challenging them. In this trait, they lack a few attributes of a hegemonic man, like being a disabled or non-white man. The last type of masculinity is subordinated masculinity; in this type, we see that they lack most of the attributes that make a hegemonic man.

Pan-East Asian masculinity is a complete contrast to Michael S. Kimmel's theory of masculinity about the west. According to Kimmel, American masculinity is consistently aggressive and provocative, but in East Asia, masculinity displayed is mostly hegemonic or soft masculinity. In East Asia, hegemonic masculinity is identified in three forms: patriarchal authoritarian masculinity, seonbi, and violent masculinity. Firstly, patriarchal authoritarian masculinity is the ability to provide and run for the family, just like traditional masculinity. Secondly, seonbi is traditional Confucian masculinity that emphasizes the separation of domestic space and labour. Finally, violent masculinity stems from compulsory military service for men, socializing men to be more damaging than a woman (Leung, 2012).

Pan-East Asian Soft Masculinity was influenced by Confucian tradition and they have their roots connected to seonbi personality as well, which is being too sensitive, polite, and kind. Confucianism is a way of life circulated by Confucius in the 6th - 5th century B.C.E. and is followed by the Chinese people for more than two millennials now. It has advanced over time and is still the component of living, the source of values, and the social code of the Chinese. This tradition doesn't belong to any particular religion, and this practice has lastingly marked the patterns of government, society, education, and families of Korea, Japan and Vietnam.

Seonbi is a symbolic word for a learned man who does not desire wealth but desires a righteous life. They believed that a man should fulfil his moral duty towards society first and live an honest life to obtain perfection of character. This type of personality usually has a tender exterior and a solid inner will. Pan-East Asian soft masculinity was first seen in Japanese anime series, and then it was slowly circulated and started gaining attention. They were tagged feminine because the male characters lacked facial hair and displayed weak, vulnerable and emotional sides i.e. their traits were in contrast to Connell's traits of masculinity which is - physical strength, muscular body, and facial hair. The biggest boy band in the world right now is B.T.S., a classic example of Pan-East Asian soft masculinity. They were criticized for their looks, their behaviour, and for applying makeup, and were tagged feminine. But they have nearly replaced Beatles in terms of fan base and music. There have been controversies where western and East Asian artists were compared. It's no joke when one says that the world is/was/

and will be ruled by the westerners. Americans are always considered the epitome of our society. In terms of fashion, music, and many more, they have been ruling the world but times are changing now and we can expect this to change.

Soft masculinity is not just seen in Korean men but also in Chinese and Japanese men as well. They say Europeans think first but Americans act first, and therefore Americans are seen as people who are reckless, rough and daring. Because of such an approach people have shifted their ideal men from being "All American Guy" to "Asian Men." In the news article "Why Asian Guys Are on a roll" by Newsweek, the publicist divorced her "All American Guy" and knew what she doesn't want in a man. So, she came up with a list of qualities that she wanted in a man: intelligent, genuine, respectful... adding up to all the qualities, and realized that she is looking for an Asian man, a group she'd never considered romantically before. That's how Asian Men have taken a toll on society.

In this research paper, the researcher focuses on how the protagonist displays traits of soft masculinity in the Korean drama "It's okay to not be okay." This drama comes under the romance genre and is written by Jo Yong and directed by Park Shin-woo. Just like the title suggests, the drama pours light on mental health stigma and how society sees them with a different eye. Jo Yong the scriptwriter of the drama was inspired by a man who had a personality disorder, which influenced her in writing the script of "It's okay to not be okay." Starring Kim Soo-Hyun, Seo Yea-Ji, Oh Jung-Se, and Park Gyu-young, the series follows a selfless psych ward caregiver and an antisocial children's book writer. This series was critically acclaimed in South Korea as well as in many other countries. The series has a total number of 16 episodes and was broadcast from June 2020 to August 2020. It was the most popular show on Netflix in the romance genre in South Korea. The New York Times named "It's Okay to Not Be Okay" as one of "The Best International Shows of 2020".

The researcher will focus on Kim Soo-Hyun's character, Moon Gang-tae, a mere caregiver of a psych ward who is selfless and always takes care of his brother who is autistic. In a world where the hero is supposed to be powerful, strong, angry, courageous, dominating, etc., our character is quite the opposite. "It's okay to not be okay" is a series revolving around mental health and describes that "it's okay" to "not feel okay." People live under the impression that we always have to feel positive and that our energy can affect others, but that's not true, and that's called "toxic positivity." (This term is coined by Dr. Jaime Zuckerman, a licensed clinical psychologist, and trained cognitive behaviour therapist) The world has changed in the past decade; we've seen psychologists and psychiatrists trying to normalize mental health. Despite such efforts, even today, it's still considered taboo in various parts of the world one of them being South Korea. South Korea's values revolve around Buddhism, and these values highlight modesty and family in the first place, and personal concerns are not the top priority of the family unit. "It's okay to not be okay" can be considered as a series that's breaking this taboo. It exclusively focuses on people suffering from mental disorders and how people around them are affected too. The title of every episode is related to Moon-young's book, and the director has done a great job by linking each of the stories.

The series revolves around two brothers – Moon Gang- tae and Moon Sang-tae. Sang- tae being the older brother is born autistic and Moon Gang-tae is a caregiver of the psych ward. Sang-tae is a very protective older brother; even though he is autistic, he tries to behave like an older brother when needed. In this drama, one can see Sang-tae's efforts of trying to be normal like others. At first, he is bothered by Ko Moon-young when she is trying to get close to Gang-tae. But slowly, he accepts Ko Moon-young into their lives, and try to stay as a family.

The series starts with narration from Moon-young's book. Ko Moon-young is a popular children's book author who suffers from an antisocial personality disorder. She often follows the gothic style in her illustrations, and we can see these gothic elements in the drama as well. Moon Sang-tae, the older brother, is a fan of Ko Moon-young. She is his favourite author. There's a scene where

Gang-tae calls his brother to let him know that his favourite author is visiting the hospital he works at and that he will try to get her autograph. Towards the end of the call, he asks his brother, "whom do you love more? Ko Moon-young or me," and Sang-tae just hangs up (It's okay to not be okay, 25.25 – 25.27). In this series, two of the main actors, i.e., Moon Sang-tae and Ko Moon-young suffer from trauma because of their dark past and, Gang-tae is the one taking care of both of them.

Gang-tae and Sang-tae spend most of their life running away because of their past; Sang-tae suffers from traumatic episodes every once in a while, so they are always on the run. Each time they move, they have to start from scratch, and wherever they move, Gang-tae works as a caregiver at the nearest psychiatric hospital. While he is working at one, there's an unfortunate incident in the hospital, and Gang-tae takes the fall for the venture, and he leaves without fighting back. In this scene, we analyze Gang-tae as a guy who endures everything and never fights back which is opposite to what we see in a hegemonic man. His character contrasts Ko Moon-young, who has a loud personality and is rude and blunt and never takes 'no' for an answer.

The first supporting character is Jo Jae-soo, Moon Gang-tae's best friend, who follows him and Sang-tae whenever they move. A naïve guy who owns a restaurant and adores and loves Gang-tae like an older brother. Second is Nam Ju-ri, a nurse and a co-worker of Gang-tae at OK Psychiatric Hospital. She has an unrequited crush on Gang-tae and is seen as a shy and jealous girl. She dislikes anyone close to her love interest. The third character is Gang-tae and Sang-tae's mother, who was murdered under mysterious circumstances a decade ago. Their mother plays a significant role in Gang-tae's personality. Because he was taught to endure everything and be there for his brother. There's a scene where Gang-tae wins the red belt in his taekwondo class, but rather than acknowledging her youngest son; she beats him up because he failed to protect his older brother, whom some thugs beat up. He vents his anger and says that "My job isn't to protect my brother... I don't belong to my brother, I belong to myself...Moon Gang-tae belongs to Moon Gang-tae!... I want my brother to die!" (Its okay to not be okay, 11.40 – 12.21) and runs off. Gang-tae grew up with a scar inside him, but when he realized that his mother indeed loved him, just that she never showed it to him, that grown man bursts out in tears for misunderstanding her all these years and ends up missing her and her warmth.

The fourth character is Do Hui-jae, the best-selling novelist and Ko Moon-young's mother. She plays a significant role in Ko Moon-young's personality. She used to abuse her daughter mentally and was obsessed with her and has been missing over a decade till Moon-young appears at OK Psychiatric Hospital. In this drama, one might think that Ko Moon- young loves her mother, but actually, she is terrified of her mother. The fifth supporting character is Lee Sang-in, the CEO of SangsangESang Publishing Company, who has been putting up Ko Moon-young's tantrums. He has been cleaning up Moon-young's mess with money until he goes bankrupt and realizes that money can't buy everything.

After the first encounter of Ko Moon-young and Moon Gang-tae, many unfortunate events follow them and with all of it going on, it's finally time to move again to someplace new. He considers Nam Ju-ri's opinion and thinks of moving back to where it all started, i.e., Seongjin City. Sang-tae and Moon-young both end up coming to the place where all of their problems started. After moving to Seongjin city, Gang-tae starts working as a caregiver in OK Psychiatric Hospital.

Gang-tae, Sang-tae, and Ko Moon-young relation go way back in the past, which is also Gang-tae's biggest nightmare. At the time, when Gang-tae gets mad at his mother and runs off his house after wishing his brother dead, Sang-tae follows him to the river of ice where they both start to play, forgetting their fight, and Ko Moon-young is sitting afar watching these boy's play. But soon there's a small mishap and Sang-tae is seen drowning and Gang-tae hesitates in helping his brother and lets him drown for a second. But soon, comes to his senses and pulls his brother out, and in this process, Gang-tae starts to drown instead. Sang-tae, terrified of this act, takes off without looking back, leaving Gang-tae to die. Ko Moon-young witnessed the entire situation and helped Gang-tae from drowning. And that little boy ends up falling in love with the young Moon-young who saved his life. This incident has been Gang-tae's worst nightmare; he was hoping that Sang-tae wouldn't remember it, but he was proven wrong. Ko Moon-young tries to consoles Gang-tae, but he realizes that he can't have both of them so he choses his brother and breaks up with Ko Moon-young.

In this series, the antagonist is Ko Moon Young's mother, i.e., Do Hui-jae. Moon-young's mother who was obsessed with her daughter and never let anyone come closer to her. She considered her daughter as her other self and this obsession led to her death. She kills Gang-tae and Sang-tae's mother, who was a maid at their place at the time. At the time of the murder, Do Hui-jae wore a butterfly brooch, and Sang-tae was the sole witness of his mother's murder and was terrified to confess because he believed that the butterfly brooch would chase him and kill him. Later, when Do Hui-jae's husband gets to know all of these incidents, he accidentally kills his wife. But Do Hui-jae somehow escapes death and came back as Park Haeng-ja and disguises herself as the head nurse of OK Psychiatric Hospital after getting plastic surgeries done. It is towards the end of the drama we realize the real antagonist is Moon-young's mother. This show breaks the stereotype structure of the series because the antagonist is a woman and a mother, and Park Shin-woo proved that even a woman could be a good villain. The whole drama seems to be breaking the stereotype.

Gang-tae is portrayed as opposite to hegemonic masculinity. We see that he is shown as someone who has equal emotional baggage, just as the female protagonist. And for a man to share his emotions is considered a sign of weakness. In the series "It's okay to not be okay," we see that Gang-tae is sensitive, kind, emotional, and enduring and makes every woman go head over heels for him. The softness of Pan-East Asian masculinity also lies in its sensitive and caring attitude towards women. We see this softness in Gang-tae, too; there's a scene where Moon-young tells Gang-tae that "I can see that you want to be loved" (Its okay to not be okay, 19.17-19.18). In hegemonic masculinity, we don't expect the man to share his vulnerable side with the opposite sex; they always hide their emotions. It's not something Gang-tae is ashamed to admit too. He admits that it feels nice and says that "I've never had someone look after me when I was sick." (It's okay to not be okay, 19.30 – 19.32)

The psychologist Robert Brannon has identified four components of the traditional male sex rules that suggest how a man is supposed to behave – The first rule is "no sissy stuff," which means a stigma is attached to any behaviour which appears as feminine. The second rule is that "be a big wheel," meaning success and status play a vital role in masculinity and that a man craves admiration. The third rule is that a man must "be a sturdy oak," which means he must be tough, confident, and self-reliant so that others can rely on him. The last and final rule is that men should "give'em hell," which evinces an aura of aggression, violence, and daring. (David & Brannon, 1976, p. 12). If we compare these rules to Gang-tae's personality, he doesn't inherit any of these traits, he is emotional, tough, and, craves love and attention and exhibits no violence.

Gang-tae is not only is a brother to Sang-tae, but he exhibits motherly qualities as well. Autism is a disorder where the person is stuck in a child's mind therefore, people who are born with autism need constant care and affection. When Gang-tae resents his mother for not loving him enough and always putting his brother first, Nam Ju-ri's mother tells Gang-tae that "You have been raising your brother, I am pretty sure you know how she must have felt," and he bursts into tears. She adds by saying, "Adults can't always be right. We make mistakes until the day we die" (It's okay to not be okay, 46.25 – 46.30). After that, he goes back to his brother sobbing like a baby hugging his brother because he misses his mother and her warmth, so he hugged his brother and cried it out. Here we see how sensitive and emotional Gang-tae is – a guy who lacks his mother's warmth, a guy who is hugging his brother and venting, and lastly, a guy who realizes how difficult it is to be a mother. He displays all the emotions a woman feels. When he realized that she always loved him, it's just that he never gave her a chance to show it to him; he regrets resenting her all these years. Through this scene, we can identify Gang-tae as an emotional and vulnerable guy despite being the hero.

When we compare hegemonic masculinity to soft masculinity, hugging and other close proximity touches in hegemonic masculinity have their limitations, especially when it's from man to man. In this series, the male characters embrace their feminine side. Whereas in American dramas or movies, we'll notice that the male characters are portrayed as macho and as someone who can never be defeated, making them look unreal, just like in the old cowboy movies. They exhibit masculine traits that rely on the action and lack demonstrated feelings and an attitude of dominance towards the woman. If we pick old cowboy movies, we'll notice that they didn't use many words but instead believed in action. But here in this series, we see that's not the case. Also, a moustache/beard is deemed to be a vital sign of masculinity. There's a scene when Lee Sang-in gets chewing gum stuck on his beard and had to shave it off, Nam Ju-ri's mother tells him that "You look so handsome without your moustache," which is odd when compared to a hegemonic man. Still, he seems happy and cherishes the compliment because he has an unrequited crush on Nam Ju-ri. When your crushes, mom compliments you, who would be pleased, so he asks Ju-ri for her opinion, "Ju-ri...Do you notice anything different...and Ju-ri replies to him saying...You looked better with a moustache. Why did you shave?" (It's okay to not be okay, 52.27 – 53.24).

Pan-East Asian masculinity is seen as 'harmless' for women because they always understand women and their feelings. Masculinity is genetically influenced, and in this series, we notice that Gang-tae was influenced by his mother as a child and then later by the woman he fell in love with. When we see Gang-tae crying like a child during his breakdowns and trying to get up after each breakdown, we empathize with him more than a man pretending to be strong. A hegemonic man mostly doesn't share his problems/ breakdown with his family because our society always portrayed him as a bread-winner of the family, who holds all the burden and should never cry.

Gang-tae's job in this drama is also controversial. Who knew that masculinities could be defined through professions as well? Gang-tae's profession also plays a significant role in his personality. He is sensitive and considerate of other people's feelings because of his job. He is loved by every patient and his colleagues wherever he goes. The amount of patience required for this job is immense, and we always see women taking up such jobs, but director Park Shin-woo is breaking that stereotype. Park Shin-woo is redefining jobs for men through this series.

The critical point of Korean masculinity is "disciplined, self-controlled, sublimating the sexual impulses and channeling them toward the nobler national good and highly militarized" (Tikhonov, 1029). In South Korea, men are obliged to serve the country and they possess not just physical but social characteristics too. During the three-kingdom war, Korea was influenced by Chinese war heroes. They practiced the traits of a Chinese war hero, i.e., "minimizing his sexual ties, always prepared to sacrifice himself and all of his family members to yi (ritual, propriety, etiquette), duty, fully concentrated on his battlefield endeavors" (Tikhonov, 1038). South Korea hasn't evolved much in terms of traditions and culture. They still put the country first and then family. Serving the country makes you stay disciplined and teaches you self-control. Despite the world demeaning East-Asians, they have paved their way to the global market. Though they are different from westerners and may seem fragile, they are indeed becoming the ideal type of every woman.

This research paper has focused on the deconstruction and restructuring of masculinity in the Korean drama "It's okay to not be okay." This research has attempted to examine the hegemonic masculinity of the west and soft masculinity from the east.

Pan-East soft masculinity is the type that is more desirable. They are the true examples of "beauty with brains," hence more desirable. If American masculinity is influenced by baseball, East Asian masculinity is influenced by their scholarly officials (seonbi). In the series as well, we see that Gang-tae and Ko Moon-young find comfort in each other. When they both realize they are broken from inside, they both embrace their pain together and comfort each other.

The softness of Pan-East Asian masculinity lies in a 'caring' attitude towards women. It is often considered 'harmless.' We expect the protagonist to be strong, not just physically but mentally, and someone who is unbeatable, but here it's quite the opposite; the main protagonist is sensitive, emotional, and doesn't exhibit signs of violence.

Gang-tae is portrayed as a character who wants to be loved and cared for. Gang-tae is the epitome of soft masculinity. He is not just sensitive and caring but also, because he has motherly qualities in him since he is taking care of his brother, which may seem feminine for an American or a westerner. According to Kimmel's theory on manhood, Americans believe that a man learns to be more disciplined and considerate of moral values by playing baseball. And in Korean masculinity, serving the country plays a major role in their personality and lifestyle. Zane Grey once said that "All boys love baseball. If they don't, they're not real boys." The roots of masculinity have ruined it for all. It should rather be "it's okay to cry, and that its okay to feel weak, it's okay if you cannot grow a moustache or a beard." Like in the series, we see Gang-tae breaking down does not make him feminine, but instead, it just assures Ko Moon-young that he is equally humane, he has emotions, he feels those emotions.

With this research, the researcher would conclude that adapting Pan-East soft masculinity is beneficial for both genders. It will be easy to communicate their emotions, and none of them will feel obligated to another. Also, women look for emotionally available men for them, so let us teach our men to be sensitive and emotional rather than pressurize them to be strong and cold.

Works Cited

Cambridge Dictionary https://dictionary.cambridge.org/dictionary/english/masculinity (Accessed on 20th May, 2021)

Brien, Jennifer. "STRESSED AND DEPRESSED: MENTAL HEALTH IN SOUTH KOREA," The Borgen Project https://borgenproject.org/stressed-and-depressed-mental-health-in-south-korea/ (Accessed on 24th May, 2021)

"It's okay to not be okay" created by Park Shin-woo, performance by Kim Soo-hyun, Seo Yea-ji, Oh Jung-se and Park Gyu-young, season 1, episode 1 to episode 11, Studio Dragon, 2020.

IPL "Four types of masculinity" https://www.ipl.org/essay/Four-Types-Of-Masculinity-FKMARC36JE86

Johnson, Sarah "It's okay to not be okay" Heart & Seoul, 2020 https://heart-n-seoul.com/2020/08/24/its-okay-to-not-be-okay/ (Accessed on 25th May, 2021)

Kimmel, Michael. *The History of Men.* United States of America "State University of New York Press."

Louie, Kam. *Popular Culture and Masculinity Ideals in East Asia, with Special Reference to China.* Association for Asian Studies, 2012 https://www.jstor.org/stable/23357427?seq=1 (Accessed on 25th May, 2021)

Mambrol, Nasrullah. "Masculinity/ Masculinities" Literary Theory and Criticism, 2017 https://literariness.org/2017/11/04/masculinity-masculinities/ (Accessed on 21st May, 2021)

Newsweek Staff, "Why Asian Guys Are On A Roll" Newsweek, 2020 https://www.newsweek.com/why-asian-guys-are-roll-162073 (Accessed on 22nd May, 2021)

Purple Clover. "13 Stunningly sexist ads from the fifties" https://purpleclover.littlethings.com/entertainment/694-sexist-ads/item/ketchup/ (Accessed on 17th June, 2021)

Salam, Maya. "What is toxic masculinity?" The New York Times, 2019

https://www.nytimes.com/2019/01/22/us/toxic-masculinity.html

Sawhney, Vasundhara. "It's okay to not be okay", Harvard Business Review, 2020

https://hbr.org/2020/11/its-okay-to-not-be-okay (Accessed on 24th May, 2021)

Song, Geng. "Changing masculinities in East Asian pop culture" East Asia Forum, 2016

https://www.eastasiaforum.org/2016/07/26/changing-masculinities-in-east-asian-pop-culture/ (Accessed on 22nd May, 2021)

"#StartWithTheBoys", created by Vinil Mathew, Vogue India, 2014.
https://www.youtube.com/watch?v=0Nj99epLFqg (Accessed on 15th June, 2021)

Steele, Megan. "Masculine" East Asia Gender, 2015

"The one with the male nanny", F.R.I.E.N.D.S. created by David Crane & Marta Kauffman, performance by Mathew Perry, season 9, episode 6, Bright/Crane/Kauffman Productions, 2002.

The Conversation, "Un-designing masculinities: K-pop and the new global man?", 2014

https://theconversation.com/un-designing-masculinities-k-pop-and-the-new-global-man-22335

Wikipedia, Masculinity

https://en.wikipedia.org/wiki/Masculinity (Accessed on 20th May, 2021)

Wikipedia, Seonbi

https://en.wikipedia.org/wiki/Seonbi (Accessed on 21st May, 2021)

Wikipedia, It's okay to not be okay.

https://en.wikipedia.org/wiki/It%27s_Okay_to_Not_Be_Okay#Cast (Accessed on 22nd May, 2021)

CHAPTER VI

STEREOTYPICAL PORTAL OF MUSLIM AS A TERRORIST AND MY NAME IS KHAN AS A COUNTER-NARRATIVE

Iram Abdul Qadar

ABSTRACT

This thesis argues that the Indian media and movies misrepresent or underrepresent Muslims as a terrorist and Islam as a violent religion which causes negative stereotypes and prejudices against them in society. They are being labelled as violent, barbaric and terrorists. The researcher tries to analyze different news article and movies with the help of cultivation theory and used the scapegoat approach to prove that Muslims has always been targeted. To counter this negative prejudice and change the negative perspective, the researcher tries to clear misconceptions with the help of the Qur'an and hadith. The researcher also analyses the scene from the movie *My Name Is Khan* to highlight the central idea of this paper. The struggle of the characters was examined, especially the analysis of Rizwan Khan's character because he represents Muslims in the movie. The aim of the researcher is to explore the problem and issue shown in the movie *My Name Is Khan*. The movie showcases the struggle of Rizwan Khan, a simple harmless man who is looked upon by the world outside as a miscreant owing to his Islamic connection and his audacious journey to convey a simple yet powerful message to the President, 'My name is Khan and I'm not a terrorist.

Keywords: Muslims, Islam, Stereotype, Terrorist, Prejudice, Media and Movie.

• • •

INTRODUCTION

Karan Johar is a well-known director of the Indian Bollywood industry. The movie that got him his second Filmfare award for the best director is *My Name Is Khan* a movie with a profound message of love. In the movie *My Name Is Khan*, the main focus is to deliver a strong message in an attempt to stop wickedness against Muslims; to eliminate Islamophobia and stereotypical behaviour towards Muslims and prejudice that unfortunately still prevails despite living in the 21st century. Karan Johar also disclosed the reason behind him making a film like *My Name Is Khan*. In a show *We the People* hosted by Barkha Dutt he explained, he was once in New York dining with six people who were well settled in New York from the Asian orientation. They were well-educated, affluent, well-travelled, had Oxford graduate degrees, were so-called liberal people but knew nothing about Islam and Muslims yet they were bold enough to talk nonsense about them. He says that he was so repulsed by their ideology and perception about Islam and Muslims that he walked off before an hour the dinner ended. He was equally disgusted by the fact that how can these educated people go against the entire community on the mere basis of information they get from the news and read in the New York Times? He thought that this was something that needs to be addressed. As a person who is a filmmaker had a platform that is impressionist. He decided to make a movie that talks about this issue, particularly about the stereotype and the prejudice the Muslims faces all over the world. The power that media has can either be misused to manipulate its audience or can be used to spread a positive message across the world.

In this article, the author tries to investigate the causes of prejudice towards Muslims in society. The main objective of this article is to educate the people and to acquaint them with the true teachings of Islam, to reduce prejudice and stereotype towards Islam and Muslims in society. The goal is to clear the misconception about Islam through the source of the Quran and Hadith.

ROLE OF MEDIA IN DEPICTING MUSLIMS IN SOCIETY

Mass Media have made a remarkable influence on society and culture by erasing the boundaries between them creating globalization. That enables people to understand diverse cultures and traditions worldwide. The main purpose of the media is to educate, entertain, and create awareness with regard to several important issues. Media plays an effective role in today's society from enhancing public awareness to accumulating views, information, and also the behaviour of the people towards certain issues. George Gerbner proposes the theory of cultivation in 1969 to demonstrate that repeated exposure to media cultivate the impression that the information transmitted by the media pertained to the real world, people's perceptions are constructed by media exposure, their thought, virtues and personalities are altered as well.

Although media is a leading influencer in today's world it cultivates both pessimistic and optimistic effects on the psyche, culture, sentiments and lifestyle of the mass audience. Matters relating to mendacious particulars, forged content has been rising. Users are being manipulated and cheated into believing anything that the media desires although what is being fed to the audience is erroneous and will misguide them. There are several instances where it has been observed that the media house is neglecting its actual role.

One of the major roles played by the mass media is representing Muslims and Islam in society. According to Sobolewskan, Maria, and Sundas Ali "Islam is misrepresented and portrayed as not a religion of peace but as a religion of terror and the root cause of the emergence of terrorism. After 9/11, 75% of media coverage in west and America was about Islam and almost 60 percent of the media content was negative" (qtd. in "Portrayal of Muslims in the Bollywood Movies", Academia.edu 97-98). Islam and Muslims are often misrepresented or underrepresented in media whether it is print media or electronic media. The stereotypical portrayal of Muslims in media has caused an increase in prejudice towards them. They are always been marginalized, disregarded and looked upon in society because media mostly represent them negatively as extremists, violent and terrorists. This prejudice further leads to scapegoating Muslims in society. Scapegoat is the theoretical approach of René Girard. Scapegoating mostly utilizes a stand-in for one's own disappointment so that one doesn't have to confront one's own shortcomings. The dominant group mostly scapegoats the minority group in society. In this case, the mass media is in the dominant state and the Muslims are in minority.

One of the examples of scapegoating by media was the gathering of the migrant workers near Bandra station in 2020. They were demanding passage back to home as they were jobless due to the pandemic and lockdown but the media represent it as a communal spin because they spotted Sunni Jama Masjid outside the station. "NewsNation asked why the venue of the gathering had to be a mosque, Republic TV too referred to the location in the same manner. ABP News also questioned the organi[z]ers of the crowd at the mosque." ("Bandra Migrant Workers' Gathering: Politicians, Media Channels Lend Communal Spin to Protesters Desperate to Return Home", Firstpost Exp 32 L 26-28). Another example is, Suresh Chavhanke who opens his show 'Bindaas Bol' by saying "In today's Bindaas Bol, I bring you a very serious issue and appeal to the Narendra Modi government that the Tablighi Jamaat be banned. If India's mosques are posing a threat to Indians, and human bombs carrying coronavirus are roaming around freely, wouldn't you call it 'corona jihad'? We should keenly monitor these jihadis and the jihadis should be strictly punished under the law" in Sudarshan News channel (qtd. in "Audit of Bigotry: How Indian Media Vilified Tablighi Jamaat over Coronavirus Outbreak.", Newslaundry Exp 27 L 21-25). The media had targeted and scapegoated Tablighi Jamaat for spreading the virus to hide the shortcoming of the government. Muslims tend to be negatively articulated to promote political agenda by some journalists in India. This can be one of the leading factors behind the upswing of Islamophobia and negative prejudices against Muslims.

This is how dangerous mass media can be when it comes to manipulating its user. Over the years, terror and detestation against Muslims and their religion have been soaring at an alarming rate, both nationally and internationally. This triggered an abrupt increase in hate crime; Muslims are being massacred brutally all around the world merely for existing. Recently, a Muslim family residing in Canada has been killed by a 20-year-old man. This clearly specifies the abhorrence and dread against Muslims have augmented to an extreme level leading to mass killing. Distrustful and gloom ridden facts are being penetrated in a child's brain against Muslims, they are brainwashed into believing Muslims as terrorists. Unfortunately, in today's society, Muslims have been degraded and brutalized thus meddling their image. Whenever anything sceptical or disastrous eventuates, the first to be accused is always a Muslim.

Movies being audiovisual mediums always succeed to grab people's attention; it paints a clear picture for the audience regarding the rigidity of the caste system, untouchability, dowry system, child labour and many more social issues. Unfortunately, movies also possess the power to manipulate public opinion towards Muslims. Indian cinema often frames Muslims as being suspicious, terrorist, aggressive, violent, dominant and anti-national. The negative characterization of Muslims in movies has been escalated since the Mumbai attack of 26/11. In most movies, Muslims are perpetually shown as terrorists, bombers and extremists. Many movies aim at degrading Muslims and exhibiting them in a bad light, for instance, Muslims were stereotypically depicted as lascivious 'nawabs' with sinful gaze, victimizing women, violent criminal, cruel, disloyal, and the atmosphere around the Muslim character is dark and gloomy. The uses of semiotics also fabricate negative visuals of Muslims on screen. "Not only superstars but Muslim superstars are also being used by Bollywood in portraying Muslims adversary for society" ("Bollywood's Anti Muslim Agenda.", The Legitimate Exp 30 L 28-30).

There is a movie 'Raees' in which Shahrukh khan played the lead role of a mobster, the mafia. This movie illustrates Islam and Muslims in a negative light as violent, criminals. The protagonist of the movie, a Muslim man, is involved in the illicit business of booze that proposed an unfavourable perspective of his religion as unethical which is against Islamic law. Such misrepresentations of Muslims in movies cause stereotypes, prejudice, disgrace and fallacy against them in society. In another movie, 'Fanna', Amir Khan played the role of a terrorist who was part of the named 'Independent Kashmir Federation' and was also involved in a bomb blast later on he was working on a dangerous mission to get hold of the trigger to a nuclear bomb which requires making the ammunition operational. Similarly, Saif Ali Khan also played the role of a terrorist in the movie named 'Kurbaan' where he deceive a Hindu lady to legitimately obtain a residence in the United States in order to plan a terrorist attack. These negative illustrations of Muslims publicize Islamophobia not only in India but also around the world.

ISLAM - THE ANSWER TO MEDIA STEREOTYPE

Islam is the second-largest religion in the world. The word Islam means 'peace' and a Muslim is a person who submits his will to Allah and is a follower of Islam. The first and foremost myth about Islam is that it was started in the 7th century by Prophet Mohammed (PBUH) however; on the contrary, it is the oldest religion of the world started with Adam (AS). Prophet Mohammed (PBUH) is the last prophet and messenger of Allah. Muslims believe that Quran is the holy book; the word of Allah and guides them towards the straight path. Every Muslim strictly abides by the rules and regulations mentioned in the Quran as well as follow the Sunnah of Prophet Mohammed (PBUH). The people, who go against the teaching of the Quran and Sunnah by treating others poorly, do corruption & mischief relating to all kinds of terror, bad things, and killing innocent falls under the category of the wrongdoers. And Allah says in Quran, "Allah does not like corruption." (The Clear Quran 2:205). Thus, the acts of terror, massacre, murder, and suicide are against the teachings of Islam. To understand any religion one must study its divine sources, for instance, the divine source to understand Islam is to study the holy Quran and hadith as defined in Merriam Webster dictionary: "a narrative record of the sayings or customs of Muhammad and his companions" ("Hadith''). Due to a lack of education and knowledge about Islam, the stereotype and negativity towards Islam and Muslims skyrocketed in society. Furthermore, media also plays an active role in misrepresenting or underrepresenting Muslims and Islam. But to contradict these inaccurate accusations upon Muslims, there is a hadith; Prophet Mohammed (PBUH) said that a Muslim is the one from whose hands and tongue no other being is hurt. A true Islamic society is where people always care for and protect each other.

Islam, under any circumstances, does not promote violence against any individual or group or even between countries. It gave the liberty to even go against parents and relatives for the sake of standing firm for justice. "O, believers! Stand firm for justice as witnesses for Allah even if it is against yourselves, your parents, or close relatives. Be they rich or poor, Allah is best to ensure their interests. So do not let your desires cause you to deviate 'from justice'. If you distort the testimony or refuse to give it, then 'know that' Allah is certainly All-Aware of what you do" (The Clear Quran 4:135).

Islam is strongly against the unjust and is a very peaceful religion. "O believers! Enter into Islam [peace] wholeheartedly and do not follow Satan's footsteps. Surely he is your sworn enemy." (The Clear Quran: 2:208). Qasim Rashid quoted "Contrary to what extremists and anti-Muslim personalities claim, the word "jihad" does not mean "to wage holy war," or "to kill the infidel," or "to commit terrorism." The word "jihad" means "to struggle." The prophet Muhammad (PBUH) said the best jihad was to speak words of truth "in front of a tyrannical leader" Muslim activist Linda Sarsour in his article "Opinion: 'Jihad' is not a dirty word" ("Opinion | 'Jihad' Is Not a Dirty Word.", Washington Post Exp 25 L 20-23). In Qur'an Allah says that "it will be as if they killed all of humanity; and whoever saves a life, it will be as if they saved all of humanity" (The Clear Quran 5:32). If this is the teaching of Islam then how one can say that Islam is a violent religion and it teaches violent activity? Islam itself is the answer to Islamophobia. The teachings of Islam are to be passed down to all the ignorant and uneducated people so as to help them get a clear picture of Islam as a peaceful and the greatest religion.

One of the major tasks assigned to Muslims is to spread the words of Allah to every corner of the world. In today's technology-driven world, mass media is a very powerful platform used by many great leaders and influencers to educate others. Unfortunately, pleasing everyone is not possible thus giving rise to haters who never leave any opportunity to negatively criticize and give hate speech against innocent scholars. Mass media, hence, can prove to be a very dangerous platform since it is also used to manipulate people.

Media and movies misrepresent Muslim men as being violent and aggressive towards women but in Qur'an, Allah said "O believers! It is not permissible for you to inherit women against their will... Treat them fairly" (The Clear Quran 4:19). Movies often depict a dominant Muslim father who forbids or rather denies his daughter, her right to marry a man she desires. In actuality, in Islam, a marriage cannot proceed without the consent of the woman who is to be married. Also, Islam gives equal rights to women as men "Women have rights similar to those of men equitably" (The Clear Quran 2:228). The portrayal of Muslim women in mass media or movies is always as submissive, a victim of domestic violence, silent women who are easily oppressed. Media creating stereotypes about Muslims does not do justice to the beauty of Islam and people around the world view Muslims as terrorists and bully them.

Terrorist is inhuman and cruel and acts upon their will but on the contrary, Muslims are the people who submit their will, desire to Allah. They strictly have to follow the commands of Allah but unfortunately, there are some Muslims who go against the command of Allah and do wrong to the people and to humanity.

"Islam is the best religion and Muslims are the worst followers" ("George Bernard Shaw Quote: Â€ œIslam Is the Best Religion and Muslims Are the Worst Followers.Â" Quotefancy). And because of some handful of people who do acts of terror, the entire community is blamed and targeted as terrorists. But the people who do such acts themselves are the enemy of Islam because they go against the peaceful and pure message of the Quran. Suicide is haram in Islam and killing innocent people is like killing the entire humanity. Islam rejects even a single act by which one can get hurt. To sum up, Islam is the religion of perfection and purity. Muslims being targeted for all the hate should become mature and set an example for everyone by practising Islam and conveying the core message of Islam.

MY NAME IS KHAN BREAKING THE STEREOTYPE

'My name is Khan' is a movie released globally striking everyone's eye around the world and the objective of delivering the optimistic message regarding Muslims and Islam was accomplished. The main focus of the movie is to highlight the major problems faced by Muslims in their day to day life and also deliver a strong message in an attempt to stop wickedness against Muslims; to eliminate Islamophobia and stereotypical behaviour towards Muslims and prejudice that unfortunately still prevails despite living in the 21st century.

'My Name is Khan' is an incredible movie released in 2010 and directed by Karan Johar, produced by Gauri Khan and Hiroo Yash Johar and penned by Shibani Bathija. Sharukh Khan and Kajol are cast in a lead roles. The film showcases the struggles of a simple harmless man who is looked upon by the world outside as a miscreant owing to his Islamic connection. Because of his Muslim identity, he faces discrimination, prejudice and violence.

The movie falls under the category of romantic drama but the major emphasis of the movie is, steering the audience towards the positive perspective about Muslims and Islam in society. In parallel with the love story of Rizwan and Mandira, a very pivotal issue has been projected in the movie i.e. Islamophobia. The life of this blissfully married couple crumbles after the 9/11 incident. They encounter hardness and obscurity, the heinous of them all is their son being inhumanely murdered because of his surname being Khan. Mandira downright blames Rizwan for her son, Sam's murder. She regrets marrying a Muslim man and claims, the switch in the surname from Rathod to Khan led to their son's demise. The drastic change in her attitude towards Rizwan was due to the gruesome terrorist attack of 9/11. This further pulls at their already strained relationship and Mandira challenges Rizwan to convey a message to the president who will reveal it to the entire State of America. This marks the start of his audacious journey to convey a simple yet powerful message to the President. "My name is Khan and I'm not a terrorist".

Throughout the journey, Rizwan Khan faces many difficulties and discrimination because of his Muslim identity. The very first scene of the movie sets the ground for the Muslims to demand respect and dignity in society. Officers suspect Rizwan's weird behaviour at the airport and hold him back for further investigation. They thoroughly examine everything in his possession for an hour's end which made him miss his flight. He blames officers for the delay in the meet up with the president as they have wasted his time with their investigation. Officers ask him about the meeting with the president to which he replies, he needs to convey a very important message to the president about him being Khan and he is not a terrorist. This particular scene highlights a very important issue faced by innocent Muslims after the 9/11 attack. After this attack, there was a sudden shift in the attitude of people towards the Muslim community. Muslims have been, since then, tagged as a terrorist and mistreated by society for a crime that they never committed.

There are several scenes where the effects of the attack are shown on society. It not only affect Muslim communities but also adversely affect others communities. This has been strongly projected in the movie as Gujarati man is attacked by haters just because his appearance is similar to that of a Muslim person. That ultimately creates prejudice towards Muslims because the Gujarati man believes that his suffering is all because of Muslims.

"All this is because of the lousy Muslims.

Six years ago, they blew up the World Trade Center

And today we bear the brunt of it.

They call for 'Jihad'

And we have to suffer the consequences...

I am going to put up a board out here. No Muslims allowed!" (*My Name Is Khan* 1:43-54-1:43:30).

Another such example is, the Sikhs has to forcefully change their identity as they are misunderstood to be Afghan Muslims. This clearly points out the prejudiced nature of society and stereotypes towards Muslims that they are terrorists. The movie tries to break this stereotype by emphasizing that the 9/11 attack affect Muslims too, they have to face prejudice and hate crime as well as their identity as innocent Muslims is lost. People look down upon them as they have done that heinous crime.

This crucial problem is showcased through the story of Rizwan Khan and his family, Mandira Khan and Sameer khan. All the characters individually suffer from the aftermath of 9/11. Because Mandira's last name is khan, the customers neglect her salon and because of that, she has to shut the salon and have to look for a new job. Someone at the university pulls Rizwan's sister in-law's hijab and says get out of his country. Muslim women have to forcefully remove their veil to protect themselves from the hate and the stereotypes, as well as men, have to shave their beards and change their names to hide their Muslim identity. Sameer has been bullied by his class fellows at school. They tease him, put photographs, sketches, and the posters of Osama bin laden in his locker. The teacher teaches in class that Islam is a violent religion and it encourages killing so all the students in the class pass look towards Sameer. This movie highlights the very fact that the world's perception changes towards Islam and Muslims after the 9/11 attack.

Sarah is Mandira's family friend and neighbour living with her husband and son. Their sons have also become good friends too, but after the 9/11 attack, her husband was sent to cover the war in Afghanistan where he dies and Sarah's son blame Sameer and particularly Muslims for his loss. As he says to Sameer

"You people are nobody's best friends.

All you people care is about your damn 'jihad' or whatever" (*My Name Is Khan* 1:19:26-1:19:24).

This showcases how immensely the attack affects the minds of the people, their relationships, their identity etc. Muslims have been, since then, blamed for the things that they never did. Sameer has to be in torment because of the hate crime since his last name is 'KHAN'. Mandira blames Rizwan for her son, Sameer's murder altogether because he is Muslim and she claims that because of his sir name she lost her son.

The movie tries to bring forth the idea that terrorism doesn't have any religion, tries to break down the standardization of Muslims to eliminate the prejudiced attitude of the society towards them and their religion through the character of Rizwan. The movie forecast Muslim's character not in a typical way as other movies but portrays Rizwan Khan being a Muslim in a positive way. He pays zakat (donation of a certain percentage of the income to the charity) to the fundraising for the family who lost their loved ones in the attack. He helps people, he even informs the FBI about the suspicious people at the mosque throughout his journey. The movie reaches its climax where Rizwan Khan reaches the college campus to convey his message to the president.

However, due to tight security and loud cheers of the citizens, he begins screaming his message. Everyone around him took it in the wrong way and started panicking. This made the security guards arrest Rizwan and put him behind the bar being falsely accused of being a terrorist without any proof or evidence. People should be careful enough while dealing with heavy words like terrorism. Without any investigation and understanding, Rizwan was arrested, this implies that the word terrorism has blindfolded people to the extent that they no longer are capable of making the right choices and decisions. This carelessness has spiked an increase in conflicts between different communities. Rizwan's innocence is proven when two research students took this task into their hands to put forth his message out in public. With lots of difficulties, the research students gathered the required information about Rizwan and with the help of media; they presented the actual truth in front of the entire world. As soon as the truth was out, many changes were observed in the movie. The fear of being judged but others started vanishing and there was a boost of confidence. A shopkeeper who was bullied started answering back to the haters. The Sikh who changed his identity didn't hide it anymore and Rizwan's sister-in-law starts wearing the hijab again. This shows the true power of media. Media do manipulate its audience but the fact that it can impact society with its positivity cannot be denied. In the movie, it's only because of the media that helped Rizwan deliver his message to the president. Media became his strength and his source for removing the tag of terrorism. This simply indicates that with the correct use of media, all the misconceptions and misunderstandings about Muslims and their religion can be tackled.

CONCLUSION

In conclusion, there is a solution to reduce the stereotype or prejudice among people towards Muslims, by clearing misconceptions about Islam and Muslims, by promoting the true teachings of Islam and the true role of Muslims in society. This task was taken forward by Karan Johar the director of the movie *My Name Is Khan.* He brings forth the reality of the Muslims on the big screen and their emotional state theirs to highlight the truth, all Muslims are not terrorists. He uses the media platform to deliver his message which reaches out to the world. It doesn't completely eliminate prejudice and stereotype but had made a small difference by broadcasting the other side of the reality i. e. the sufferings of the Muslims all over the world after the 9/11 attack.

Indian media, especially Bollywood movies, are a big source to spread the message as it reaches not only the domestic audience but also those overseas. After the 9/11 attacks, the media turns out to be negative towards the Muslim community. It portrays Islam and Muslims in an unfavourable, stereotypical way. It misrepresents or underrepresented them cause an increase in Islamophobia, prejudice, hate and an overall negative impact on the minds of the people. The true meaning of jihad is misrepresented in the mainstream media that making the audience believe that all Muslims who do jihad are a terrorist. On the contrary, jihad means 'Struggle' this word has different contexts in Quran. Terrorism or act of terror is not acceptable in Islam. It is strictly prohibited to harm the innocent, to do corruption on earth and any kind of mischief that hurt others. Conversely, the act of terrorism includes mass killing, violence, bombing etc.

The attacks of 9/11 also affect the mind and the life of the Muslims which is amazingly depicted in the movie *My Name Is Khan*. The character of Rizwan Khan is not stereotypically portrayed as other movies portray the Muslim characters in the movie. In the movie, the director cleverly shows the significance of using journalism in a positive way as the story of Rizwan khan was shown on the television news channel which influences the audience and results in spreading his message to the world that is "My Name Is Khan and I'm not a terrorist".

Works Cited

Johar, Karan, director. My Name Is Khan. Disney+ Hotstar, Fox Star Studios, Fox Searchlight Picture, Dharma Production and Red Chillies Entertainment, 2010.

Aamir, Altaf. "Bollywood's Anti Muslim Agenda." The Legitimate, 14 Sept. 2020, https://thelegitimatenews.com/bollywoods-anti-muslim-agenda/ June 8, 2021.

Bernard Shaw, George. "Islam Is the Best Religion and Muslims Are the Worst Followers." George Bernard Shaw Quote, 2021.

Dr. Mustafa, Khattab. "The Clear Quran." https://quran.com/

Gupta, Chahak, and Ayan Sharma. "Audit of Bigotry: How Indian Media Vilified Tablighi Jamaat over Coronavirus Outbreak." Newslaundry, 27 Apr. 2020.

"Hadith." Merriam-Webster.com Dictionary, Merriam-Webster, https://www.merriam-webster.com/dictionary/hadith 18th Jun.

2021.

Qasim , Rashid. “Opinion | ‘Jihad’ Is Not a Dirty Word.” The Washington Post, WP Company, 1 Apr. 2019.

Staff, FP. “Bandra Migrant Workers' Gathering: Politicians, Media Channels Lend Communal Spin to Protesters Desperate to Return Home” Firstpost, 16 Apr. 2020.

Zafar, Abid. “Portrayal of Muslims in the Bollywood Movies.” Academia.edu, 2021, https://www.academia.edu/37595907/Portrayal_of_Muslims_in_the_Bollywood_Movies . 4 th June 2021.

CHAPTER VII

VOICE OF UNTOUCHABLE MORTALS BORN FROM THE FEET OF THE CREATOR: THRICE MARGINALIZED DALIT WOMEN IN INDIA IN SELECTED NOVELS OF URMILA PAWAR

Jennifer Dias

ABSTRACT

In the traditionally contrived caste system or caste echelon, the life of Dalit people is inconsolable they are considered to be untouchables and are subjected to bestiality, vehemence and dehumanization. Particularly asserting about Dalit Women who are oppressed among oppressed, their lives are thrice sombre. Women are always considered to be marginalized gender, but when it comes to Dalit women they are placed at the bottom of the caste edifice where they are been thrice marginalized and exploited on basis of caste, gender and class. Another demeanour is that the struggles and sufferings of Dalit women were consistently over sighted by mainstream male-dominated literature which also includes mainstream feminist writers. To some extremity, they were also been evade by Dalit men writers. So, Dalit women writers by themselves started articulating their own as well as other Dalit women's experiences. Where they also converse about marginalization, gender configuration and also question casteism. Notably, in Bama's and Urmila Pawar's autobiographies they not only share their toils to conjure their idiosyncratic mishaps but specifically pivot on thrice marginalization of Dalit women in India.

Keywords: Marginalization, Writing of Dalit women, Dalit Women, Caste, Gender and Class.

INTRODUCTION

The term marginalization means to propel an individual or a group at the brim, give them lesser importance and also exclude them from all their virtues. According to the Varna System, a Hinduism society is divided into four Varna's or Castes on basis of their birth, aptitude and vocation. Where it is firmly believed that Brahman was born from the mouth of the creator, whereas Sudra was born from the feet of the creator as said in "Purushasukta" and so Sudra becomes of lower rank in the caste hierarchy and this is the reason why Dalits are always considered to be a marginalized caste in India. Due to this vicious caste system, folks belonging to the lower caste are been deprived of all prerequisites of life and they are also been callously brutalized.

On the contrary, Dalit women faces immoderate quandaries of themselves for the last so many centuries, which still today even in this contemporary world has not completely remould. Dalit women to some extent moieties the muddles of gender exploitation and economic destitution with other women but unfortunately they also have to bear caste differentiation which other women did not face. Dalit women have to undergo treble depreciation due to caste, gender and class and this thrice marginalization create a vital problem for Dalit women, it becomes formidable for them to prevail over this marginalization. They also have to suffer from caste-based segregation and atrocities. Dalit women are harassed due to their lower caste whereas the upper-caste males can sexually assault Dalit women. Whenever there is conflict among the upper and lower castes. Dalit women always become a victim as they are facile prey.

Voice of Untouchable Mortals Born from The Feet of The Creator: Thrice Marginalized Dalit Women in India in Selected Novels of Urmila Pawar's *The Weave of My Life: A Dalit Woman's Memoirs* and Bama's *Karukku*

Dalit women are not only subjugated because of their caste identity but also because of their gender. Under patriarchy, these women face violence in their own communities. Dalit women are brought to demean by their own family, especially by the men of the household who due to their subdued status shed their vexation on these women. Dalit women also have to suffer because of their class as they are been denied all the equities and property rights. They remain aloof from all the assets and affluence they are denied their rights not only because they are women but predominantly as they are lower caste women.

Dalit women writing shared similar issues of all the Dalit women with respect to caste, gender and class in their works. This Dalit women writer becomes the voice of Dalit women's agony, suppression and scuffles which was never been dilapidated. Similarly, Pawar's The Weave of My Life: A Dalit Woman's Memoirs and Bama's Karukku are Dalit autobiographical texts. Pawar talks about her personal as well as her community struggle in the state of Maharashtra. Similarly, Bama also talk about her and her communities struggle in the South of India. But they also precisely hub on Dalit women grapple in their own communities and how they are been triply deprived on account of caste, gender and class.

***The Weave of My Life: A Dalit Woman's Memoirs* and *Karukku*.**

Urmila Pawar is a Dalit Indian feminist writer belonging to the Mahar (Dalit) caste of Maharashtra. She is a Marathi novelist and short story writer. In her works, she delineates the experiences of Dalit people of her community and especially the experiences of Dalit women. Urmila Pawar was born in Adgaon Village of Ratnagiri district and later with her husband she shifted to Bombay. Pawar at an early age experienced marginalization in her region, in her school. When she was still a teen her family members along with the other people of the village converted to Buddhism under the influence of Dr. Babasaheb Ambedkar. Later Pawar received an M. A. degree from the University of Bombay. She has also worked in the Department of labour welfare for the government of Maharashtra. She was also a member of the Dalit women's organization. She has also written two short stories collections, 'Sahava Bot' and 'Chauthi Bhint'. Pawar was also a former actor in Marathi theatres.

> *"My mother used to weave aaydans, it is Marathi*
> *Term for all things made out of bamboo. I find that*

Her act of weaving and my act of writing
Are organically link. The weave is similar.
It is the weave of pain, suffering and
Agony that links us."(Preface).

These are the quotes From Urmila Pawar's autobiographical novel 'Aaydan' or The Weave of My Life: A Dalit Woman's Memoirs. This novel was first written in Marathi and then was translated into English by Dr. Maya Pandit who is pro-vice-chancellor of English and Foreign Languages University, Hyderabad. The title means the things made out of the bamboo and weaving the bamboo baskets was traditionally the job assigned to nomadic tribes. In the Konkan region, however, it was the Mahar caste that undertook this task. Where Pawar's mother also did the same and Pawar compares her mother's weaving with her writing which sketches their struggle as Dalit women. And which reveals different aspects of the everyday lives of Dalits, and manifolds the ways in which caste exert upon Dalits and pulverized them. Through the novel, Pawar not only talks about her own personal experiences but she recites three generations of Dalit women who struggled to overcome the burden of their caste. She also outlines how Dalit or untouchables are forbidden due to their caste and forced to live in quarantined communities. Bama was born in 1958; Bama was not born as Hindu. She was born in a Christian – converted family she was a Roman Catholic her name is Faustian Soosairaj. She used Bama as a pen name. Bama is a Tamil Dalit women writer. She has published three works Karukku (1992), Sangoti (1994) and a collection of short stories, Kisumbukkaran (1996).

Karukku is Bama's first novel and it is also the first autobiography of its kind to appear in Tamil. The novel was first written in Bama's own mother tongue and was translated into English by Lakshmi Holmstrom who is an Indian British writer, literary critic, and translator of Tamil fiction or works into English. The novel is written in a non-linear manner. And there Bama narrates her experiences: The driving forces that shaped this book are many events that occurred during many stages of my life, cutting me like karukku (Saw-edged Palmyra) and making me bleed, unjust social structures that plunged me into ignorance and left me trapped and suffocating, my own desperate urge to break, throw away, and destroy these bonds, and when the chains were shattered into fragments, the blood that was spilt all these taken together. (*Author's Preface to the First Edition*)

There are various synonyms for the word Karukku. One such meaning is the double-edged Palmyra leaf. Bama has used it as a metaphor for her novel. She says that there are many congruities between the saw-edged Palmyra and her own life. When Bama was a child she uses to play with Palmyra leaves and due to the sharp edges of the leaves she use to get hurt on her hand and it used to bleed. When Bama was growing up due to the injustice, caste-based discrimination she got the same cuts on her heart and her heart used to bleed and there was no medicine to heal these scars on her heart.

Bama was Catholic but still, she and people from her community have to face this caste prejudice. She also reveals that they were not only discriminated against by the upper caste but also by the people of the holy order. She simultaneously writes about many incidents from her childhood to adulthood about her life, her family, friends about her community and especially about the Dalit women of her community and about the oppression they faced due to their caste, gender and class. Bama wrote to change hearts and minds and as Gayatri Spivak Say "Surrender to the special call of the text" similarly the readers of Bama's work are asked to enter her world and experience her world and her perspective through her own lens.

Dalit woman Autobiography always focuses on Caste-based dilemmas in the Indian context. But it also accurately seats the spotlight on caste-based discrimination of Dalit Women. Where Dalit Women due to their caste identity is subjected to harassment and violence by upper caste men the molestation might be in various forms. Dalit women will be addressed in pejorative language, can be sexually abused, they are also been exploited by upper-caste women. This caste-based discrimination can also see in Pawar's and Bama's autobiographies. "The Weave of My Life: A Dalit Woman's Memoirs" or "Aayadan" is written in chronological order and shows the experiences of Dalit women from her childhood to womanhood. In the first chapter of the novel writer don't start with person 'I' but in fact, she indicated the women of her village the first chapter is from the child's perspective. Where women of her village have to make the long-distance journey through the mountains carrying a lot of burdens of various stuff to sell in Market. Because people belonging to Mahar(Dalit) community have to choose the 'place of the settlement which is not close to the place where upper caste people resides. Residence of this Mahar caste was so, at the fringe that it was extremely difficult for them to travel to the main district of Ratnagiri they have to face various strains to reach Ratnagiri and especially women of this community have to face duplex plights as Pawar writes:

Women From our village travelled to the market at Ratnagiri to sell various things. They trudged the whole distance with huge, heavy bundles on their heads, filled with firewood or grass, rice or semolina, long pieces of bamboo, baskets of ripe or raw mangoes. Their load was heavy enough to break their neck. They would start their journey to Ratnagiri early in the Morning Between our village and Ratnagiri the road was difficult to negotiate as it wound up and down the hall. It was quite an exhausting trip. (1)

Karukku is not written in chronological order. But then to Bama evokes the aspects, reality of the Dalit Women's life through her own experiences as a Dalit Christian woman. Karukku manifests Bama's life from childhood to adulthood. The novel also exhibits that though Bama and most of her community members were Christians then do they have to encounter belittlement because of their lower caste. Bama had got early experience of caste discrimination. Through the people of her caste and through the women of her caste who were demarcated because of their caste, she describes that most of the people from her village were agricultural labourers. When people of her community did not have work in fields they have to go to the mountains to gather the firewood for selling so that they might get some money. She also tells that people of other better of caste never had this problem. They had their own land, wells they eat well and live a comfortable life. This shows how lower rank people were diminished under caste halo where their job opportunities were mitigated and they were forced to live impecunious life. Even lower-caste settlement was discrete from the upper caste settlement as she says, "I don't know how it came about that the Upper caste communities and lower caste communities were separated like this into different parts of the village. But they kept themselves to their part of the village and we stayed in ours. We only went to their part if we had worked to do there. But they never ever came to our parts" (7).

There are various lower castes in regions and states of India. Bama and Urmila Pawar belong to different lower castes from different states of India. But as Dalit women they both as well as their communities unequivocal the women of their caste are been marginalized due to their Dalit caste.

Issue of Gender based marginalization of Dalit women in: "The Weave of My Life: A Dalit Woman's Memoirs" and"Karukku".

In Dalit literature, the cynosure is caste-based tyrannizing. But Dalit women's literature pivot on the double subjugation they face due to caste and gender. Where in their work issue of gender is more conspicuous and eminent than that of caste. Patriarchy and the issue of ancillary treatment by the men of upper as well as of their own community create a great predicament for these Dalit women who have to undergo caste and gender-based manipulation and marginalization. Pawar in her autobiography, such kinds of quagmire and muddles that Dalit women had to bear illustrate in a very relevant and unequivocal manner. Women were not only exploited by the men but by the women of her own community where daughter-in-law was always despised and bashed up. There was a common expression that mother-in-law would use about their daughters-in-law's treating than like trash.

On the whole, Dalit women were invariably treated with the same degree of exclusion in the Brahmin community. Although Pawar does not touch on the issue of widow remarriage, she gives us a small linguistic essay on the interesting term "rand kisooj", which translates as widow's swelling or widow swelling Urmila has heard the phrase from her Mother, who claims that, although she is a widow, she does not have the "randkisooj", Urmila asks her elder sister about it and gets the following reply. "Youknow, for some women, when their husband dies, it is a release from oppression. Then they look a little better, fresh, so people say they have got the "randkisooj". Then she grew grave and said, "But let me tell you, I have always been like this, same what plump, even before my husband died" (9).

This explanation is perhaps an adequate comment on the nature of Dalit patriarchy. The earthy phrase more so because the word raad means both the widow and a prostitute in Marathi - tell us that many a woman is so badly treated by her husband that she blossoms out after his death. And yet, the freedom to joke about it, the common use of such a phrase, also signifies that windows are not completely suppressed. Urmila also explains that in name of traditions and rituals that a Dalit woman was always subdued Bama exhibited and exposé twofold segregation of lower caste women of her community owing to their caste and specifically their gender under patriarchy structure. Bama recalls various incidences that how on basis of lower caste, women's gender under the patriarchy have to suffer. Women were been suppressed by their community chiefly by the men of their own caste and family. Bama also Show how in her community rules for men and women were different. Bama and Pawar through their experiences try to expose this false patriarchal order that has made women's life ludicrous particularly the lives of lower caste women.

Issue of Class-Based Marginalization Of Dalit Women in: "The Weave of My Life: A Dalit Woman's Memoirs" and "Karukku".

Class is undeviatingly affiliated with caste. The individual belonging to the lower caste under the caste-based stipulation is repudiated from all the legal rights and basic necessities such as the right to have property, good education and jobs and due to this hideous practice, it has a tremendous impact on the development of the people allied to Dalit communities. Where Dalit women have to face double denial, where she is untouchable person, denied of all property rights, they lack any kind of income assets and have to depend on their husband and fathers who made their condition more shellac and worst. Urmila Pawar in her novel illustrates the class-based marginalization of Dalit caste people and primarily of Dalit caste women. Pawar said that in her village children of Dalit caste were gainsaid of education, another reason was also that this Dalit person was poor and did not have enough money to educate their children but still boys of lower caste were taking education but when it came to a girl they were completely negated. Pawar also explains how due to the lower class, poverty women of lower caste were exploited twice. The author says that always due to their class, their poverty they had to suffer.

Pawar and her siblings sometimes used to play imaginary games of eating food when there was no food in the house. They never had good sanitary conditions, when her mother was sick she never got good medication. In fact, this was the tale of every lower-class family and if they were lower caste they were poor among poor and lower caste women had to bear twice due to poverty and lack of money. In "Karukku" also we see class-based discrimination of Dalit women. Bama says that in her village most of the land belonged to the Naicker community as they were the upper caste. Whereas people from Bama's community did menial jobs they have to work in the fields of the Naicker community and got terrible pay for their work. This Dalit person worked tremendously hard but in return got very less remittance because of their caste and so due to the meagerness of money this person had to face insolvency. Bama and Pawar both had to struggle due to their class and through their experience, they also reveal the experiences of another Dalit woman of their community who had faced the same struggle due to their class.

CONCLUSION

Dalits are been marginalized for centuries where Dalit women were oppressed among oppressed due to caste, gender and class. Even Dalit women feminists were tarnished and debilitated by mainstream writers. So the Dalit women took it upon themselves to outlet their own experience as Dalit women, descending from the circumference to the core. The Dalit women originated volumes of literature such as autobiographies, poetry, short stories etc. Their work spoke for the Dalit women's identity and promoted the source of the Dalit movement. Substantially the Dalit women's autobiographies spoke distinctly from male correlative and upper-caste women, they expropriate and misdemeanour the enclave dominated by mainstream writers. Their autobiographies highlighted the triple oppression of Dalit women where they tried to crack this manacle. These autobiographies eloquent the whole span of paroxysm, indigence, indignity and rage which they had to bare due to caste, gender and class. These autobiographies renovated the conception of Dalit women; this works gave the voice to the Dalit women where they placed their own panorama without any misinterpretation. These women became active characters in the autobiographies, where they also celebrate their womanhood. Their work also accommodated other majority of women; they were never biased while presenting something or someone. Bama and Urmila also in their autobiographies endure their personal tribulations but also presented the experiences of other Dalit women in their community they became their voice and also tried to emancipate them. Their testimonies become voice of one who witness for the sake of another, who were made voiceless.

As it is said the remodeling start from home indistinguishably the folks of lower caste should stop considering themselves beneath or inferior to anyone. And even the upper caste should stop patronizing these false caste ideologies. Every individual is equal and independent and most importantly identity is not based on anyone's birth every individual should make their own identity on basis of their aptitude.

Works Cited

a) Primary Sources:

1. Pawar, Urmila: translated by Dr. Maya Pandit as [*The Weave of My Life: A Dalit Woman Memoirs*], Columbia University Press, New York, 2009.

2. Bama: [*Karukku*] translated from Tamil by Lakshmi Holmstrom, Oxford University Press, New Delhi, 2012.

b) Secondary Sources:

1. Rege, Sharmila: [*Writing Caste / Writing Gender, Narrating Dalit Women'sTestimonios*], Zubaan, New Delhi, 2006.

2. Kanakaratnam, N. &Varaadarajulu, G. et al, [THE EMERGENVE OF DALIT AUTOBITAPHYIES IN INDIA], [INTERNATIONAL JOURNAL OF MULTIDISCIPLINARY EDUCATIONAL RESEARCH ISSN]: 2277-7881, September 2015.

3. C.S., Lakshmi: Serrated Palmyra leaf, Bamboo Baskets and Brocade Saris: Life and Stories of Two Writers, from SPARROW Archives, 2017.

4. Isalkor, Umesh&Shinde, Swati: Voices and views from margin, ITNNI, 03.33, Feb 22, 2009.

5. Shodhganga: [URMILA PAWAR'S "AAYADAN" – A NEW PERSPECTIVE], chapter 12, (3).

6. International journal of Multidisciplinary Education Research: Volume 4, Issue 9(3), Sucharitha Publication, Andhra Pradesh, September 2015.

7. Rao's: (*The Caste Question*), 2009.

8. Indian Institute of Dalit Studies: Dalit Women Rights and Citizenship in India, Delhi, 2010.

9. Wankhede, S.M.: A Study of Bama's (*Karukku*) in light of Subalternity, Literary Herald: An International Refereed English e-journal, www.TLHjournal.com, 2017.

10. Limbale, Sharankumar (2010) (*Toward an Aesthetic of Dalit Literature*), New Delhi: OUP.

11. Zelliot, Eleanor: (2010) (*From untouchable to Dalit*), New Delhi: Manobar.

12. Nayar, Pramod: Bama'sKarukku: (*Dalit Autobiography asTestimonio*), University of Hyderabad:
https://www.researchgale.net/publication/240713501,2015.

13. Jangaiah, k.: [Exploration of Dalit and Christian Identity: Karukku on Autobiography by Bama] Hyderabad, Telangana – state k. jangaiah66@gmail.com, 2016.

14. Haider, Nishat: Other Tongues: A study of Bama'sKarukku and Sangati: http://tandfonline.com/loi/raut20 29 Oct., 2015.

15. Guru, Gopal: "Dalit Woman Talk Differently" [*Economic and PoliticalWeekly*] 14. 21 (1995): 2548-50, print.

16. Limbale, Sharankumar: Akkarmashi [The Outcaste], Trans. SantoshBhoomkar, New Delhi, Oxford UP, 2008.

17. Pandian, M.S.S.: "A Dalit Woman's Testimonio.", Rao,129-35.

18. Rao, Anupama. Ed., [Gender and caste] New Delhi: Kali For Women, 2003. Print.

19. Rege, Sharmila: "'Real feminism' and Dalit Women: Scripts of Denial and Accusation." (*Economic and Political Weekly*),5.11 (2000) : 492-95.

20. Spivak, GayatriChakravorty: "Can the Subaltern Speak?: Marxism and the Interpretation of Culture.", Chicago : Illinois University press, 198.

21. Cast(e)ing Gender in Dalit Literature : An International conference at Savitribai Pune University, 14-15 December, 2015.

22. Althusser, Louis: Ideology and Ideological State Apparatuses (Notes towards an investigation), (Lenin and Philosophy and other Essays), Monthly Review Press, 1971.

23. ^Parkin, E Marx's Theory of History: A Bourgeois Critique. New York: Columbian University Press, 1979.

24. Beauvoir, Simone (1971). [*The Second Sex*] Alfred A Knopf.

25. Beauvoir, Simone de (2002). [*The Second Sex*] (SvenserUppl0ga) ,p. 325.

26. Woolf, Virginia: A Room of One's, Literary Criticism and Theory, MEG 05, IGNOU, New Delhi, (Virginia Woolf n.p.).

27. Devi, Mahasweta: The Breast Stories. Seagull Book Private Limited: Calcutta, 1997.

CHAPTER VIII

NOT STRAIGHT OUT OF THE CLOSET

Miss. Madhura Sudhir Walavalkar

ABSTRACT

A boy or a girl is the first thought that comes to mind when someone hears the word 'gender'. People, oftentimes, mistake sex for gender. Gender is a social construct while sex is a biological construct assigned to a person at birth. Many-a-times, some individuals feel that the sex that they have been assigned at birth does not align with their gender and they cannot identify themselves as a male or a female. They are not attracted to people of the opposite sex rather are attracted to the people of the same sex as their own, or both. At times, these individuals do not even label themselves as male or female. This is where the theory of LGBTQ comes into the picture. The LGBTQ theory that is, the Lesbian Gay Bisexual Trans and Queer theory has aided many individuals of society to identify themselves other than the conventional heterosexuals' labels. This concept of the LGBTQ theory has been hilariously explicated intertwining with their personal experiences since childhood by Jacob Tobia in their *Sissy- A Coming-Of-Gender Story.*

Keywords: LGBTQ, gender studies, society, sex, gender nonconforming.

INTRODUCTION

Contemporary society is aware of the acronym LGBTQ and its full form to be as Lesbian Gay Bisexual Transgender Queer. But are the individuals cognizant and conscious about the meaning and significance of this acronym concerning society? The answer that would be derived is partial. The generation of the modern times is the one very well mindful about the LGBTQ community where it can be seen functioning. The reason is they are not gazed at with a prejudice making them uncomfortable. The ones who are ignorant of the fact that the LGBTQ community is an integral part of society, make them feel like outsiders in their own homes. Nevertheless, the individuals of the present generation encourage the LGBTQ community to freely identify themselves as lesbian, gay, bisexual, transgender or queer making them experience a sense of belonging in society. In the present scenario, the LGBTQ community has transformed the way that non-LGBTQ individuals perceive them and has redefined the view of humanity.

The autobiographical novel *Sissy* presents Jacob Tobia's personal experiences, challenges, discrimination and rejection that they had to face since childhood to be a gender nonconforming individual. Jacob Tobia- an author, an LGBTQ activist and a T.V. producer and performer- prefer the pronouns they, their and them. Through their autobiographical novel *Sissy*, they condemn the stigma faced by the gender-nonconforming group, the stereotypical stories of coming out of the closet and the society's gaze and/or ignorance towards them as an individual not belonging to the group. They have revealed their true identity of being more feminine and how they were looked down upon and were bullied for it. *Sissy* also uncovers how individuals are made to feel negative about their incoherence with the so-called normal people. This novel is an answer to all the genuine questions about LGBTQ and a back answer to all those who still consider it as an abnormality.

OVERVIEW

The Concept of LGBTQ:

LGBT is an abbreviation for the terms Lesbian Gay Bisexual and Transgender. There have been additions made to this concept with the evolution of time and with an increase in the field of studies around it. The Queer Theory forms a part of the LGBT concept and includes individuals that do not identify themselves either as heterosexual or as cisgender. Though the queer theory now forms a part of the concept of LGBT, it first emerged in the 1980s as a framework for evaluating gender issues and sexuality.

To describe each term individually, L stands for lesbian that is, a homosexual female with a sense of romantic or sexual attraction towards another female; G stands for gay, a homosexual male that is attracted to another male romantically or sexually. To elucidate about bisexuals in the initialism, they are individuals attracted romantically and/or sexually towards both males and females. And finally, T stands for transgender. The individuals who label themselves as transgenders have a different gender identity from the sex they are assigned at birth.

In the yesteryears, queer was considered to be a congregate label for homosexual individuals and individuals of other sexual orientations and sexualities. But in modern times, queer has become a more widely defined concept and is not restricted to these labels. It deals with all the other emergent notions of the LGBT theory. Society has assigned every individual a gender role based on the sex assigned at their birth and this gender role is given validation by society if she/he performs the duties accordingly. Nevertheless, the LGBTQ community does not seek the validation of society and hence are seen as distinct from the rest. It does not follow the ostensible gender norms and their framework.

According to the queer theory, gender is not confined to males and females; it changes or transforms itself into divergent forms which are universally followed and are standard. The term queer is often used to indicate gender variability and in modern times, can be interchangeably used with LGBT, as an umbrella term. The queer theory rejects the social constructs coerced upon individuals so that society can identify them as distinct from each other. Those who do not follow and raise their voices against these supposed gender norms laid down by society are frowned upon and are considered to be anti-socials subjugated to social oppression.

People who identify themselves as queer and a part of the LGBT community are afraid to profess their true identity or as it is called come out of the closet due to the gender obligations enforced by society. After their coming out, the first thing that their family members should do is support them and accept them. But this is often not the case. The individual is made to believe that this confusion of identity as LGBTQ is just a phase and it will pass.

Accepting the individual as they are is an extremely important factor in the development of their personalities and this is what is portrayed by Jacob Tobia in their autobiographical novel *Sissy.*

The Journey of Identity (Crisis):

Sissy is an autobiography of Jacob Tobia a T.V. performer, producer and author about their personal experiences of coming out as a gender nonconforming individual. The pronouns that are preferred by them are they, them and their. Through this novel, Tobia has portrayed the challenges that they had to face for being effeminate as a young child. They have revealed their confusion, deprivation of warmth and emotional connection to their parents, the bullying that they faced for being a little different, the comfort that they found in the company of other girls, the lack of acceptance and in turn depression and thoughts of self-harm and suicide as a young kid.

As a young child, Tobia had always known that they experienced the world differently than their elder brother. At the time when their elder brother enjoyed playing football and soccer along with other boys, Tobia played dolls with their best friends who were girls. In the novel when the author reminisces about their childhood, they find more bitter memories than the sweet ones. They remember one specific incident from their childhood that occurred while playing with their pre-school girl best friends, which now makes them realize that they and other children have been indirectly falling prey to the gender-related propaganda of society. The three friends had decided to choose a character to play from their favourite "Japanese cartoon about five sailor girls who fought evil" (Tobia, 4) named *Sailor Moon.*

When my friend got to me, she said matter-of-factly, "And Jacob can play Tuxedo Mask since he's the only boy!" I remember my heart sinking. It felt like an indictment, like a verdict. I didn't want to play a boy character that wasn't part of the core group of girls. I wanted to be one of the groups like everyone else, but as the only boy, I had no choice in the matter. I couldn't play a girl. (Tobia, 4)

Since childhood, it is imbued upon children's minds that an individual should always observe the decorum set by society may it be concerning overall behaviour or gender. A boy has to be strong and a girl has to be delicate. Any individual found not observing these rules is called rebellious and misanthropic. Children at a young and tender age should be made aware of the fact that it is perfectly alright to not follow the so-called gender norms.

As a young kid, Tobia's choice of games was different from that of the other boys; boys of his age were more inclined towards sports like football, baseball, etc., whereas they were more inclined towards games like dress-up which were and still are considered to be played only by girls. For them, this was "a sense of longing." (Tobia, 5). They wanted to experience sequined clothes and "cover my lips with bright lipstick." (Tobia, 5). But due to societal pressure, they were forced to involve themselves in baseball. Although they were not interested in playing baseball, they were forced to at least watch the game that their brother was playing so that it might create an interest in their mind.

Another aspect of society's gender obligation is that if a man does not conform to the norms laid down by society, he is made to feel that he is not man enough and cannot fit into the institution named society and its confines. Tobia has explained this in their autobiography when talking about their journey of healing and the trauma that they had to go through for self-acceptance as a gender nonconforming individual. As a result, there are millions of cisgenders, heterosexual people - particularly men - who have never coped with the trauma they've experienced, who don't even recognize their experiences *as trauma* in the first place. They've spent a large portion of their lives being told that they are not man enough if they do this or aren't masculine enough if they do that, and none of these imperatives are even recognized as gender policing. (Tobia, 7-8)

Tobia, as a child with a confused gender identity, remembers an incident from the past. After they learnt of the destruction of their only barbie doll by their elder brother and his friends, they had thoughts of self-harm and suicide. They thought of self-harm and self-destruction as the only way to cope with the kind of trouble they were facing. The thought of homicidewas the only way that they could find to cope with such a stressful situation as a child. This scenario of dilemma, to have to choose between life and death should not have been existent for a child so young. Were there more awareness about identity and gender, a child of such a tender age would not have gone through such trauma?

The Straight Gaze:

Sissy portrays the way straight people or cisgenders perceive the gender-nonconforming individuals of society. Cisgenders support the queer community but expect them to be a certain way. They also expect the coming out stories of the queer individuals to be filled with trauma, emotions and melodrama. But this is not always the case. There has been an increased awareness about this fragment of society but their coming out stories have been stereotyped. The assumption of cisgender members of society is that it must have been difficult for queer members to be accepted as a part of their family let alone being a part of the society. They must have to beg for them to be accepted as individuals. And Tobia is tired of hearing such exclamations. This can be evident from the following extract from the novel. It seems to be the only trans narrative that cisgender*_ people want to hear; the only trans story that cisgender people can comprehend. (Tobia, 13)

Transgender peopleand their coming out stories and journeys have been generalized by cisgender people and authors in their works. But unlike other novels about the LGBTQ members of society where hyperbole is the only figure of speech used, *Sissy* gives its readers an unexaggerated outlook on the lives of these individuals. Tobia, through their autobiographical novel, state that they are exhausted of people forcefully trying to fit the stories by re-editing them according to the expectation of their cisgender readers. The reason behind this is these cisgender authors and editors "pressure trans people into fitting into one of the two binary genders." (Tobia, 14), glamourizing the wounds and trauma of the trans individuals. It has become the perception of society that if the coming-out stories are not packed with drama, rejection and emotional outbursts, then the struggles of trans people are no real struggles. And this is what Tobia wants to erase from the minds of the cisgender people and they have been successful in doing so in this novel.

Growing up, Tobia had a confused gender identity. They knew they were a boy bodily but were not able to align their behaviour and mind to it. They always felt that, like a jigsaw puzzle, some part of them was not a proper fit, making their life incomplete. The knowledge of they being different from the other children was grasped by them but could not identify it distinctly. And this is true with respect to most transgender people. The identity or its lack thereof is what makes them aware of their perception from the lens of society they live in. They are not expected to have this uncertainty or confusion regarding their identity. Transgenders are expected to give answers like " "I've always known I was a girl" or "I've always known I was a boy" " (Tobia, 16). They were not sure of their identity and this is portrayed from the following excerpt from the novel: I didn't know that I was a girl. And forgive the double negative, but I wasn't sure that I *wasn't a boy*, either. (Tobia, 16)

Media and its Perception of LGBTQ:

Media is one of the most influential and important aspects of today and plays a paramount role in portraying the LGBTQ community. But the question of 'is media portraying the correct picture of the LGBTQ?' arises. The answer to this question is provided to the readers by the author in this novel. Tobia is of the opinion that the depiction of the LGBTQ community in the media is partial, along with the history of transgenders being concealed by the media of modern times. They believe that the concept of transgender has been put forth to the audience without acknowledging its antiquity. It has been propounded as a concept of modern times and without there being any transgender individuals in the hitherto. The author conveys that gender nonconformity is "as old as gender itself" (Tobia, 17), and that the concept of gender itself is imprecisely rendered.

Tobia also expounded that gender non-conforming individuals of colour need to get equal exposure in the media if not more, than that of the gender-conforming and/or straight individuals. They should be encouraged to showcase their talent with equal enthusiasm and should not be looked at as exotic and mystical beings. Inclusivity of not only gender but also of colour should be encouraged by and in the media. These gender-nonconforming individuals of colour should be given equal opportunities in all work fields.

CONCLUSION

The minds of children are like clay which can be moulded into nothing but a blob of mud or can be sculpted into a beautiful sculpture. It is the responsibility of the elder- their parents, teachers and other adults that they come in contact with- to help them understand these concepts and ideas of gender in their true sense. Besides instilling moral values and good conduct in the children, which are essential for them to become a member of society, they should also be exposed to sensitive topics like gender and identity. Rather than imbuing the outdated and rusted gender norms on children they should be taught equal opportunity for every individual, irrespective of their gender, colour, class, caste, etc. These life lessons of embracing and treating everyone as human first regardless of their social and personal identity and status should be taught in school together with the usual subjects. The idea of individuals following gender binary rules strictly being granted a social standing and glorifying this act should be erased from the unsaid social rules. Now is the time to eradicate all the prejudices and misconceptions about the LGBTQ community and celebrate their identity and acknowledge their presence as important members of society.

Works Cited

1. Tobia. Jacob. *Sissy- A Coming-Of-Gender Story*. 1st ed. G.P. Putnum's Sons New York; 2019.

2. https://sheridancollege.libguides.com/lgbtq/theory
3. https://ythi.net/abbreviations/english/what-does-lqbtq-mean-what-is-the-full-form-of-lqbtq/
4. https://literariness.org/2019/03/04/queer-theory/
5. https://literariness.org/2016/10/10/judith-butlers-concept-of-performativity/

Bio-Note

Miss. Madhura Sudhir Walavalkar is an amateur poetess and writer with a post-graduate degree in English Literature from Mithibai College, Mumbai. She is currently working as a visiting staff member at Sydenham College, Mumbai in the department of English along with plans to pursue PhD in English. She has one other research paper published in a Peer-reviewed journal named Knowledge Resonance. Besides being a lecturer and a research Candidate, she also is an Indian Classical Vocalist.

CHAPTER IX

THE DRAMATIC MONOLOGUE AND ITS UNIVERSAL NATURE: A CASE STUDY OF ROBERT BROWNING AND FRANK BIDART'S POEMS

Manjari Nagori, (B. A. Hons, M. A. Hons)
Assistant Professor, Department of English
Thakur College of Science and Commerce.

ABSTRACT

Since its conception during the Victorian Era, the dramatic monologue has been in constant use in the ages that followed. It evolves along with society and captures the nuances of the complex human psyche. Along with capturing the nuances of the human psyche, the dramatic monologue also enchants its reader by positioning them into the world of the subject, which is achieved by making the reader directly emotionally involved by giving them the role of a silent observer or put, "overhearer". Robert Browning is the pioneer of this form of poetry, and Frank Bidart takes this form a step further with this unconventional punctuation. In this paper, I aim to point out the differences and similarities between the two poets, who are a century apart to prove their universal nature, by analysing their thematic similarities and their structural uniqueness.

Keywords: Dramatic Monologue, Frank Bidart, Robert Browning, Characterisation, Unconventional use of Poetry, Universal Nature of Dramatic monologue, Psychology.

• • •

INTRODUCTION

The Dramatic Monologue has been consistently in use ever since its conception by Robert Browning, it's the universal nature of this type of poetry that keeps it trending throughout the ages. To understand its universal nature, one must first track its origin, development, significance and how it manages to stay relatable and relevant a century later. To prove this, I will exercise a comparative case study between the poets Robert Browning and Frank Bidart. Although the two poets are a century apart, their style, content and subject matter are similar, they both write dramatic monologues with a special focus on characterization and the complexities of the human psyche, society and psychology. They both are pioneers in this format, Browning for conceptualizing it and Bidart for his unusual and different use of typography, punctuations, linguistic and prose to provide different voices.

The Conception and Development of Dramatic Monologues

The dramatic monologue was a new style of poetry invented by Robert Browning. This new style of poetry is defined by many aspects such as its form, content and structure. These poems have 3 major parts: the occasion, the speaker and the hearer (Howard, 3). They often revolved around a particular occasion which prompts the speaker into a monologue that is of course dramatic in nature. These poems often focused on the psyche and inner-most thoughts of the speaker, particularly a character and not the poet themselves. The hearer or the audience in these poems played a minor but impactful role as they provide the foundation to the poems. Structurally, these poems were often written in blank verse. The progression and ultimate concept of the dramatic monologue were also influenced by the Victorian Era. This Era was often referred to as the "Age of Science and Technology", it was during this time the "Innovations of the nineteenth century transformed philosophical psychology into scientific psychology." (Psychology in Nineteenth-Century, Exp 18 L 38).

This influence of psychology was reflected in the literature of the era, especially in the gaining popularity of the novel and the decline of drama. The Modern era has its own impact on the dramatic monologue which was followed by Post-modernism, they reject modern optimism, while still employing the stream of consciousness, fragmented, experimental form, unreliable narrator and focus on character psychoanalysis from the modern era, but also makes use of metafiction, intertextuality, irony, dark humour and parody. Both modern and post-modern eras make use of innovative stylistic and linguistic experimentation. During this time, Confessional poetry often made use of the interior monologue which is believed to be derived from the dramatic monologue (Litgalaxy, Exp 26 L 45). These writers often focused on subjects that were considered taboo such as mental illness, suicide, sexuality and social politics. The confessional writers focused on the "I", personal trauma and individual memories.

The Universal Nature of the Dramatic Monologue

This article argues that the universal nature of the dramatic monologue comes from a deep, continued focus on the complex human psyche, characterization, psychoanalysis of character and the role of the reader as a secondary listener. The reader plays an important role in the continued success of the dramatic monologue, they act as a secondary listener or an "overhearer" due to the fact that the listener in the poem is often ghostly or not present. This results in a more complex and connected reader-response from the audience. According to John Maynard in, *Speaker, Listener and Overhearer: The Reader in the Dramatic Poem*, this relationship between the reader as an overhearer and the speaker, results in an exciting experience for the reader as they have to choose between a sympathetic or a judgemental approach to the speaker, leading the course of a direct interpretation based on particular viewpoints (108).

Thematic comparison of Browning and Bidart's poems

Browning and Bidart pose as mirrors to one another in terms of their focus on psychoanalysis and fictionalisation of a character, these poets not only make use of the same genre of poetry but also similar, themes, motifs and characters. The poems, "Herbert White" and "Porphyria's Lover", both have themes centred on violence, murder, sin, control and obsession. Both of the poems go into the gruesome details of the why and how of the murders committed. "Porphyria's Lover", describes how the insecure unnamed lover killed Porphyria, he was insecure about her love and commitment towards him, regarding her profession of love as "murmuring", he believes her lack of commitment stems from vanity and her higher class status, he believes that Porphyria will break-up with him, which is evident in the lines "*I listened with heart fit to break*", although she seems to be doing the opposite by comforting and loving him (L 10).

The unnamed lover decides to kill Porphyria when he is finally assured of her commitment when he realises that she has left a party and braved a storm to come be with him, he is desperate for control and he finally kills her by wrapping her hair around her neck 3 times. Similarly, "Herbert White", begins with the speaker giving descriptions of the feelings that were aroused when he committed the murder of the little girl. There are two versions of Herbert White being portrayed in this poem, one of them is a necrophiliac, paedophile and a murderer and the other one is horrified and in denial about these actions, there are two descriptions of this murder. The first description is quick, emotionless and casual, which is evident when he refers to it as "funny" and describes it quickly in the lines, "*and saw a little girl – who I picked up, hit on the head, and screwed and screwed and screwed and then buried in the garden of the motel*" (153). The second description is more emotional, longer and remorseful which is seen in the lines "*kept circling the block as she walked along with them, saying "You're going to leave her alone." "You're going to leave her alone.*" (156).

The themes of control and obsession are significant in both of these poems. It is clear that the motives of both the speakers is control and obsession over their subjects. Porphyria's lover is obsessed with her, he wants complete control over her and so he kills her and treats her body like a doll when he props her up and adjusts her positions, evident in the lines "*I warily oped her lids: again*" and "*I propped her head up as before, Only, this time my shoulder bore her head which droops upon it still*" (L 54). He goes as far as to assume that she felt no pain when he killed her, evident in line "*I am quite sure she felt no pain*" (L 47). Herbert White is a troubled character who is obviously going through some sort of mental illness, his subject of obsession and control is not only the little girl but also his childhood trauma and his inability to cope with his father's new life.

The pattern of rape and murder in order to gain some control over his feelings is adopted by him since childhood, when he rapes and murders a goat, evident in the lines, "*—Once, on the farm, when I was a kid, I was screwing a goat; and the rope around his neck pulled tight;-and just when I came, he died...*" (155). He uses this same pattern to gain control of his feelings after he meets his father and realises that he is ready to play the role of "papa" and a family man now, a role that Herbert was deprived of, this is evident in the lines, "To think that what he wouldn't give me, he *wanted* to give to them" (156). His father's apology does not make him feel better, it makes him angrier and triggers his self-hate, trauma and deflection on his mother, evident in lines, "*and he asked me to forgive him for all he hadn't done–: but, what the shit? Who would have wanted to stay with Mom? With bastards, not even his own kids?*" (153).

The theme of sin is expressed very differently in both of the poems. Both the murders in the poems are not premeditated, they happen in the heat of the moment, but both the speakers have very different reactions to it. Porphyria's lover is happy and satisfied, he plants a kiss on her cheek and is not remorseful, in fact, he believes that Porphyria herself would be pleased, is evident in the lines "*so glad it had its utmost will*" (L 58). He taunts the belief in God in the last line of the poem when he expresses, "*And all night long we have not stirred, and yet God has not said a word!*" (L 64 – 65). Herbert on the other hand cannot digest the fact this gruesome act was committed by him, he stays in denial and tries very hard to believe that it was someone else who murdered but the facts were undeniable, he finally wishes that he fries in hell, evident in the lines "*I hope I fry. –Hell came when I saw MYSELF... and couldn't stand what I see...*" (157).

"Porphyria's Lover" and "Herbert White" aren't the only two poems by the two writers that are similar to one another, the poems "Fra Lippo Lippi" and "Ellen West" hold many similarities in terms of themes and motifs. The themes of toxic aestheticism, identity and mental sufferings are found in these poems. West suffers from body dysmorphia and an eating disorder, her "ideal" body reinforces toxic beauty standards, she wants to be "*thin, all profile and effortless gestures, the sort of blond elegant girl whose body is the image of her soul*", moreover, West is disgusted when she witnessed her mother and her grandmother growing old and loathes "nature" and "*the "natural" process of aging*", because it made them gain weight in their abdomen and made their skin blotchy. West is also seen admiring a woman at a restaurant; who meets her ideal beauty standards, the woman is beautiful, elegantly dressed and most importantly she has a good "bone structure" and skin so clear that even without makeup she would look beautiful (132).

West's goal in this poem is to beat "nature" and achieve her ideal look and she attempts to do this by starving herself and abusing the use of laxatives. West becomes a personification of the toxic beauty standards by observing the world. Lippo on the other hand is against censorship, he doesn't like the fact that he was asked to censor his paintings to fit the image and narrative of the church, he was a realist painter and wanted to depict society as is. His depiction of the Prior and his "niece" struck a nerve and he was asked to mimic the style of another painter called Gitto and redo his painting. Lippo tries to argue that "*A fine way to paint soul, by painting body*", and questions that "beauty" can be used to symbolise hope, fear, sorrow or joy but is ultimately denied. Lippo questions the purpose of art, is it to examine, observe or to be passed down to the next generations? He further laments that to paint any of God's works such as man, child, woman, nature, one must be careful to not "let truth slip" as it may be considered as a crime (L 206). He comes to the conclusion that the purpose of art is to depict the "perfect" world, as paintings last longer, showing one's perfect version, this is evident in the lines, "*And so they are better, painted –better to us, Which is the same thing. Art was given for that;"* (L 311). Both Lippo and West are inhibited by social norms, while Lippo resists the norms set by church authority, West succumbs to the toxic beauty standards.

The theme of identity is central in both of the poems. West reveals her "true self" in the first stanza of the poem, she beings with the description of her perfect death which would be, "*I love sweets, --Heaven would be dying on a bed of vanilla ice cream …*", she immediately changes tone focusing on her "ideal" beauty standards. She is also seen struggling with gender identity and her sexuality, she questions why she is a girl because she cannot deal with its "implications" and states that "*and sometimes, I even feel like a girl*" (132). Her struggles with sexuality are noted in the prose portions of the poem, these portions contain the voice of her doctor who psychoanalyses her, and he notes that she had become particularly attached to another female patient in the facility, he finally notes that the conclusive suicide letter in the poem is addressed to this patient and West's husband.

The suicide note states that West has finally lost the battle between her "ideal" self and a healthy lifestyle, she considers this lifestyle to be a "compromise", "sterile" and "unreal", she is unable to let go of her toxic ideal and it costs her, --her life. West is not only fighting her demons but is also dealing with a dismissive doctor, which in turn makes her struggle even more real. When West questions her gender identity, she is told that it is a "given", they do not dive deep into her gender dysmorphia, leaving it untreated, this is evident in the lines, "*Why am I a girl? I ask my doctors, and they tell me they don't know, that it is just "given".*" Moreover, her doctor declares that "no reliable therapy is possible" because her symptoms do not line up with any other typical mental diseases, he makes assumptions and does not focus on her ongoing problems, not only does he dismiss her gender dysmorphia but he is also dismissive of her sexuality, he only focuses on her symptoms such as her eating disorder but he ignores the causes of these symptoms leaving her vulnerable and untreated, which results in only more pain and confusion for West, leading her to take drastic measures to end her life (132).

Lippo struggles with his identity as a monk, he is caught in the middle of the night in front of a brothel by police officers, and he attempts to persuade them to let him go by declaring that he is a monk and by throwing big names like Medici. Lippo feels very stuck in his life, he believes that it was not fair to make an 8-year-old to take the vow of a monk and be celibate because he did not have the understanding of what he was giving up, all he cared about was the "mouthful of bread" that was his food that month since his parents passed away and he had to scavenge to survive. In the lines, "*The world and life are too big to pass for a dream, and I do these wild things in sheer despite, and play the fooleries, you catch me at, in pure rage!*" Lippo expresses that he does not want life to pass him by with his dreams unfulfilled. Both of the characters feel that their identity and life is controlled by others, for West, it is controlled by societal and gender norms, while Lippo is controlled by the Church (L 257).

Structural Analysis of Browning and Bidart's poems

The dramatic monologue is often written in free verse, it is dialogue-based and often uses literary devices such as unreliable narrator, non-linear narrative structure and use of punctuation to denote speech and dive deep into the psyche of a character. The free verse as a form lifts the restrictions of rhyme, metre and lyric allowing the poet to freely portray a psycho-analytic characterisation of their subject. This allows the dramatic monologue to bridge the gap between poetry and short stories, similar to the elements of the short stories, the dramatic situation, character analysis and the addition of prose act as plot and climax in a dramatic monologue. Narrative techniques are an important aspect of the dramatic monologue, not only do they set the tone of the poem but also entice the reader to adopt the role of "overhearer", as mentioned before. The dramatic monologue makes great use of nonlinear narrative and an unreliable narrator. The nonlinear narrative is a structural technique that does not follow the chronological order of events, instead, it gives information in bits and pieces for the reader to unfold, and it helps in establishing the mental state of the character and keeps the reader on their toes.

Bidart makes great use of this technique, in "Herbert White", the narration of events alters between the two voices, White moves back and forth in time throughout the poem, the poem begins with a description of the murder and the course of the poem moves between snippets of traumatic childhood memories, the day of the murder and the events after the murder in a haphazard manner. Similarly, in "Ellen West", the course of the events in the poem moves back and forth between her midlife, childhood, a time before she was married and her dearth. Even the voice of the doctor moves in a nonlinear fashion, jumping from the start of West's 32nd birthday to specific dates in January and February and then finally a big jump to March 30th, followed by her suicide three days later. Browning also makes use of subtle nonlinear narrative in his poems, in "Fra Lippo Lippi", Lippo attempts to make his bizarre actions understandable to the police by explaining how he got to where he was caught by them, he begins by telling them of his frustration of being locked in a room to paint saints for three weeks and he ends up pouring out his life frustrations, from his childhood events to his conflicts with Church authority, to his plans for a grand future painting. He jumps from topic to topic until his frustrations get to him, this long unprovoked rant by Lippo shows the reader his tired mental state. "Porphyria's Lover" is an exception to this narrative technique, as the events and their portrayal happen in a linear fashion.

The dramatic monologue makes distinctive use of punctuation, such as enjambment, line breaks, semicolons, exclamation points, colons, parentheses, dashes, ellipsis, white spaces, italics and capitalisation. This unconventional use of punctuation is essential to capture all the nuances of speech and the core identity of the character and their intense emotions. Browning makes subtle use of enjambment in "Porphyria's Lover", the line breaks in the poem happen at distinct moments: when he makes a decision. For example, he has decided that he is listening to the storm "*with a heart fit to break*", even before Porphyria has arrived, this decision making is most visible, in the lines, "*No pain felt her; I am quite sure she felt no pain.*" here he decides on Porphyria's behalf if she felt any pain while dying (L 10 & 47).

This combination of line breaks and enjambment are in line with a confessional or a rant and reveals the lover's mental state of what his insecurities and priorities are. In "Fra Lippo Lippi", Browning makes use of a lot of exclamation points to denote the dramatic and the heated altercation between Lippo and the police, these exclamation points are used to convey Lippo's mental state, especially his annoyance and frustration with life, for example, they are used when he was caught by the police, when he is describing his childhood experience of learning Latin at the monastery or when he is simply frustrated with the Church authority censoring his art. Browning also makes use of dashes frequently in this poem, these dashes are used to bring attention to something important, this is most visible in the lines, "*I'm my own master, paint now as I please—Having a friend, you see, in the Corner-house!*", here Lippo declares that he is free from censorship by the Church authority since he has influential connections with Medici who lives in the corner house, Browning highlights Lippo's connections because they signify that Lippo is no longer a child in need of food and shelter, he is a grown man and he can fend for himself by selling his paintings to these connections (L 93).

Bidart takes this unconventional use of punctuation a step further, he makes conscious use of elements such as capitalisation, semicolon, dashes, line breaks, commas, italics to add depth to the voice, emphasizing their emotional expression, he states this in an interview with Mark Halliday, "Punctuation allows me to "layout" the bones of a sentence visually, spatially, so that the reader can see the pauses, emphasis, urgencies and languours in the voice" (Halliday, 23). In Herbert White, Bidart makes use of dashes to differentiate between the two voices of the same speaker, the one who feels guilty and disgusted and the one who does not, this is clearly evident in the first stanza of the poem, " "*When I hit her on the head, it was good, and then I did it to her a couple of times,-- but it was funny,-- afterwards, it was as if somebody else did it...*", here the dash is followed by a change in perspective, it is used in two places indicating the different voices, the first voice of White finds the murder funny, moving forward to the second voice of White who is in denial and is trying to separate himself from these actions (153).

He also frequently makes use of italics and capitalisations for a dramatic emphasis on the emotional state of the speaker, this is best seen in the lines, "*—Hell came when I saw MYSELF... and couldn't stand what I see...*" " here the word "MYSELF" is capitalised, indicating that the speaker is longer in denial about his actions, he is finally accepting his crimes and is horrified with them, condemning himself to "fry in hell" (157). In "Ellen West", Bidart makes use of prose to differentiate between the two speakers in the poem, the voice of West and the voice of her doctor, this is indicative of their personalities and their mental states, West speaks in poetry not only because she is a poet herself and is artistically inclined to do but also because she is mentally suffering from her struggles, moreover, it adds an amplified dramatic effect when contrasted with the prose sections of the poem.

The doctor's prose sections are simply the notes or a case study that a doctor makes on their patient, they portray the detached, cold, apathetic clinical observations of her which are often dismissive of her struggles, and moreover, they also provide an authoritative objective to West's unreliable narration. Similar to "Herbert White", Bidart also makes use of capitalisations and italics frequently in this poem, these are used to portray her emotional state, her refusal to accept therapy and her innermost perceptions of her "disease". In the lines, " *–My doctors tell me I must give up this idea, but I WILL NOT... cannot.*", here she is refusing this treatment, as mentioned in her suicide letter, she considers giving up her ideals as a compromise that make her "sterile" and "unreal" (132). Bidart also makes curious use of three separated dots in between every stanza, they separate West's flow of thought, jumping from one thought to another and also jumping back and forth with prose and poetry sections to portray West's mental instability and the contrast of the doctor's authoritative voice, it also displays a non-linear progression to West's story (138).

CONCLUSION

In conclusion, the dramatic monologue has an overarching function that gives us poetry in a form of character-centric drama which bridges the gap between short stories and poems. The form evolves and adapts its structure according to the changes in society and literature because the core of it remains constant: a deep analysis of the unexplored and unuttered psyche of a character. In addition to psychoanalysis, it also connects the reader to the poem by eliciting their role as an "overhearer", leading the course for interpretation of the character through their personal viewpoints. By examining the poems of Robert Browning and Frank Bidart, this combination of constant and evolution is quite clear, their poems have similar themes, motifs and characters but their ever-changing structure portrays the change in era. Even though Browning and Bidart are writing a century apart, their work displays the ability of the dramatic monologue to be universal beyond the grasp of time, showing the depth of the human mind.

Works cited

Primary Sources

1. Bidart Frank, "*Half-Light: Collected Poems 1965-2016*," United States, Farrar, Straus and Giroux, 2017
2. Browning Robert, "*Fra Lippo Lippi*", accessed on 2nd May,2021

   Fra Lippo Lippi by Robert Browning | Poetry Foundation

1. Browning Robery, "*Porphyria's Lover*", accessed on 2nd May,2021

   Porphyria's Lover by Robert Browning | Poetry Foundation

Secondary Sources

1. Anderson Crystal L., *"The Coagulate and 'Not Simply a Case': Frank Bidart's Post-Confessional Framing of Mental Illness, Typography, The Dramatic Monologue and Feint in "Herbert White" and "Ellen West""*, 2015

FULL_TEXT.PDF (manchester.ac.uk), accessed on 6th May, 2021

2. Halliday Mark, *Frank Bidart- An interview (with Mark Halliday),* 1983

Frank Bidart—An Interview (With Mark Halliday) on JSTOR, accessed on 2nd May, 2021

3. "History of Psychology in the Nineteenth Century",

History of Psychology in the Nineteenth Century (iresearchnet.com), accessed on 10th May,2021

4. Howard Claud, "The Dramatic Monologue: It's Origin and Development", 1910,

The Dramatic Monologue: Its Origin and Development on JSTOR, accessed on 2nd May, 2021

5. Litgalaxy, "Stream of Consciousness and Interior Monologue", 8th September, 2020,

Stream of Consciousness and Interior Monologue - Lit-galaxy (litgalaxy2019.com), accessed on 4th June, 2021

6. Maynard John, "Speaker, Listener, and Overhearer: The reader in the Dramatic Monologue", 1987,

Speaker, Listener, and Overhearer: The Reader in the Dramatic Poem on JSTOR accessed on 13th May, 2021

7. Moldaw Carol, “Frank Bidart’s Poetry: The Substance of the Invisible”, 2004,

Frank Bidart’s Poetry: The Substance of the Invisible on JSTOR accessed on 13th May, 2021

Bio-Note

Manjari Nagori, (B.A. Hons, M.A. Hons)

Manjari is a teacher based in Mumbai, currently working as an Assistant Teacher at the English Department of Thakur College of Science and Commerce. She graduated from Mumbai University with a Bachelor’s Degree in English Literature in 2019 and then went on to pursue Masters in English Literature. She has a wide variety of interests ranging from world politics, philosophy, arts, fine arts to sci-fi.

CHAPTER X

CULTURAL BONDING, WOMEN EMPOWERMENT, AND ECOFEMINISM IN SUDHA MURTHY'S NOVELS HOUSE OF CARDS AND GENTLY FALLS THE BAKULA

Pallavi Kadam

ABSTRACT

The purpose of this research paper is to study the cultural bonding, women empowerment, and ecofeminism in Sudha Murthy's novels *House of Cards* and *Gently Falls the Bakula.* Sudha Murthy's novel women present powerful feminine characters that are compassionate, exuberant and charming in their way, yet simple and innocent. Indian history, culture, and tradition are eminently rich and three thousand years old. Indian women enchantingly preserve as well propagate Indian culture, tradition, and ethical values which are centuries old.

The main objective is to study various challenging aspects revolving around present Indian women and to explore their role in cultural bonding, their relationship with their surroundings, and their power to make decisions. Sudha Murthy through her novels make attempts of unwinding the recurring chapter of Indian women's life, also the complexity of her life and her efforts to adjust to different culture and structure of values. The most appreciable and overwhelming thing about Murthy"s female characters compared with the female characters of other Indian women novelists, are that Murthy's women have a positive attitude to life. They are educated, have a good intellect, and believe in hard work. They don't disregard the Indian culture and values but cherish them. They are exceptionally optimistic in their approach to life, ambition and believe in a leading ethical way in the profession as well everyday life. At the same time, they are not ignorant toward their country's environment and common people surrounding even after acquiring wealth and certain status.

Keywords: Indian culture, Sudha Murthy, relationships, environment, culture, Indian women and commercialization.

INTRODUCTION

Sudha Murthy is a prominent name in Indian women novelists who represent the pain struggle and conflict of the modern educated women that tussle between culture, tradition, modernity, rural and urban of India, and between individuality and independence on the other hand. The leading woman characters in novels choose to fight and protest against the traditional, culturally accepted norms and taboos of society. They are also facing responsibilities by trying to adjust themselves in the socio-cultural modes of the changing society. Women character in Sudha Murthy's novel are Intelligent and decision-makers, blending within the Indian culture and values. Her maternal home is a cocoon where she is guided by her parents and has the independence to choose the educational stream. After marriage circumstances represent the image of a woman who struggles between tradition and modernity, commercialized and normal ethical lifestyle. Her battle within herself to establish her own identity by being economically independent and without depending on her male counterpart. Murthy in her novels delineates the image of a new woman who demands to hold the same position and status as that of man in the society with equal sexuality and rights. Though initially, they are a supporter to their Husband both financially and emotionally when they find themselves stuck in unacceptable family life they are the rebellious women who seek self-discovery, self-respect, self-autonomy and self-govern as they are caught between declining values, marriage bonds, and the fast-approaching new life.

Unconventional remark on Women by Great Philosopher

In most cultures and traditions, women have always been considered subordinate to men, typecasted as homemakers, caretakers, and subservient of men. Aristotle the great Greek philosopher declared that "the female is female by virtue a certain lack of qualities". Nietzsche, the German philosopher, insisted that "woman is the source of all folly and unreason" and "woman is God's first mistake". *Freud* also insisted" women are weaker than men and women envy the private parts of a man". In this way, women somewhat were not only marginalized but denigrated in all traditions.

On the contrary, the following is Swami Vivekananda's quote on women and womanhood.

"Can you better the condition of your women? Then there will be hope for your well-being. Otherwise, you will remain as backward as you are now."

Female comprises fifty percent of the human population, both male and female are the prominent and essential components of human society. They depend on each other, regenerate together; life and society can only be sustained if there is a balance between these two components of society. For human evolution and the existence of humanity, both men and women are important, mother nature has provided each individual strength and potential same can be said about other creatures too, researchers agree to this fact that one is not bigger or better than the other. Still, have witnessed inhumane, unethical, and immoral practices against women and the environment in a larger sense. Commercialization has become so predominant in men's minds that less involvement of women in generating and supporting the economy has put her in the second status and less significant to society.

Social status and importance of women in Vedic and Post-Vedic Period of India.

In the Early Vedic period, there was no discrimination between men and a woman. Sometimes the birth of a female child was desired as can be seen from some texts in *Rigveda,* 'praying for a birth of girl child. The birth of a female was not seen as a misfortune and treated with tenderness and benevolence. Preference was given to girls' education. They were sent to Gurukuls to master various subjects such as theology, philosophy, medicine, and so on.

Initiation ceremony or Upanayana, Hindu ritual marked as acceptance of the student by a guru was performed for girls as well. To get a deeper insight into the past, we can look into *Vedas, Gita, Mahabharat, Ramayana, Arthashastra, Dharmashastra*, and several similar ancient literary works.

In the Vedic times too, the women had to face a world full of paradoxes, taboo induced on them on basis of religious beliefs and customs. Manu, the father of Indian political theory describes the position of women of the Vedic age as a place of dependency and subordination. Apparently Manu, himself has assigned a high status and dignity to women. His dictum is evidence of this in "*Yatranaryastupujyante,*

Ramantetatradevata"(III,56), says, "God exists where women are respected' but very few women in our state exercise their freedom, most of them are either oppressed or neglected to a secondary position. Sudha Murthy presents the bold, intelligent and confident woman who has the right to education, has the freedom to choose the educational field she wants to pursue, is confident to select a partner and at last strives for her values and individuality. Without any complaints, she accepts her fate, tries her best for the happiness of others, her husband, the greedy in-laws, relatives and guests. For their sake, she overlooks her own life, comfort, and ambition. In her every sphere of life, she was perfect, a perfect daughter-in-law, sister-in-law and wife. She was the same Shrimati, the village girl, who always liked the Bakula flowers and the same Mridula of the house of card who use to be pampered and caring daughter.

Status of Women in the Buddhist Period:

In the Buddhist period, the position of women improved to some extent. In the religious field, women came to occupy a distinctly superior place. for equal opportunity of women, in all aspects like education, employment culture and politics became very popular in the western world called feminism. Feminism as a movement gained potential in the 20th century, marking the culmination of two centuries' struggle for cultural roles and socio-political rights. This movement gained increasing prominence across three phases/waves - the first wave (political), the second wave (cultural) and the third wave (academic).

French existentialist Simone de Beauvoir in the book *The Second Sex* stated, "one is not born, but rather becomes a woman" - a statement that highlights the fact that humans are result of their choice as built by resources surrounding/her and those which society imposes on them. Second-wave feminism broadened the debate to include a wider range of issues: sexuality, family, the workplace, reproductive, and official legal inequalities. In the third wave, feminism was actively involved in academia, with its interdisciplinary associations with Marxism, psychoanalytic and post-structuralism, dealing with issues such as language, writing, sexuality, postcolonialism, ecological studies, representation, and so on.

In a simple style, she has analyzed the significant current-day issues in her family, society, and community in her novels. She has explored in-depth, various women characters through her works. She has projected in a simple style and explored in-depth the feeling, intellectuality, and identity of the women characters in her works.

House of Cards (2013)

Sudha Murthy sticks to her favourite theme - the clashes between the husband and wife when the husband becomes highly successful and rich. The story starts with a dedication "*To all the Mridulas who suffer silently.*“. House of Cards is a story about a simple village girl Mridula, who migrates to Bangalore city along with her husband Sanjay. Mridula is a school teacher and Sanjay is a doctor (gynaecologist). Sanjay to leave his government job and start a private hospital along with him. Sanjay's behaviour and attitude change when money flows from the nursing home. Their son Sishir was a spendthrift and Sanjay and Sishir ignored Mridula. Mridula assumes that she knows all about the management of Sanjay clinic, but her trust thrashes when she comes to know that Sanjay has given lakhs of rupees to his sister and mother and always lying to her regarding their poor conditions. Her husband had manipulated her completely due to her ignorance and foolishness.

Mridulla disappointed with their husband's ignorance and of hiding things from her goes into a depression she starts consulting a psychiatrist. The doctor asks Mridula to bring Sanjay with her, Sanjay completely ignores her and assumes this is her trick to get his attention. Finally, Mridula decides to leave her luxurious house and move to her native place and breathe in fresh air when Sanjay tried to stop her. She said, "No, I have spent twenty-five of my most important years with you, and yet, I never felt like I belonged to you or your family. I'm still an outsider. Now, I want to live for myself. I have my job, my school and my village. You don't have to worry about me any longer. You and Sishir can visit me whenever you want" (HOC, 218).

Summary "Gently Falls the Bakula"

Shrimati and Shrikant are two intelligent competitive classmates. They hail from a small town in Karnataka, are neighbours and their families are involved in an ancient feud. Shrimati is very intelligent and could ace anything she put her mind to, but she loved history and studied for the love of the subject. Shrikant wanted to be an acheiver. Both follow their dreams and fall in love and get married. But with success comes a high price. The couple slowly starts drifting apart. Shrikant's meteoric rise to the top makes him ambivalent towards his wife. He wants to achieve more and more and treats Shrimati like his secretary who is there to do everything to run his life smoothly. Being childless too makes Shrimati lonelier, adoption is not an option as Shrikant does not support the notion Shrimati who put her career on hold and even gave up her chance to a full scholarship for a PhD program in the US now is second-guessing her choices

Shrimati goes into depression, tries to convince Shrikant to give her some time, but he completely ignores her. She sobs and realizes this marriage lack compassion and tenderness of the relationship. There is no existence of her in this relationship. Their residence had no room for a relationship. Since she cannot return to Hubli, she decides to do her PhD with Prof. Collins and follow her passion and ambition, as this marriage had left her empty-handed. The Bakula flowers as a symbol of their love had lost all their fragrances and power, there is no essence same as Shrikant and Shrimati relationship. The present paper also focuses on ecofeminism, cultural bonding and women empowerment in Sudha Murthy's novel *House of Cards and Gently Falls the Bakula*

Ecofeminism

Ecofeminism opens many aspects of suppressed elements, it not only links women with vegetation, plants but also with animals, land, and water exploitation. Ecological destruction and industrial catastrophes threaten daily life, and the maintenance of these problems have become the responsibility of women. Sudha Murthy cherishes motherland by mentioning the following lines through the protagonist of 'Gentle fall of Bakula' highlighting ancient poet Pampa's line

"This land is so pious and sacred, that
If I am not reborn as a human being in this land,
God then please make me a singing
cuckoo or humming bee at least."(4)

Shrimati mentions these lines to Shrikant praising the place where she was born and presents her feeling and compassion with the land she is born in, and grown-up, her connection with land and environment. Sudha Murthy connects women with the environment with a positive aspect as caretakers. In the novel *House of Cards* protagonist Mridula is compassionate toward Champa Bai Kamitkar's flower garden spread in the backyard.

`capabilities compared to other animals, but the human being has dominated and suppressed existence of all others for his/her materialistic views, for example, cutting trees for materialistic purpose, converting jungle to farms and real estate properties. Ecofeminism as materialist is another common dimension of ecofeminism. A materialist view connects some institutions such as labour, power, and property as the source of domination over women and nature. Men dominate the commercial world and exploit every other animal, land for his betterment and selfish desires. He exploits farm animals; cows and buffalo for self-use, commercialization of milk and its products at cheaper rates have tremendously reduced the life span of these animals by almost one-third. Men dominate women and humans dominate nature.

In *Gently Falls the Bakula* Sudha Murthy has used the Bakula tree as a symbolism of spirituality, romance, beauty, union, engaging aroma. She describes throughout the year the blooming of Bakula flowers even in diverse climatic conditions, its stability in weathering conditions. Bakula tree stood gracefully as usual and spread its fragrance. In the evening time, the flowers lay on the ground forming a carpet. Not only does the female protagonist 'Shrimati' have a great attachment with the Bakula tree but her school friend and later her husband Shrikant recollects many ancient stories that connected the Bakula flowers with attraction and romance, the Bakula flowers were one such memento of love that these young men carried, even though it would dry up, it would still give out the fragrance summoning the beloved's love.

Cultural Bonding:

"You have to maintain a culture of transformation and stay true to your values" (Jeff Weiner. *0eb73e-jeff-Weiner-quotes)*Above quote asserts that to remain true to our roots, which certainly includes our values, and we need to remain open for new experiences, new ways of looking and the world and new beliefs that may influence our way of looking at the world. Developing a culture of transformation both inside of yourself and also within your company is very important in the sense that it is the contrast to stagnation.

Culture consists of the beliefs, behaviours, objects, and other characteristics common to the members of a particular group or society. Through culture, people and groups define themselves, conform to society's shared values, and contribute to society. Thus, culture includes many societal aspects: language, customs, values, norms, mores, rules, tools, technologies, products, organizations, and institutions. This latter term **institution** refers to clusters of rules and cultural meanings associated with specific social activities. Common institutions are family, education, religion, work, and health care. Popularly speaking, being **cultured** means being well-educated, knowledgeable of the arts, stylish, and well-mannered.

Culture is that sense of relationship that makes each person of one society feel that they belong there. Bonding and interaction commence at the family level and grow in a community, women play a greater role in bonding at family. Society, according to what we know so far, is any group of people who tend to share the same region, biological and cultural characteristics and have the same system of behaviour and action. One society must be able to be self-sufficient to continue existing while the culture exists beyond the term of sufficiency. Sudha Murthy's works carry a lot of historical influences and a strong cultural bonding. Her novels make a lasting impact in the minds of the readers which make them think and rethink.

Sudha Murthy cherishes Indian culture and values in her novels, same time believing in the liberalization and individuality of women which society should accept. Her principle-based writings assert immensely on simple and ordinary lifestyles of rural India wherein the readers can identify themselves in some character. Her writings grasp Indian culture and incidents are drawn from day-to-day realities, events, and experiences. Any society could not be formed without a cultural bond, Sudha Murthy's novels portray common people with simple lifestyles and minutely analyses day to day activities at the family and community level. The culture of a community is the result of the present past and history of that territory, In Sudha Murthy's novel, we find numerous examples of eminent features of Indian culture and history. The author has got this cultural-socialism from the smallest thing like a relationship among family members such as the relationship between daughter in law and mother in law, mother and daughter, husband and wife, between cousin, village and urban people, between two friends, educational system and to the universal thing like the Noble Prize.

For example in the *'gental fall of Bakula's* the author describes emperor Ashoka as a great human being about Kalinga war, his decision to become tolerant compassionate and dedicate the rest of his life to practice and preaching dharma. She mentions great Ashoka's kingdom expanded from Karnataka in the south to Pakistan Border in the north, he inscribed Pali, Prakrit. Brahmi and Aremic scripts so that dharma messages would reach the common man. Unknowingly Shrikant expresses doubt on the intelligence level of girls though Shrimati was always ahead of him at school and higher secondary level. The author wants to address how female interest and intellect was not worth for male borne in a patriarchal society.

In*House of Cards*, the Protagonist female character Mridula belongs to a family which is economically affluent and the owner of very fertile land in the village. Bheemanna Mridula's father is a kind and gentle father, he gives Mridula all independence to choose any education stream at the college level, of her choice and liking, though her teacher and mother insisted to study Medicine, Mridula choose to be a teacher. This also explains the Indian culture and the empowerment of women at a young age, the freedom families grant to their children to decide on their own though financially they are still dependent on them. Once Bheemanna questions Mridula: "Why god has given a speech to humans and not to animals" Mridula answered childishly, "to talk, Bheemanna says no child not just to talk, it is to share, so whenever you face difficulties or you receive joy, you must share it with others, but other poor animals can't even share their difficulties".(*HOC*,3) The author through small dialogues in her novel asserts on the humanitarian view of sharing and bonding with one another is a human necessity and duty too.

Murthy in *House of Cards* mentions a wedding atmosphere where the first encounter of Shrikant and Shrimati happens dramatically and they are attracted to each other. During the Mehendi ceremony, the bride goes into the emotional transition of getting married to an unknown man and getting into a different household. The author describes an arranged marriage situation in which the parents of two people, typically of similar cultural backgrounds, are predetermined to be married by their parents or a third party. Arranged marriages are a part of many different cultures, both old and new. They present a very logical approach to the institute of marriage and are influenced by both cultural and economic factors. The author insists that women play a greater role in bonding two families and taking a step ahead in the growth of bond between both families. In the same circumstances Murthy describes different emotions the rainy season brings in every person, for Mridula rain was blissfulness and joy, it was nature's gift, she thought the earth is full of dirt and still makes the world green. It inspires creativity in artists and poets. Sudha Murthy fashionably presents Indian culture through wedding descriptions of rituals performed, colourful silk sarees, variety of flowers used , the fragrance of havans, and mouthwatering wedding food.

Food is one more medium of cultural bonding in India whether it is homemade spices, veggies, or sweets like laddo jalebis, people love to share the same with neighbours, relatives. Whenever a guest visits he/she carries homemade sweets or snacks, this quality is inherited from generation to generation. Mridula after her wedding, when she first time visits her mother in law house she carries saree and fruits for her and even to sister-in-law's house, the same is not well received by both of her relatives. When Mridula arrives in Mumbai she finds the culture of the city very different, the crowd, pollution, people juggling from one station to another, Author tries to describe the mechanical life of humans and the psychological impact on the human mind. Also, the author mentions the culturally rich places of Maharashtra like Pune, Ajanta Elora, Aurangabad, Nasik, Nagpur through Mridula's school trip.

Culture is learnt through the process of socialization. Culture is a social heritage as it is transmitted by, and communicated to, members of society. When an individual is born into a society, the social symbols, artefacts, and so on of his/her culture are passed on to him/her. Culture is gratifying as it satisfies the needs of its individuals. Example: The need for love and security is satisfied by the institutions of family and marriage. The structure of culture is transmitted from one generation to the next, and every generation adds, subtracts, or changes what it inherits. This aspect of change and continuity shows that it is a dynamic process and is not stagnant for example marriage, customs, and traditions. Culture is super-organic, it is above society. People and societies are born and perish too, but culture continues to survive. Culture is, therefore, super-individual and super-organic. Sudha Murthy professes the role of women in propagating Indian culture and tradition. Women not only performed the tasks assigned to them as per tradition but also pass on values and expertise to their daughters and son, in short, the next generation.

Women Empowerment

In her book, *Gender Trouble*, Butler uses a central concept that gender is something that is not always based on social construction but rather is created through repetitive performances throughout one life. It is not a fixed notion that one is born with but rather keeps changing through time till it constructs the self altogether. Women are considered weaker in most of society including India, she is protected by her father in childhood, her husband in adulthood, and by her son in old age. Somehow in this caring and protection phase, women lose their power of standing as independent individuals with their own identities.

Women empowermentcan be measured through the Gender Empowerment Measure (GEM), which is a measure of inequalities between men's and women's opportunities in a country. It combines inequalities in three areas: political participation and decision making, economic participation and decision making, and power over economic resources. Empowerment means social and political independence in the decision-making process. Individuals' right to participate in political structures and formal decision-making and the economic sphere, once ability to obtain an income that enables her participation in economic decision-making without any sort obstruction. Empowerment is the process that creates power in individuals over their own lives, society, and their communities. People are empowered when they can access the opportunities available to them without limitations and restrictions such as in the right education, profession, and lifestyle. Feeling entitled to make decisions for the self, family and larger scale while participating in a community, creates a sense of empowerment.

In Sudha Murthy's writings, it is always asserted that a woman has to break the barricades of psychological and social constrain situated within and by the community. Researchers minutely observe various women characters in Sudha Murthy's novel, they are economically independent and are decision-makers too. For example, in *House of Cards* Sanjay's mother, Ratnamma has a small shop and believes in saving every penny she earns. Champa Bai Mridula's neighbour is travelling frequently for her business, Bheemanna asks Mridulla to take whichever branch she like to pursue in college disregards her being a rank holder he doesn't allow his wife to impose any sort of pressure on Mridula to pursue Medicine. Even intently Falls the Bakula the protagonist's mother is shown as a working woman, apparently owning less power to decide for her family. Even Shrimati has the right to choose the educational stream and later life partner she wants to marry.

Apparently the scenario of both Protagonists changes after their marriage. In one of the chapters Murthy doesn't confide protagonist to the kitchen, for instance, Mridula had never cooked a complete meal at her parent's place in Aladahalli, she helped mother but never maid main course but responsibility increased after marriage she had to cook a full meal, lock the house and go out to work. Similarly, Shrimati is also presented working in Mumbai, doing household and longing for their husband at the same time just to help her husband economically.

The author explores the relationship in depth; Mridula, Shrimati are simple, hardworking, innocent also intelligent throughout, whereas the male depiction of Sanjay and Shrikant is strongly influenced by the power of luxury, comfort, and materialism, steadily climbing up the corporate ladder without realizing the value of family life. The family class difference, the rift between in-laws relationship, misconception, lack of understanding, loss of faith, and compassion, holding male domination stands are prominent features in both the novels taken for study. Both lead female characters to have much-untapped potential but are left as doormat types by their respective partners.

Women's empowerment certainly means equal participation of women in the economy and politics, apparently, in reality, it has increased workload on women, the heavy stress and strain she faces while combing outside world and domestic work, child care makes her tiresome, in society, she is just valued as an idol of sacrifice, her devotion is never considered or given any status. The point to be noted is even in Hindu Mythology and culture women is depicted as a symbol of sacrifice. Working women face many problems related to health, psychology, and family in association with their time allocation. It is true that with a tight schedule in-between market work and domestic work, the majority of working women even have significant turmoil on their physical and mental health. The whole patriarchal system needs transformation, to empower women at work, men should support them in household responsibilities, which is not easy in the case of India at least, although many men support their wives at home the overall responsibility of children and house lies on her shoulder. Sudha Murthy asserts that women have to distinguish themselves from their patriarchal constructed social ties. To reconstitute herself, she goes through a saga only to unfold as an individual.

CONCLUSION

"Self Revelation is a cruel process.
The real picture, the real you never emerge.
Looking for it is as bewildering as trying to know
how you look "ten different mirror show then different.
(Shashi Deshpande, *That long silence*)

It is evident that women play a crucial role in the development of society and the nation. Women are fifty percent of the world population, still subservient to men in all societies. The unpleasant marriage experience of these female characters reveals their experience of cluelessness, demotion, exploitation, continuous persuasion still facing just ignorance then breaks the silence. Man-Woman relationship, social acceptance, estrangement in modern life, and Indian values, capitalism forms the core of all these novels. In spite of all complaints Indian wife adhere to cultural values, she goes on compromising. The baggage to keep home and family intact, present the Indian concept of marriage. The agony and helplessness of the Indian wife are suggested through an ironic situation which she accepts as her destiny. The writer tries to present the bitterness of the husband and wife relationship Sudha Murthy covers a wide range of characters, mixed incidents, different scenarios, larger involvement (gallery) of characters depicting a realistic context, restricted mindsets, stereotyped judgments, and unfulfilled expectations. Sudha Murthy embarrasses her protagonists who emerge victorious as successful individuals, flouting all fears, dilemmas, contradictions, taboos, frustrations, and long-suffering endurance. Behind the silence of every woman, there is a voice that remained voiceless but turn to her jest. The Protagonist remains predisposed and vulnerable to society, which has used her to remain like a statuette, emotionless and in vain, an illustration of beauty only

The author explores the relationship in depth; Mridula, and Shrimati are simple, diligent and virtuous throughout the novel, whereas the male depiction of Sanjay and Srikant is strongly influenced by the power of luxury, competitiveness and materialism. The compassion, trust from their partners slowly becomes insignificant to them. The family disjoint/class misbelief, mistrust, unprogressive thoughts, strangled male egos stands similar in both the novels taken for study. All these female characters have much-untapped potential but are left as doormat types. Symbolism prevails in a large representation of each character as a symbolic behaviour, Bakula is related to Shrimati's, charming sweet and attractive nature. But these qualities go unnoticed as the story progresses. The flower symbolizes true love which remains constant but shrouded in their self emphasizing world and priorities. Male protagonists fail to realize that a home is a place of feelings, and every individual relationship is eminent, partner's views are quintessential. As goes the age-old proverb: "A House is made of brick and stone, a home is made of love and compassion and trust" (99).

Here in these novels, realization sets-in in the male inconsiderate characters like Shrikant and Sanjay who fail to establish an equal bond. At end of the novel, they do realize their incompleteness and inaccuracies in developing a strong relationship in partnership and providing equal opportunities in the household are the key ingredients of a happy marriage. They observe life from a different angle, away from their self-centric perspective. Social and Ethical values are declined in the novels as Shrikant and Sanjay accomplish their capitalist endeavours and ignored their partner's effort and love in making them wealthier. The female protagonist is presented as having great willpower while unfolding the chapters of life and facing the obstacles of the marriage journey.

This ignorance and deduced importance of protagonists by their life partners make us realize the aftermath of the whole struggle as depicted by Sudha Murthy. Their choices were tough; they gathered courage, strong will, carried the bruise of their marriage to create a new horizon. Getting to know our real worth is a relentless task, it helps us to toughen our values and passion. Self-discovery is not an easy ride and its journey of pain and understanding. The characters portrayed, faced many twists and turns, disappointments and setbacks yet decided to live a purpose-driven life. I conclude with these lines

I sprouted in tenderness in a warm abode.
I dream to flutter high in the sky.
I had fallen in love to rise high.
I choose my nest to thrive and
I just expected adoration and assurance,
but my dreams were thrashed as never
left me aloof forever,

I have sub versed now, to create my own new sky. (8)

Works Cited

Primary Text a)Murthy, Sudha. *Gently Falls the Bakula.* New Delhi. Penguin Books,2008.

House of Cards. New Delhi.Penguin Books, 2013.

Staal, Fritis,. *Discovering the Vedas,* Penguin Books,*2009*

Manuscript, The Oxford International Encyclopedia of Legal History,

Carl, Olson. *The Many Colors of Hinduism*, Rutgers University Press, 2007d) Shiva,Vandana, Mies, Maria. *Ecofeminism*, London and New York ,Zed Books, 1993

Cargill and the Corporate Hijack of India's Food Agriculture

CHAPTER XI

A HISTORY OF FOOD: EXPLORING DALIT POETRY

Priyanka Corda

ABSTRACT

Food and culture are noodled together in a dish that runs deep and continues to owe to the eternal impacts that various visitors like religion, politics, colonialism, displacement, class, caste bring to the table. The opportunity to examine the twain presents itself in the form of literature. This paper serves as an investigation of the works of three Dalit poets which delivers a semblance that food has in poetry in order to unearth several areas such as the poet's cultural identity, dining etiquettes and eating habits, political implications, food memories, cultural and religious altercations, the time period the poem presents as well as the connotations implied during it. Tracing the purpose of using food imagery in poetry transforms the text into an entity that survives beyond its creation. Progressing along with this paper, the use of food language in Dalit poetry unlocks a portal of knowledge that helps study the behaviour of food, the grasp it has on an individual and, or a community as a whole and, as the pivotal key, the ruthless impacts the Dalit community has been inflicted with.

INTRODUCTION

The presence of food in literature has been thriving organically since ancient times. The acknowledgement and examination of this presence are owed to the recent studies of food in literature from religious texts to cookbooks to poetry to fiction. The use of food in literature can conjure up in the forms of dining practices, feasting, fasting, diets, eating and drinking habits, the preparation and, or preservation processes and many others which materialize into opportunities to examine its correspondence with cultural, political, sociological, historical, economical, religious domains.

The bread and wine in Biblical scriptures is a notable example of food in literature. The Last Supper is an important and symbolic crux in Christianity where the breaking of the bread and drinking of the wine during the Passover meal symbolises the acceptance of the body and blood of Christ not only into the body but also in the lives of the people. From a literary analysis standpoint, the Passover meal also foreshadowed the death of Jesus. The bread and wine have such a mammoth prominence that the re-enactment of the last supper is practised during almost all religious Christian gatherings, for instance, during a regular Catholic mass which is known as the Eucharistic celebration. It is through the recognition of the vitality of the bread and wine that results in the traditions, customs and celebrations in the Christian community. Other literary texts include John Milton's *Paradise Lost* (1608–1674), Lewis Carroll's *Alice in Wonderland* (1865), Geoffrey Chaucer's *The Canterbury Tales* (c. 1387 and 1400), Edmund Spencer's *The Faerie Queen* (1590), William Langland's *Piers Plowman* (c. 1370–90) are conducive and notable examples amongst many to study not only the symbolism, imagism, allegorical and metaphorical contexts of food but also to deduct the origins, influences and impacts of food on civilisation as well their art. Therefore, food in literature has a very special role as it helps investigate the history of a people and understand their practices. For instance, the diversity of religion is so vast that there are often major differences.

These differences extend to the food habits of respective communities. While these differences can be politically and humanly questionable, the tension and its effects seep into literature which is noteworthy. The dynamics of these differences as well as the brotherhood of a multicultural nation such as implementations of certain unfair laws (beef ban) or the communal practice of fasting in relation to religious customs ('roza') have valuable scope in the study of food culture in literature. Food and culture are interconnected to the extent that a shift in the diets of a small community implies a change in the culture of that community.

> Food becomes culture when it is prepared because, once the basic products of his diet have been acquired, man transforms them by means of fire and a carefully wrought technology that is expressed in the practices of the kitchen. Food is culture when it is eaten because man, while able to eat anything, or precisely for this reason, does not in fact eat everything or precisely for this reason, does not in fact eat everything but rather chooses his own food, according to criteria linked either to the economic and nutritional dimensions of the gesture or to the symbolic values with which food itself is in-vested. Through such pathways, food takes shape as a decisive element of human identity and as one of the most effective means of expressing and communicating that identity (Montanari, 11).

Now, how can you stay connected to a culture that feels real these days? A country blessed with its colourful ingredients in the form of people and their backgrounds has transformed into a toxic potion that has conjured a vicious partitioning. Culture will create an image of richness in the essence of the word but that richness has always been compromised. Culture has shaped itself into a field that strenuously ventures upon picking apart the subalterns and separating them from the masses. This paper aims to demonstrate the undeserving discrimination against the Dalit community culminating in the most major and inhuman means of subordination imposed: food. Food functions as a vital source of energy to sustain life. This natural access to sustenance deprived to the masses belonging to the Dalit community finds its evidence through the poetry of Dalit writers which serves as documentation of the inequitable treatment imposed upon them in the form of literature.

FOOD AND THE BIASED

Meena Kandasamy is the first Indian Dalit woman poet penning down Dalit poetry in English. Her scathing words are unremorseful and the sentiments channelled are sharp, clear and graphic. The underlying stations of her poems speak of the sordid realities of women and Dalit people but one stop after another her poetry splashes into one face the wake-up call to recognize the true unashamed identity they possess. A ruthless contemporary voice like Kandasamy disenchants the assumption of the simple struggles and identities inflicted upon the marginalized section. A relevant, contemporary voice, as opposed to classic writers, is dire in these times to not only remind one of the discriminatory treatments that occurred towards them then but how it has worsened in the present decades.

In an overtly Ram Rajya ideological nation, one may have an inclination to believe that if you do not "naturally" lounge in the first-class Hindu gents' section you might as well just be a visitor in their world, merely existing to wipe shit stains off their latrines. Access to unquestionably basic needs such as water is forcibly transformed into the questionable when laid in regards to the Dalit community. In her poem, "Liquid Tragedy: Karamchedu 1985", published in her first collection of poetry *Touch*, in 2006, structured artfully into a matka or pot:

Buffalo Baths. Urine. Bullshit
Drinking-Water for the Dalits
The very same Pond.
Practice for aeons.
A bold Dalit lady
dares to question injustice.
Hits forth with her pot. Her indignation
is avenged. Fury let loose. Violence. Rapes.
Killings. Self-seeking politicians shamelessly
consult History—"If there was a way out then,
there shall be a way out now." Succor arrives with
Esteemed Father of our Nation. His Samaadhi speaks:
If Harijans don't get water in this village, let them
set on a sojourn elsewhere. The rotten example
is obeyed. Casting behind cruel memories
Dalits exit—weary of the persecution
And wander all over the nation.
Again, a Dalit Exodus.

Total Surrender. (Kandasamy, 52)

which symbolizes the monstrous treatment of the Dalits and the undignified conditions they barely survived in: "Buffalo Baths. Urine. Bullshit", who were not deemed human enough to access clean drinking water, is based on a real incident that took place in Karamchedu, Andhra Pradesh, on July 1985 where six Madiga (lower caste Hindus), men were killed and three Madiga women were raped by the Karmas (upper-caste Hindus) while many were injured irrespective of whether the victims were pregnant or children, displays the prevalent dire conditions that have been a "Practice for aeons." She lashes out at Mahatma Gandhi's so-called pro-Dalit ideologies, recognizing the hypocrisy in them: "If Harijans don't get water in this village, let them set on a sojourn elsewhere. The rotten example is obeyed," in turn the hypocrisy of the system of a so-called secular state.

Water, the source of life, a creation inseparable from culture, food that is rudimentary to all life forms finds itself in negation, in a realm forcibly and separately created for the subalterns. Water is not only used to survive but has an essential purpose in the preparation of food. It also presents itself as a spiritual and physical entity in various religious beliefs such as Hinduism, Buddhism, Islam and Christianity, for example, in the form of ritual acts such as sprinkling holy water, the purifying river Ganga. The universal presence, value and vitality of water since the dawn of time need not be overexplained. Water in itself functions as a cultural identity of a people. It is the single most commonality that binds humanity. The separation of a person, a people or community from this binding power, that water is, is to separate them from the human. To lynch the right to water is to lynch the right to cultural identity and life in itself. The poem is a direct charge against these undeserving cultural practices imposed on the Dalit community and unflinchingly exposes the cultural bias existing in the present-day life of the discriminated.

FOOD AND POLITICS

Sukirtharani is a Dalit poet from Tamil Nadu. Her poem "Beef is My Right" which was written after the beef ban imposed on the nation on 26 May 2017, by the Bharatiya Janata Party is a protest against the cultural imposition that took place by the "upper" caste Hindu mentality. The poem has been translated and published in a few articles that display the underlying discontent with the political party's agenda:

When I grew hungry and licked my lips
That beef juice
Cooked in the night stove
Was mother's milk for me.
Drying that yellowish fatty pieces
covering the meat
in the noon sun
And roasting it in its buttery fat
That melts like snow
Is my snacks.
It is my pass time
to chase away the crows
with the piece of black cloth
when the pieces of beef are cut at length and dried
in the courtyard of the house
over the thorny bushes cut into clusters
Clad in folk costumes
That local dance of men and women
For rituals and deaths
Is my dance
Cutting good bovine meat
Spreading the pieces on fresh coconut strips
Shared into ten and twenty
Collecting them in a bamboo basket
polished with dung
carrying the deep red beef
on those Saturdays and Sundays of the week
Is my festival.

This is my life.
This is my celebration.
This is my festival.
This is my living.
This is my food.
If you want
you to decide your shit
My Food. My beef.
I will only decide. (Sukirtharani Exp 29)

A nation that is meant to flourish in its multiculturism time and again submits itself to the Hindutva forces. The BJP, in their election manifesto, set forth their entitled notions of cattle slaughter as unholy as well as a non-Indian cultural practice even though consumption of meat, mainly beef for that matter, was prevalent even before Buddhism entered the picture which intervened with the case of abuse towards animals and where the consumption of beef by a great number population of the nation, for ages, goes against the anti-cultural belief. The excuse propagated by the party was to retract the influence of minority communities like the Muslims and Christians who consumed beef. But the consumption of beef is done mainly by the SCs and STs due to their lack of access to different dietary lifestyles. There have been historical evidence of the SCs, STs and OBC's consumption of beef along with cattle rearing which does not equate to their hatred towards animals. Therefore, the premises on which the manifesto is based is inequitable, serving only the Brahminical ideologies. The basis of the enforcement of the ban is unfair as these beliefs of cows or buffalos being sacred are not shared by the nation as a whole.

Food rights, food habits and culture are tightly knit as the food habits are large aspects that define important cultural aspects of communities and the basis to having food rights emerge from them. The large aspects of food habits are what contribute to history, help communities grow in harmony, as meals and feasts are the ignitions to socializing, factors that carry the food industry and so on. To device laws that take away the food rights of people are not only a step towards the destruction of food culture but also the omission of space for basic human rights of an individual and a community as a whole.

The poem exposes the dietary inequality against Dalits who have been tormented by their imposed caste status for years. Caste discrimination has been prevalent for decades. Various Dalit poets, writers, activists have come forth to expose the plight they have been subjected to while asserting their identity through their works. Poets like Meena Kandasamy and N.D. Rajkumar has used their fearless words to detonate the caste system and its bias by claiming their identity in society. Sukirtharani is one such writer whose words are a weapon against the never-ceasing caste discrimination and carry a torch for expressionism of dissent. Her use of 'beef' and 'rights' held in such proximity of the title itself exhibits the mangling of politics in food culture.

Food in language denote several implications and can symbolize matters or sentiments that leap beyond its literal usage. Beef is the central character of the poem. Comparisons of beef consumption to sentimental metaphors project the importance of personal freedom. Beef represents the poet's way of living. She compares the ordinariness in her right to consume beef with ordinary acts that portray a universal relevance in the lives of any given individual such as enjoying snacks, doing household chores, delicate moments of being comforted, frolicking in the air of festivities with loved ones and even the most basic routine of bathing. She tactfully slips in the meaty metaphor in these acts to represent the vitality that her dietary choices in their most regular form signify.

The food language in the poem embodies basic human expression in all its forms. Food encompasses an immortal magnetism that draws an individual or community hailing from any walk of life as food is a permanent requisite for the nourishment of the body and the life of it. "Beef is My Right" sentimentally and assertively tries to restore her right to food which is central to her means of subsistence. The energy for life is supplied from the liberation of suppressing forces that bludgeons the quality of life. While these forces are inexorable and can take shape in the form of government laws or religious customs it is in the service of literature, in this paper, poetry, that produce impressions of the complexities and instabilities that exist within a society and especially in a multicultural and multireligious nation like India.

FOOD AND RITUALS

N. D. Rajkumar's "He will sing and dance the Original Song", translated from Tamil by Anushiya Ramaswamy, from his poetry collection *Give Us this Day a Feast of Flesh,* was first published in December 2010. This collection contains poems from Rajkumar's *Kal Vilakkugal* (2004) and *Odakku* (1999). The poem speaks of the poet's love for the god, Sudalai Madan. This area of focus of this paper is to be on the diet of the god.

He will sing and dance
The Original Song.
His tongue withered with a steady diet
Of butter and boiled vegetables
Sudalai quarrelled and left his abode
For earth
And joined the group leaving for a sacrifice
The black male goat bathed and placed
Under the knife, cooked
And offered to the god;
After eating the meat spice with love
Sudalai in gratitude
Promised to protect
When called with such love. (Rajkumar, 57)

Sudalai Madan is worshipped by the people living mainly in the villages of Tamil Nadu. Any knowledge in regards to his birth or character has been the consequence of various versions of oral narratives passed down to the people from ancient times or certain folklores, folksongs (*Kayathar*) and even literature (Jayamohan's "Madan Motcham") (Maadhava Exp 30). A general understanding of the god is he was born of Lord Shiva and Goddess Parvati. He detested vegetarian food which made him a gigantic meat devotee.

Sudalai means protector while Madan means burial grounds. It is said his hunger for meat originated from the burial grounds at Kailasa. Sudalai in appeasement with the food offerings by people is believed to deliver his protection to the villages in Tamil Nadu from evil forces.

The dishes mentioned in the poem are "butter and boiled vegetables" and (goat) "meat spice". The people have taken into consideration, as one does for any guests that are about to visit, the dishes most favoured by the god. To take note of the likes and dislikes in regard to the dietary preferences of one implies the immense regard one holds for the person or entity in question. The peculiarity of this poem also lies in the preparation of the offering. The offering in question is the animal sacrifice of a black, male goat. It is not cutthroat, brutal, horrid or gory depiction. The meal is "meat spice with love" which is a display of genuine worship of the god Sudalai. It is in response to this love that Sudalai performs his service in the protection of his people.

The correlation between food and culture expands beyond the boundaries of earthly human relationships. To understand the practice of food within a culture it is of certain worth to consider how people perceive its value in association with a dominating portion of the lives of a people: religion. Dietary lifestyles like vegetarianism and non-vegetarianism are often reflective of the food habits that were practised or believed to be practised by the deities in question. What contributes to the food consumption practised by people is the food offerings done during religious rituals. These food offerings symbolize various things such as surrender, worship, imploration, penance and so on. Often, these food offerings which are prayed over during rituals, are believed to have transformed into sanctified food. An example and a term for this transformed food are "Prasada" in Hinduism.

Animal sacrifices have been prevalent throughout history for religious purposes. For instance, in the Old Testament, the sacrifice of animals (as well as people) was practised for various reasons like to attain reconciliation with God or the atonement of sins. In some cultures, animal sacrifices were done so that the gods in question would be pleased in turn changing the course of nature. Often these animal sacrifices were consumed after the rituals, especially by priests and sometimes even their slaves. While the poem does not state any consumption of the food offered by the poet or the people from his community it is a high probability that it took place considering the non-vegetarian diet of Dalit people as well as the preparation style. Naivedyam in Tamil culture often culminates with the consumption of the food offered by the devotees.

The use of food in the poem is not of the consumption by people but by a god which holds significance as its presence in poetry serves as an area for speculation of evidence in literature in relation to the prevalence of cultural and religious practices. The portrayal of this ritual function in the poem serves as a recording of the religious customs and beliefs of the Dalit community residing in thc villages of Tamil Nadu. The worship of this deity is not practised in urban areas or cities. These indirect documentations of a food culture found in poetry is necessary as there are not many resources that provide an accumulated pool of information.

It is estimated that 80% of the people of South India address their worship almost exclusively to minor deities and yet these deities receive little attention in studies of Hinduism (Elmore, 1915). Meyer (1986) notes that more studies dealing with folk tradition are needed before the older patterns of worship have totally disappeared and before the minor local deities have all become absorbed by the great gods of Hinduism. (Periyaswamy, 2)

The interference of other religious communities or political authorities works as factors that contribute towards the shrinking of the culture in the particular region. It is to be noted the researcher does not intend on taking a moralistic approach but rather to estimate, as the topic suggests, the massive scope food has in poetry to explore and contribute, through the correlation it has with, different fields of studies. On 27th August 2003, Chief Minister J. Jayalalitha of Tamil Nadu had declared a ban on animal sacrifice in Hindu temples which constituted a hindrance in these ritualistic practices of a community. These fluctuations in the cultural and religious practices of a community may not be avoidable but the preservation of these practices is indirectly recorded in literature like the chosen poem "He will sing and dance the Original Song" (8).

CONCLUSION

The thriving interlacing of food with literature has proven itself to be an ever-nourishing source of knowledge. A tremendous reconstruction of intimations and implications occur in the inquiry of food language in poetry. When poets find purpose in their pain, struggles, anger, passions through the medium of poetry blended with a dash of edibles the literary community and other various fields of studies, such as sociology, politics and religion, find the opportunity to engage in the enquiry of food and culture. This paper, which exhibits the engagement of food with Dalit poetry, creates a paradigm illuminating the realities of the community which have presented themselves in their works of art: poetry. Poetry is a weapon that has proven itself a medium of intense expression for, especially the discriminated, to voice out and assert their identities to the universe.

Works Cited

Rajkumar, N. D. *Give Us This Day a Feat of Flesh.* Translated by Anushiya Ramaswamy, Navayana Publishing, 2010, p. 5

Sukirtharani. "Blogarama.com." *Blogarama*, 31 May 2017, Accessed 15 May 2021.

www.blogarama.com/education-blogs/330186-tronbrook-blog/20591923-beef-right-poem-sukirtharani.

Kandasamy, Meena. *Touch.* Peacock Books, 2006, p. 52

Montanari, Massimo. *Food is Culture.* United States, Columbia University Press, 2006. Accessed 13 May 2021.

https://www.google.co.in/books/edition/Food_is_Culture/NlSsAgAAQBAJ?hl=en&gbpv=0

Priyaswamy, Laxmi. *Caste and Worship – A Study of Folk Gods of Tamil.* Pune Research Discovery, vol. 2, Issue 2, Accessed 16 May 2021.

http://puneresearch.com/media/data/issues/591b4dac5ca12.pdf

CHAPTER XII

SEARCH FOR IDENTITY, IMMIGRANT PSYCHOSIS AND SUBALTERN VOICES IN SATHNAM SANGHERA'S DIASPORIC MEMOIR THE BOY WITH THE TOP KNOT

Manmit Kaur Chadha

ABSTRACT

Diasporic identities face a constant struggle between retaining their original culture and adapting to and accommodating host cultures. The diasporic search for identity is an ambivalent course not bereft of psychological anxieties as the subject is stretched between two different worlds. This project examines Sathnam Sanghera's memoir The Boy with The Top Knot to show how the diasporic experience of re-forming identity is often confusing involving difficult decisions about social, cultural and religious traditions as well as love and familial ties. It can be understood as an attempt to gain control over one's own life and this difficult balance between the old and new is a test of resilience often resulting in immigrant psychosis. The project examines the influence of multiculturalism on diasporic identity and how the diasporic search for identity resembles the disconnection and difficulties faced by the schizophrenic. It also scrutinizes the reasons why immigrants are at a greater risk for developing schizophrenia and how myths and shame associated with mental illnesses prevent their timely detection and treatment. It further examines the text to throw light on subaltern voices of women's experiences in diaspora, particularly those who are uneducated and have relocated as dependent migrants.

Keywords: Identity, immigrant psychosis, schizophrenia and subaltern.

INTRODUCTION

Diaspora is a vast field that has so far not been successfully constrained within the limits of any one single definition. One of the most widely accepted understandings of Diaspora refers to the temporary or permanent migration of people away from their homeland A major part of the Indian diaspora post-independence was due to better employment opportunities.

In his diasporic memoir The Boy with the Top Knot, Sathnam Sanghera born to Sikh parents who had migrated to the midlands of Wolverhampton in England in the 1960s brings out the dilemmas of acculturation or adapting to the culture of the host country. His reminiscence is not just the voice of one immigrant family but a mirror to the experience of Asians who migrated to Britain in the 1960s and 70s. They were immersed into a foreign western society that was industrialized as opposed to the agrarian societies they formerly belonged to, urbanized in contrast to their rural way of life and largely individualistic in outlook -a far cry from their former conformity to strong community ties. Apart from the basic challenges of learning a new language they had to reconstitute a new sense of identity trying to fit into and be accepted by the host country. Sanghera was raised as a devout Sikh in his family embedded in ethnic traditions.

• • •

Search for Identity, Immigrant Psychosis and Subaltern voices in Sathnam Sanghera's Diasporic Memoir *The Boy With The Top Knot*

He attended Wolverhampton Grammar School and graduated from Christ's College, Cambridge, with a first-class degree in English Language and Literature and this was the catalyst for his transformation from a part-time worker in a sewing factory into a successful journalist with the Times liberating him from his family ghetto in the midlands of Wolverhampton. In London, he lived a secret life quite contrary to his traditional existence back home. Thus, the second-generation diasporic subjects experience a unique struggle of coming to terms with their dual identity- the conflict between their ethnic inheritance and individual identity. This issue is at the crux of the conflict between generations, parents desiring to preserve their ethnicity, and children desiring free will and individuality.

Sanghera's search for his own identity reflects his desire to escape the tradition-bound society of his Eastern roots for the more individualistic society of the West. However, before he could find a solution to this dilemma he wants to know more about his past and his parent's history. Helping his mother with her packing before her trip to India he comes across a medical note from his father's general practitioner Dr. Dutta leading to the chance discovery that his father, Jagjit, had been suffering from paranoid schizophrenia, later realizing that same was the case with his eldest sister, Puli. He was oblivious to these facts till the age of twenty-four. He gives up his job in London to live with his family in Wolverhampton and come to terms with his unsettling past. Further probing his mother on her past life, he gets a disturbing insight into the way most Indian families are in denial of diagnosis of mental disorder. The shame and taboo associated with mental illness, lack of education and awareness are reasons it remains a closely guarded secret in most families.

Though genetic predisposition is one of the prime factors in the case of schizophrenia there is enough research to suggest that migrants are at a higher risk and more susceptible to the illness. Sanghera's own search for identity and the stress of keeping his two lives apart is a kind of immigrant psychosis that strangely resembles the symptoms and struggles experienced by his schizophrenic father and sister. In the course of delving into his family's past history, Sanghera feels a renewed respect for his mother who, as a young wife was transported into a completely alien environment and the traumatic experience of dealing with a schizophrenic husband. She withstood pain, poverty and violence in this painful journey. His anger is at the way Indian families deal with mental illness not revealing it to the prospective spouse often blaming her for the circumstances. This is the subaltern voice that echoes throughout the novel.

Search for Identity and Assimilation in First and Second-Generation Diaspora.

The ancient human question who am I?' leads inevitably to the equally important question 'Whose am I?' - for there is no self outside of a relationship. - Parker J. Palmer

Let Your Life Speak: Listening for the Voice of Vocation

Identity is one of the most common themes in diasporic literature. Formation of identity in diasporic arrivals is a confusing process as Stuart Hall explains, 'defined, not by essence or purity, but by the recognition of a necessary heterogeneity and diversity; by a conception of 'identity' which lives with and through, not despite, difference; by hybridity. (Hall, 401). Diaspora identities are those which are constantly producing and reproducing themselves anew, through transformation and difference.' Diasporic identities are constructed by hybridity and assimilation. Assimilation refers to the gradual blending of diasporic identities into their new surroundings. The way and the extent to which the first and second generation assimilates into the host country and construct their identities differ. In the case of first-generation diaspora, they maintain strong ties to their homeland through cultural practices. They do not readily accept the customs and traditions of the host country and maintain their ethnicity. They experience loneliness, alienation and longing for their homeland. Hence, they can never completely assimilate into the new culture.

In contrast, the second generation who are born or grow up in the host country identify that as their home. They have a secondary connection with the homeland and do not feel the same sense of belonging or connect towards it as in the case of their parents. In addition, the parents or the first-generation immigrants perceive themselves as the custodians of traditions, values and customs but the second generation considers these norms outdated and often question them. Sanghera, a second-generation diasporic has a divided identity and experiences existentialist traumas of being torn between two worlds. Having grown up in Wolverhampton in the eighties he was fed on George Michael music, Dallas on TV, Elton John's 'Rocket Man' and in contrast was his traditional Sikh upbringing, a wardrobe of tartan smocks, attempts at tying the perfect top-knot and superstitions like burning red chillies to ward off the evil eye. As a solution to this Sanghera learns to lead a dual life. One part of his identity is preserved for his family home at Wolverhampton and the other for his friends and peers at his workplace in London.

Born and brought up in London like most of the second generation he cannot comprehend his parents' nostalgia for Punjab and its culture. 'I swayed on the spot psyching myself for what was to come. The switch from West to East, North to South, English to Punjabi, rationality to superstition, smoke almonds to salted peanuts' (Sanghera, 8) He suffers from inner turmoil, loss of self-esteem and failed relationships because of the fear of criticism, from his mother for his deviant behaviour. Another key problem a diasporic community faces with regard to identity is race and religion. The second-generation considers the country in which they are born and brought up as their own, therefore, when they experience discrimination with regards to their roots it leads to internalization of a position of subordination. These experiences are painful and humiliating. Sanghera recalls his ordeal at Grammar school where he was bullied because of his top knot, '.... I was one of just a few topknots in the whole school, and my days were marked by taunts of 'Oi turbinate 'and 'Is your lunch packed on your head?'....' (174). In another instance, he recalls 'I dreaded the sweet wrappers and paper balls hurled at my top knot' (175)

Discrimination played an important part in the formation of his identity, 'I became timid and speechless, my unhappiness measured out in numbers in my end – of term reports' (175). Having freed himself of the top knot and jettisoning cultural practices, his greatest turmoil now is to do away with the idea of an arranged marriage imposed by his coercive mother. He attributes his fear of confronting his mother to his strong Eastern roots -' it was made clear that our parents word-or rather, Mum's word, as Dad didn't have many to offer-was the word of God.' (100) Sanghera further expresses his condition saying 'They say it normally takes a death or birth for someone to want to know about their family history. In my case, it was six failed relationships and the prospect of an arranged marriage.' (61)

Immigrant Psychosis and Schizophrenia

At some point, I believe one has to stop holding back for fear of alienating some imaginary reader or real relative or friend and come out with personal truth. - May Sarton

Journal of Solitude

Schizophrenia is a mental 'disorder characterized by delusions, hallucinations, disturbances in thinking and communication and withdrawal from social activity. (Rays of hope 14). Some schizophrenic experiences include 'disorganization of thought/ perception apathy, lack of interest, lack of attention, social withdrawal. Thinking may be coloured by delusions and false beliefs that resist logical explanations.' (Rays of Hope, 15). Sanghera's attempts to know more about his parents and their past so that he can reconcile with his identity leads him to a chance discovery that his father and sister are suffering from schizophrenia – a fact that he had been oblivious of till the age of twenty-two. His knowledge of schizophrenia was restricted to the biopic of John Forbes, the math prodigy who overcame schizophrenia to win the Nobel prize and as he reveals in his memoir-

'I regarded the mentally ill as a distant, difficult and sometimes even amusing aspect of other people's lives' (87). Mental illness is never taken seriously and the terms associated with it are loosely used to denote eccentricity. 'I occasionally used the word as an adjective- to describe ex-girlfriends and colleagues and also ironically my split life between Wolverhampton and London.' (88). In order to find out more about the illness, Sanghera started reading extensively. However, Sanghera's research only filled him with strange and uneasy thoughts. He could not help thinking he himself was experiencing several symptoms of the above. - 'If anything, I seemed to exhibit more of the symptoms than he did. I lacked mental energy, had anxiety, was a hypochondriac, had inner (and outer) hostility, was interested in religious themes meanwhile, the second point- deviations from the common ways of thinking expressed by bizarre association or looking at the cards from unusual angles- could have been my job description" (90). He was often addressed as neurotic by friends and family, always too quick to anger with his family and quick to tears in confrontation. Yet another book titled Surviving Schizophrenia: A Manual for Families, Patients and Providers by E. Fuller described the lives of schizophrenics as 'chronicles of constricted experiences, muted emotions, missed opportunities, unfulfilled expectations. (91)

His sister Puli's (who is suffering from schizophrenia) description of her own state of mind can easily pass off as his own,' I was a zombie. Drowsy, Withdrawn, Moody, Depressed. Nobody understood me, not even me.' (142). Genetic predisposition or heredity is one of the important causes of schizophrenia' There is a 10-15% chance of developing the illness when a sibling or one parent has schizophrenia; when both parents have schizophrenia, the risk rises to approximately 40%-50%. '(Rays of Hope 16). Hence, Sanghera's fears were not unfounded. However, his condition can be more appropriately referred to as immigrant psychosis. Factors like loneliness, alienation, social adversity, racial discrimination, family dysfunction, unemployment and poor housing conditions have been proposed as contributing factors for immigrant psychosis.

Research conducted on immigrant psychosis suggests that immigrants are at higher risk for schizophrenia. Immigrants experience psychosis at rates two to five times higher than non-immigrants. (The Conversation, 6). "research and theorising suggest that discrimination and social exclusion may lie at the heart of the immigrant psychosis problem" (8). These difficulties induce psychological distress which can lead to immigrant psychosis. Immigrants are separated in space from their loved ones and in time from memories of the past resulting in schizophrenic tendencies. "Two rifts in the mind of the schizophrenic are defence mechanisms against a world too hard to bear" (Sheng-mei, 44).

Hence learning about schizophrenia, how it had impacted his family and his own formative years forms an important of Sanghera's search for identity and reconciliation with his past. However, the possibility of immigrant psychosis has not been tapped by either him or any of the medical practitioners his father and sister visited though it needs due recognition in diagnosis and treatment of mental illness in immigrants.

Subaltern Voices in Sathnam Sanghera's The Boy with the Top Knot

There's really no such thing as the 'voiceless'. There are only the deliberately silenced, or the preferably unheard. - Arundhati Roy, The Ministry of Utmost Happiness. The term subaltern was first coined by Italian activist Antonio Gramsci to refer to the hegemonic domination of a ruling elite class that subordinates peoplc of lower socio-economic ranks and denies them their basic rights. Gayatri Chakraborty Spivak further elaborated on the problems of the subaltern by looking at it from the point of gender and of Indian women in particular - 'in the context of colonial production, the subaltern has no history and cannot speak, the subaltern as female is even more deeply in shadow'. (Spivak, 28)

In Sanghera's memoir The Boy with the top Knot we can decipher several Subaltern voices through narratives of his parents and his sister Phuli -firstly of migrants, secondly migrants suffering from mental illness and thirdly the plight of women migrants. Migrants are often discriminated against and are not able to exercise their rights in the host country. Though Sanghera himself was an educated journalist his own attempts to get information on his parent's past faced several roadblocks. His letter to the manager at the office of the Crown Court Mr. Robinson is indicative of the second-hand treatment meted out to immigrants-

I'm not asking wrong questions, or submitting my requests on the wrong type of paper. The problem is that there is an array of obstacles, ranging from the fact that my parents come from an oral culture to the fact that they do not speak English....to the fact that my father is an illiterate, uneducated, unemployed mentally ill Asian man. You see, I have reluctantly and bitterly concluded that ....my father doesn't matter in the eyes of society; he is not worth producing background information on. (277)

Migrants are often unable to speak the language of the host country putting them at a great disadvantage for many things. This can be especially daunting as far as medical care is concerned. As Sanghera reminisces. I 've long despaired at the consequences of my father's illiteracy and my Mums lack of English.... not being able to read about a condition that has defined and restricted your entire adult life was the worst consequence of them all. I'd learnt more about the science and incidence of schizophrenia in a few hours of reading than my parents had picked up in more than thirty years of living with the disease. It was bewildering to think that even the word 'schizophrenia' remained foreign to them. (96)

Inappropriate diagnosis because of cultural misunderstanding and language difficulties often goes unnoticed. Sanghera went through his father's medical records only to realize that initially his father too had been misdiagnosed and treated for depression instead of schizophrenia. Valium, Tofranil and ECT treatment generally used to treat depression are all ineffective in the treatment of schizophrenia. Sanghera has brought out her predicament in his memoir- "So, I started taking them(medicines), not knowing they were for schizophrenia. I didn't know my name had been added to the 'severely mentally ill register. I found this out when I read through my medical records recently" (141). Additionally, migrants with financial constraints also have fewer choices in obtaining mental health care treatment.

However, the primary reason that mental illness continues to remain a closed book is due to the shame and taboo associated with it. Mental illness is still equated with "madness". The myths and lack of awareness associated with mental illness often become a barrier that holds people and their families back from seeking professional help. In some societies, mental illness is often mistaken for black magic as happened in the case of Sanghera's great-grandfather who was thought to be possessed hence, he was tied to a bed until he died. People with mental illness are often misjudged due to a lack of awareness and face discrimination and flak from society.

The subaltern position of women especially in relation to marriage is very obvious in Sanghera's memoir. Right from a very young age, Indian women are prepared for life after marriage. Sanghera's mother reveals "almost every task she'd been given, from making cow dung cakes for cooking fuel at seven to embroidering at eleven had been suggested with a view to preparing her for the prospect of getting married to a strange man and moving to a strange home" (155).

After marriage, she was forced to go to a strange land which was culturally a total contrast to her country of origin 'the grief of leaving everything she'd ever known seems to have blotted out the memory of her journey.' (158) Not only are women often unaware of their husband's illness but feel obliged to stay in spite of abusive issues as 'there's only one thing more unacceptable than a divorced woman in Punjab; a single mother' (252). In the case of his sister Puli who was schizophrenic marriage was seen as a solution to her problems. As Sanghera says of his mother,'...in her urge to get Puli married off, she was, in a strange but very Indian way, trying to save her.' (233)

Diasporic issues like racism, poverty, illiteracy as well as other social, cultural and political factors often place immigrants in a socially disadvantaged position. These multiple inequities intersect and have a great influence on the life of immigrant's leading to the internalization of a position of subordination. Women and diasporic subjects with mental illness are doubly marginalized. These subaltern voices form an important part of Sanghera's memoir.

CONCLUSION

The nature of immigrant experience and diaspora opens doors to a number of social, political, economic and psychological implications. A key problem a diasporic community faces is the ambivalence with regard to identity and the inner turmoil of being pulled between two worlds. In addition, social inequities such as racism, sexism, and class relations influence the treatment given to immigrants often leading to loneliness and alienation.

Sanghera's memoir is a painful and enlightening insight into the harsh reality of mental illness like schizophrenia and the impact it has on all concerned. It also brings out the strange similarities between the symptoms of immigrant psychosis and schizophrenia. Immigrant psychosis has been the subject of research in the recent past. However, most of this research is restricted to African, European and Middle Eastern subjects. Very little material is available in context to the Indian diaspora and the rate of psychosis among immigrants. Illiteracy and lack of awareness, stigma associated with mental illness also result in it being a closely guarded secret among Indians. Another interesting area of study is whether the rate of psychosis differs in educated and non-educated immigrants.

A very interesting fact brought to light by the memoir is that one of the reasons why Indian families are able to cope with psychosis is the close-knit Indian family system and strong community ties which actually provide insulation against and major support for psychosis. As revealed to Sanghera by the Indian doctor treating his father 'Indian families manage to cope somehow, because the whole family rallies around to give the necessary support. In the Western population- families break up like mad and the outcomes are bad. A similar individual of white origin would be in a nursing home by now.' This is an eye-opener for Indians as we take our family system for granted and undermine its strength.

The attitude of the host society towards migrants also influences how these problems are understood and treated by health care providers and society. Often immigrants internalize a position of subordination and fail to voice their concerns. The position of women immigrants can be said to be doubly marginalized as many of them are economically and socially dependent on their spouses. Sanghera's mother is a living example of the extraordinary struggle of Indian women to make their marriages work at all costs.

Sanghera's brave attempt to bring his family secrets to light shows the necessity for the first generation to accept the hybridity and continuously evolving nature of diasporic generations with regard to assimilation and the need for subsequent generations in the diaspora to reconcile with the past.

WORKS CITED

Sanghera, Sathnam. The Boy with the Top Knot. Penguin, 2008.

Ezzeldin, Hend. "(Un)Representations of the Subaltern in Three Victorian Novels." International Journal of Humanities and Cultural Studies, vol. 3, no. 4, 2017, pp. 2356–5926., ww.academia.edu/ 32088166/ Un_Representations_of_the_Subaltern_in_Three_Victorian_Novels. Accessed 9th April,2019.

Frye, Northrop. Educated Imagination and Other Writings on Critical Theory, 1933-1962." University of Toronto Press, 2006.

Hall, Stuart. Cultural Identity and Diaspora: Identity: Community, Culture. Lawrence and Wishart, 1990.

Howell, Geralyn, editor. Schizophrenia Society of Canada. 3rd ed., 2003, www.easacommunity.org/PDF/Rays_of_Hope.pdf.

Ma, Sheng-mei. Immigrant Subjectivities in Asian American and Asian Diaspora Literatures. State University of NewYork Press Albany, 1998.

McIntyre, Jason, and Richard Bentall. "Immigrants Suffer Higher Rates of Psychosis – Here's How to Start Helping Them." The Conversation, 21 Apr. 2017, //theconversation.com/immigrants-suffer-higher-rates-of-psychosis-heres-how-to-start-helping-them-73552. Accessed 9th April,2019.

Palmer, Parker J. Let Your Life Speak: Listening for the Voice of Vocation . 1st ed., Jossey-Bass, 1999.

Palmer, Parker J. "The Heart of a Teacher Identity and Integrity in Teaching." Change: The Magazine of Higher Learning, vol. 29, no. 6, 25 Mar. 2010, pp. 14–21. 29, 6, doi: 10.1080/ 00091389709602343.

Spivak, Gayatri Chakravorty. Can the Subaltern Speak? Basingstoke : Macmillan, 1988.

Roy, Arundhati. The Ministry of Utmost Happiness. Hamish Hamilton, 2017

Sarton, Mary. Journal of a Solitude. W. W. Norton Company, 1992.

CHAPTER XIII

HYBRIDIZATION OF CULTURE AND IDENTITY IN JHUMPA LAHIRI'S THE NAMESAKE

Umang Jangid

ABSTRACT

Jhumpa Lahiri in her novel The Namesake explores the intricate process of constructing the identity of diasporas, who find it difficult to assimilate with a foreign culture and shows initial resistance towards acculturation. Lahiri demonstrates this complexity through the migration of a Bengali family, from India to America. This paper aims to explore the complexity of the constant formation of identity and how amalgamation or collision of two different cultural values impact the transformation of identity through Stuart Hall's essay "Cultural Hybridity and Diaspora". In his essay Hall explains, how identity is always in 'process' and it is a matter of 'being' as well as 'becoming', and also suggest that the cultural identity of the diaspora can be understood through the dialogic relationship between two axes: the vector of 'similarity and continuity and the vector of 'difference and rupture'. In Lahiri's The Namesake two axes are Bengali culture and American culture, dialogical relationship between these axes affects the identity of the Indian diaspora. This paper attempts to understand how in The Namesake, through the integration of Bengali rituals, ceremonies, food habits and language into daily American life, the Indian diaspora assimilate with American culture by making necessary sacrifices and become hyphenated American or acquire hybrid culture and identity; which shows the intricate process of forming identity; how it is in constant formation and explains what Hall meant by, "The diaspora experience as I intend it here is defined, not by essence or purity, but by the recognition of necessary heterogeneity and diversity by a conception of 'identity' which lives with and through not despite difference, by hybridity".

Keywords: Identity, Diaspora, Heterogeneity, Hybridity, American-ness, Acculturation, Integration, and Assimilation.

• • •

INTRODUCTION

In the opinion of Lahiri, "The question of identity is always a difficult one" as it is always in production, "...but especially so for those who are culturally displaced, as immigrants are, or those who grow up in two worlds simultaneously, as is the case for their children" (Lahri Int Exp 1 L 23). Similarly, the premise of Hall's essay is that, "Identity is not as transparent or unproblematic as we think" and he suggests that, "...instead of thinking of identity as an accomplished fact..." identity should be perceived, "...as [always in] 'production', which is never complete, always in process..."(Hall 222). To dwell more on the layers of complexity of identity formation, this paper aims to study the complexity of hybridization of identity and cultural practices of people migrated from their homeland to foreign land and the impact of assimilation of different cultures.

Cultural identity in the case of diasporas is complicated as it develops between two different cultural worlds. Culture is cultivated through daily habits, food habits, language, rituals and ceremonies. These practices of any particular culture or cultural environment, in general, makes the identity. First-generation diaspora sees the amalgamation of different cultures more clearly than the second generation of diaspora, as they are dislocated from their homeland and relocated to a foreign land, they can see this transition phase more accurately. On the other hand, the second generation of diasporas are in a more complex situation, they grow between two different cultural practices which creates a conflicted identity from the start, and while growing up striving for 'essence or purity' in any direction results into failure. As Hall suggest this complexity can only be understood as the dialogic relationship between these two worlds. In The Namesake two different worlds are Bengali culture or Heritage that diaspora brings from their home land and American culture or system into that they want to integrate. The integration process and conundrum of 'purity of identity have been studied in this essay.

The author of The Namesake, Jhumpa Lahiri had a similar experience in her personal life, the dilemma of living in America where she has to live a dual life and have the baggage of expectations from both sides. She expresses this sentiment in her interview, "I wanted to please my parents and meet their expectations. I also wanted to meet the expectations of my American peers, and the expectations I put on myself to fit into American society. It is a classic case of divided identity" (Lahiri Int Exp 2 L 16). This conundrum she explores in Gogol Ganguli, the protagonist of the novel, second generation of diaspora. In the case of Gogol, it becomes more complex as he strives for pure 'American-ness' by cutting his past roots of Bengali identity, which is not possible as Hall's theory opposes the idea of purity and suggests it needs heterogeneity and diversity. Whenever Gogol wants to escape from his Bengali identity by rejecting his past, either his past memories or tradition or family expectation pulls him back.

Explanation of Professional Terms: Migration and Immigration

The terms migration and immigration have a slight difference which arises from the basic question of what has been the purpose of movement? Was it temporary stay or conscious settlement? These terms are considered synonyms in European countries. However, these terms differ and give a different meaning. The term migration simply means, "...movement from one country to another country..." and immigration means, "...coming as a permanent resident into a foreign country..." (Gautam 2)

Cultural Hybridity

Cultural hybridity is a mixture of two or more different cultures. In other words, a cultural hybridization is a new form of culture created from combining two or more forms of culture. Enculturation is a process of socialization where a person becomes part of another person's culture. A person can become enculturated through processes of acculturation and assimilation. Cultural hybridization is a complex process it is no longer represented in binary form, as Hall describes, "...its complexity exceeds this binary structure of representation"(228). The immigrants pass through a stage of in-betweenness and sometimes they ride two cultural boats at the same time leading to what is called hybridity in cultural theory which is mixing up the features of the host cultures to native cultures.

Assimilation and Integration

When an Indian migrates to a foreign country to settle down he becomes aware of the surrounding host culture. He adopts the ways of the host culture by communicating with people. He starts with integration when his group is very small he just adopts the customs of the host society. "He does not assimilate completely..." by learning the language and culture of the county he socially integrates. In order to integrate he retains its culture, language and religious values. On the other hand, "Assimilation of a group into another group is a process where immigrants lose visibility as they adopt the culture of the new surrounding culture. In a way, it is a sort of acculturation" (Gautam 2 & 3). The process of hybridization starts from integration and then turns into assimilation.

Acculturation

Acculturation is a process through which a person or group from one culture comes to adopt practices and values of another culture, while still retaining their own distinct culture. This process is most commonly discussed in terms of a minority culture adopting elements of a majority culture, as is typically the case with immigrant groups that are culturally or ethnically distinct from the majority in the place to which they have immigrated.

Diaspora

The word diaspora has been taken from the Greek, meaning "to disperse." Bill Ashcroft, Gareth Griffiths and Helen Tiffin define diaspora as "...the voluntary or forcible movement of peoples from their homelands into new regions..." (Ashcroft 61).

Stuart Hall describes the complexity of diasporic identity as they are in constant formation, "Diaspora identities are those which are constantly producing and reproducing themselves anew, through transformation and difference..." (235).

Theoretical Premises Framework

The novel starts with Ashoke's migration to America for future career opportunities, for a better standard of living. After getting married he takes her wife Ashima to America. Initially, Ashima feels alienated and wants to go back to India, but she continues to live with resistance to assimilate with foreign cultural practices. Later, both Ashima and Ashoke have to make necessary sacrifices to incorporate American culture into their lives. In people of diaspora, the first generation of diaspora find the problem of assimilating with alien culture, goes through trauma, alienation, feels isolated and nostalgia, while the second generation migrants attempt to assimilate by embracing this alien culture and they find it difficult to cope with their parents' native culture. In this case, first-generation diaspora, born in America, Gogol goes through a series of experiences which makes him hate his heritage culture and he sees that as a burden and strive for foreign cultural values but ultimately pulled back by family expectations and attachment to his parents. Ashoke and Ashima work as mediators between Gogol and past heritage. According to Hall past speaks to us, "...through memory, fantasy, narrative and myth..." (225). The identity of main characters of The Namesake, especially Ashima and Gogol goes through the constant formation and as Hall asserts, "Diaspora identities are those which are constantly producing and reproducing themselves anew, through transformation and difference"(235). Ashima and Gogol both go through constant transformation by constantly producing and reproducing themselves, and through the gradual process, their identity becomes Bengali-American identity. Thus, the hypothesis of this essay is that the process of identity creation is an intricate process and hybridization of culture and identity causes through 'integration' and 'assimilation' of foreign culture, which is inevitable in people living abroad. The hybridization of culture and identity of diaspora is studied through theories of cultural theories of Stuart Hall in the lives of the Ganguli family.

Literature of Diaspora and Fluidity of Definition of 'Home' for Diasporas.

Homi K. Bhaba, Avtar Brah and Stuart Hall talk about how the floating nature of home and fluid identity changed the narrative of age-old concepts of fixed 'home' and 'identity'. People who have migrated to foreign land develops a conflict about where is 'home'. Hall suggests that beyond the spatial territory, 'home' is associated with emotional territory. Bhabha explains this situation, points out hybridity as the 'third space', identity as impure identity rather than fixed identity. This dual or hybrid identity construct an identity crisis in one's creating home of familiarity in the overseas country. This leads to conflict information of identity.

Post-colonial writers like V. S. Naipaul, Salman Rushdie, Bharti Mukherjee, Agha Shahid Ali, Kiran Desai and many others in their diasporic writings have incorporated themes of immigration, exile and expatriation, identity, nostalgia, memory, isolation and alienation. Similarly, Jhumpa Lahiri's works focus on dislocation and displacement, cultural conflicts, loneliness, language barrier, loss of identity, sense of belonging, and the generation gap between the first and the second-generation immigrants. The cultural dilemmas experienced by them and their American born children in different ways, the spatial, cultural and emotional dislocations suffered by them in their effort to settle "home" in the new land. Insights of diasporic writings shares "...diaspora experience and its narrative of displacement..." (Hall 223), which creates a discussion about how the culture of diasporas and natives assimilate with each other as Jasbir Jain says about diasporic writing, "Language and cultures are transformed as they come into contact with other languages and cultures. Diasporic writing raises questions regarding the definitions of 'home' and 'nation'. Schizophrenia and/or nostalgia are often preoccupations of these writers as they seek to locate themselves in new cultures" (Jain n.p).

Initial Resistance to Accepting New Culture.

The Namesake tells the story of the Ganguli, a Bengali American family grappling with loss, love and identity. Ashima and Ashoke are dislocated from India and relocated to America. Both have different approaches to dealing with displacement, Ashoke who has come to America for new opportunities does not feel isolated and alienated in a foreign land. On the other hand, Ashima feels isolated. Migration to America for Ashima is the dispersal of roots which involves pain, alienation, identity crisis as Dubey puts it, "...a sensitive immigrant finds himself or herself perpetually at a transit station fraught with memories of the original home which are struggling with the realities of the new world..."(Dubey 22). Lahiri shows, how in order to stick to their cultural values and beliefs in a foreign system, immigrants have to face cultural dilemma but eventually has to imbibe their cultural ways to host country.

Ashima feels isolated, alienated and uncomfortable with American culture and the American way of life. For instance, Ashima's isolation is visible at the time of her pregnancy in hospital she wonders, "In India...women go home to their parents to give birth, away from husbands and in-laws and household cares, retreating briefly to childhood when the baby arrives." But soon she accepts the situation and realizes, "It's the consequence: motherhood in a foreign land" (Lahiri 10).

Bengali tradition one should have two names one 'a daknam' pet name and 'a bhalonam' good name. But according to American rules to get discharged from the hospital name should be given to the child but they were waiting for Ashima's grandmother's letter which contains the name. Ultimately they had to sacrifice to assimilate into the foreign system and they had to choose names. Any diaspora has to make necessary sacrifices to assimilate into the foreign culture. In this case, they have to sacrifice with the Bengali tradition of choosing the name. Ashoke would have named it differently anywhere else, but now in America, he has to abide by the rules and regulation.

"Every pet name is paired with a good name, a bhalonam, for identification in the outside world. Consequently, good names appear on envelopes, on diplomas, in telephone directories, and in all other public places. (For this reason, letters from Ashima's mother say "Ashima" on the outside, "Monu" on the inside.) Good names tend to represent dignified and enlightened qualities. Ashima means "she who is limitless, without borders." Ashoke, the name of an emperor, means "he who transcends grief." Pet names have no such aspirations. Pet names are never recorded officially, only uttered and remembered. Unlike good names, pet names are frequently meaningless, deliberately silly, ironic, even onomatopoetic. Often in one's infancy, one answers unwittingly to dozens of pet names, until one eventually sticks (Lahiri 32).

Ashima is resistant to assimilating into different cultures, she wants to go back to India "I'm saying I don't want to raise Gogol alone in this country. It's not right. I want to go back" (Lahiri 39). Ashima and Ashoke continue to have Bengali traditions to follow that it is taking effort by Gogol and Sonia who are growing up in America hard to find following Bengali traditions. Children born in America speak in a native accent, insist on celebrating Christmas, they identify more with American traditions. Ashima and Ashoke become less resistant towards adopting American culture as they realize the inevitability of retaining 'essence or purity, they start incorporating foreign values in their lives which leads to their hybrid culture or identity.

Integration of Bengali Culture into American Culture and Vice Versa; Dialogical relationship Between Two Axes.

Discussion about culture and identity is pivotal in post-colonial studies. In the case of Diaspora and immigrants, the cultural encounter of the migrant culture with host culture is inevitable which creates "infinite postponement of meaning" (Hall 229) of culture and identity as two cultural beliefs, rituals, ceremonies, habits and language assimilate with each other. Lahiri shows the encounter of cultural values and rituals of Bengali tradition with American tradition, this encounter creates disjuncture in the creation of the identity of diaspora. Hall suggests that "The cultural identity of diaspora is can be understood through the dialogic relationship between two axes: the vector of similarity and continuity [i.e Bengali tradition] and the vector of difference and rupture [i.e American tradition]" (226). Marry Louise Pratt, describe this collision as a 'contact zone', in this 'contact zone' immigrants experience identity issues, sometimes they assimilate with the American tradition, which is inevitable in most cases and sometimes they want to preserve their ethnic identity. This leads to a chaotic situation where for preserving the ethnic identity they have to grapple with promoting their Bengali culture as well as adapting to the American culture.

People of diaspora try to 'integrate' their cultural values in the American system or American way of life by 'space-claiming' a concept given by Susan Koshy. In The Namesake the space is claimed, by incorporating Bengali rituals and ceremonies related to birth, death and marriage; imbibing Bengali habits and language they try to express or promote their cultural and ethnic identity but due to the presence of the American system in the environment they are bound to 'assimilate' or hybrid their culture and identity. Ashoke and Ashima go through an intricate process, "...in order to make this cultural claim possible and negotiate their space among other diasporic cultures along with the standard American culture" (Siber, 276).

Rituals or Ceremonies

Rituals or religious ceremonies are a crucial part of creating identity, "Ceremonies are an expression of culture" (Bone Exp 5 L 3). Rituals are used as mechanisms that express and generate love and establish and identify community or culture. In The Namesake,

Lahiri shows the celebration of the birth of a child as "The occasion: Gogol's annaprasan, his rice ceremony". This is a replacement of baptism ceremony in the Christian tradition as Lahiri explains, "There is no baptism for Bengali babies, no ritualistic naming in the eyes of God. Instead, the first formal ceremony of their lives centres around the consumption of solid food" (Lahiri 44). In addition to that, for the death ceremony, "For ten days following his father's death, he and his mother and Sonia eat a mourner's diet, forgoing meat and fish. They eat only rice and dal and vegetables, plainly prepared. Gogol remembers having to do the same thing when he was younger when his grandparents died, his mother yelling at him when he forgot one day and had a hamburger at school" (184). Marriage of Gogol and Moshumi is also seen as promotion of Bengali values i.e marriage in the same caste.

Integration of cultural values happens in both ways, Bengali traditions are creating space in the American environment through rituals/food habits/language which is transmitted by their Bengali parents, but the U.S born children also alters the Bengali values by transferring American values to them. For instance, Ashoke accepts the celebration of Christmas and ThanksGiving after initial hesitation, when he realizes the inevitability of it. He prepares for the celebration of Christmas:

For the sake of Gogol and Sonia, they celebrate, with progressively increasing fanfare, the birth of Christ, an event the children look forward to far more than the worship of Durga and Saraswati. During pujos, scheduled for convenience on two Saturdays a year, Gogol and Sonia are dragged off to a high school or a Knights of Columbus hall overtaken by Bengalis, where they are required to throw marigold petals at a cardboard effigy of a goddess and eat bland vegetarian food. It can't compare to Christmas, when they hang stockings on the fireplace mantel, set out cookies and milk for Santa Claus, receive heaps of presents, and stay home from school (70).

Food Habits and Language

Food in the lives of human beings functions as a symbol of cultural identity. "Food habits are an integral part of cultural behavior and are often closely identified with particular groups..." (Fieldhouse n.p). Food habit expresses the cultural side of immigrants and plays an important role in claiming a cultural space. In the house of the Ganguli family, Christmas or any other occasion is celebrated with Bengali food, "...lamb curry with lots of potatoes, luchis, thick channa dal with swollen brown raisins, pineapple chutney, sandeshes molded out of saffron tinted ricotta cheese" (77).

Language is another key component in establishing the cultural space for migrants' cultural values. Ashima and Ashoke, as Bengali parents living in America, make Gogol, "perfectly bilingual" (63). They talk in their native tongue at home but have to address in English in school and other places, they have to abide by the rules. As Gogol grows he is more drawn towards American culture as his learning affects my schooling and other extra-curricular activities. Ashima and Ashoke's deliberate attempt to teach Gogol Bengali language to sound more like them, but they are bound to fail as American educational institutions will assimilate their children linguistically and culturally. Thus, Gogol is drawing aspects of his identity more from his outside home environment.

When Gogol is in the third grade, they send him to Bengali language and culture lessons every other Saturday, held in the home of one of their friends. For when Ashima and Ashoke close their eyes it never fails to unsettle them, that their children sound just like Americans, expertly conversing in a language that still at times confounds them, in accents, they accustomed not to trust. (71)

Intricate Process of Becoming Hyphenated American.

Throughout the novel, Ashima and Gogol struggle to adjust to find their identity to place it on one side of the spectrum. In the case of Ashima, she is afraid of becoming too American as that would be a betrayal of her Bengali heritage. On the other hand, Gogol goes away from his past heritage and strive for the 'American-ness' as he sees it as liberation. This becomes problematic as Hall negates the idea of "fixed essence" and suggests that identity is "...not once-and-for-all..." (Hall 227). Though it seems that the second generation of diaspora has a more clear picture of what to choose, Mcleod suggests that the first generation of diaspora and, "their sense of identity borne from living in a diaspora community [is] influenced by the past migrant history of their parents or grandparents" (McLeod 207). Being a child of immigrants Gogol begins in a kind of nowhere place. Gogol's identity lies on both sides, "[it] belongs to the future as much as to the past. It is not something that already exists, transcending time, place, history, and culture. Cultural identities come from somewhere, have histories. But, like everything that is historical, they undergo constant transformation" (Hall 237). the Second generation of diasporas are constantly had an identity crisis, they struggle between future and past, in this process, they try, "to rediscover his roots, his self, his hyphenated identity and to revitalize the in-betweenness of cultures, the alternate culture." (Qtd in Jindal 728)

Name and Identity

Ganguli family struggles to understand how to reconcile life in America with Bengali culture and heritage. As Lahiri on the complexity of identity creation says, "the question of identity is always a difficult one, but especially so for those who are culturally displaced, as immigrants are, or those who grow up in two worlds simultaneously, as is the case for their children" (Lahiri, 23) In case of Gogol, he strives for American-ness as he sees, Bengali heritage as a burden. The novel raises the question of what is Gogol's identity. As upbringing, he has an American presence, his becoming identity. In relation to blood, he has Bengali presence, his past memories and connection through his parents. Gogol comes to hate his name and decides to change it, unknowingly about the connection of the name with his father, hoping to leave both his former name and his Bengali heritage behind. As he strives for

American-ness to have one pure identity changing his name to Nikhil helps to cut away past roots, eventually helps to become a new person. He loses his virginity, with his new identity and, "Gogol has nothing to do with it..." (100). Changing his name helps Gogol to cut away from his roots to become a new person. Rejection of name symbolizes the rejection of past roots. Nikhil can work as a fresh start for distancing himself from his heritage. Gogol denies the existence of past identity.

The rich history of the name "Gogol" is also part of the heritage Gogol receives from his father. In the end, Gogol's choice to be at peace with his own past is also a choice to begin reading about the original Gogol who changed his father's life. When Ashoke tells the story of his tragic accident, Gogol realizes the importance of his name. "And suddenly the sound of his pet name, uttered by his father as he has been accustomed to hearing it all his life, means something completely new, bound up with a catastrophe he has unwittingly embodied for years" (127).

Striving for American-ness

Gogol starts to live with Maxine, his American girlfriend, He sees Maxine's parents as liberated and free from the burden that he sees in his own Bengali culture. By cutting away from his Bengali roots he adopts their cultural values. Thus, Gogol with his relationship with Maxine tries to establish his American Identity and views his relationship with Maxine as the height of his "American-ness". He tries to fully assimilate with American culture want to forget his past roots. Gogol still has a hold over his transformative identity Nikhil, Gogol is not just a name but it signifies all his discomfort to fit into two different cultures as he grew up. He tries to live away from his family heritage as much as he can.

Gogol's identity of Bengali heritage is transmitted through his parents, he is not directly connected to his roots. For that reason, when stumbles on panellist discussion he is startled by a description of the second generation of diasporic immigrants: He eventually gathers that it [ABCD] stands for "American-born confused deshi." In other words, him. He learns that the C could also stand for "conflicted." He knows that deshi, a generic word for "countryman," means "Indian," knows that his parents and all their friends always refer to India simply as desh. But Gogol never thinks of India as desh. He thinks of it as Americans do, like India. (121)

Gogol isolates himself from his family to completely dwell on American identity. When Maxine visits the house is a significant scene where values of both American and Indian culture clash and Gogol feels uncomfortable with his Bengali identity. Maxine's lunch with Ashoke and Ashima is the external embodiment of the cultural tensions that Gogol has been feeling internally.

Whenever Gogol wants to escape from his Bengali identity by rejecting his past, either his past memories or tradition or family expectation pulls him back. Ashoke's death forces Gogol to come face to face to his past. This creates a change in Gogol, now he no longer feels or needs to escape from his Bengali heritage. He accepts all the traditions and does all the rituals where he has to eat vegetarian food. At the time of his grandparents' death he sees his father getting bald which he did not understand at that time, "Years later Gogol had learned the significance, that it was a Bengali son's duty to shave his head in the wake of a parent's death" (184). He had disguised himself as Nikhil, which separates from his Bengali heritage, to be in a relationship with Maxine. This sudden change in his identity gets difficult for Maxine to understand. When she suggested taking a trip to New Hampshire to get away from all this. He replies, "I don't want to get away..." (187). Gogol falls on an attempt to "purity", instead his identity is defined, "by the recognition of a necessary heterogeneity" (240). In addition to that, Hall asserts that "This identity must be discovered, evacuate and bring to light...this is a very powerful force, helps to connect with roots" (236). This final loss forces Gogol to come to grips not only with his multiple names but also with his multiple identities.

After this traumatic incident, he experiences "a sudden need to reconnect with lost Bengali rituals; this desire to return culminates in marriage to an Indian American woman". He breaks up with Maxine, sees his Bengali tradition in a different way, starts to embrace Ashoke and Ashima's sacred relationship. To follow his Bengali tradition, he marries Moshumi to give it a try that Bengali is the best way to build a lasting relationship. Though his marriage ends in divorce he comes near, "to the bosom of his ethnic community by marrying an Indian American woman in a traditional ceremony, returning again to his home and family after" (Qtd in Siber 278).

Lahiri does an excellent job of juxtaposing the autonomous assimilated American way of life in a manner that avoids suggesting the superiority of one over the other. Gogol does not have to choose one over the other; he is made up of both and it should strengthen his pride instead of weakening it. He has assimilated himself into American culture and values at the same time retaining his parents' Indian heritage.

CONCLUSION

Jhumpa Lahiri's personal experience of living in-between two worlds and her keen observation of the hybridization of diasporic culture and daily lives of diaspora people brings authenticity and legitimacy to the plight of the Ganguli in this foreign land. Lahiri does an excellent job of juxtaposing Bengali values and American values without showing the superiority of one over the other. The Namesake does not propose the importance of either fully embracing one's cultural heritage or completely assimilating into American culture; instead, it encourages to embrace both words and asserts with what Hall says, "The diaspora experience as I intend it here is defined not by essence or purity, but by the recognition of a necessary heterogeneity and diversity; by a conception of 'identity' which lives with and through, not despite, difference; by hybridity," (235)

To conclude, in The Namesake, through the integration of Bengali rituals, ceremonies, food habits and language into daily

American life, the Indian diaspora assimilates with American culture by making necessary sacrifices and becoming hyphenated American or acquiring hybrid culture and identity; which shows the intricate process of forming identity.

Works Cited

Aneja, Anil K. "Alienation to Acculturation in Jhumpa Lahiri's The Namesake" International Journal of English, Language, Literature and Humanities, Volume 3, Issue 3, (May 2015): 479-485.

Ashcroft, Bill, Gareth Griffiths and Helen Tiffin. The Post-Colonial Studies: The Key Concepts Second Edition. 2000, New York: Routledge, 2007.

Bhabha, Homi K. The Location of Culture. London: Routledge, 2004

Bone, Alison. "Why rituals are still relevant". "https://www.sbs.com.au/topics/life/culture/article/2016/06/27/why-rituals-are-still-relevant". SBS, 27 June 2016.Web.01 May 2018.

Dubey Ashutosh. Immigrant Experiences in Jhumpa Lahiri's Interpreter of Maladies. Journal of Indian Writing in English. 2002; 30(2):22-26.

Fieldhouse, Paul. Food and Nutrition: Customs and Culture. London: Taylor & Francis, 1986.

Gautam, Dr. M.K. Indian Diaspora: Ethnicity and Diasporic Identity, CARIM-India RR 2013/29, Robert Schuman Centre for Advanced Studies, San

Domenico di Fiesole (FI): European University Institute, 2013.

Hall, Stuart, "Cultural Identity and Diaspora", Contemporary Postcolonial Theory: A Reader, Ed. New Delhi: Oxford University Press, 2009.

Jain, Jasbir. Writers of the Indian Diaspora, Jaipur: Rawat, 1998.

Jaya, K. "A Study of Immigration and Diasporic Sensibilities in the Novel of Jumpha Lahiri's The Namesake" Asian Journal of Applied Science and Technology Volume 1, Issue 1, (February 2017): 158-159.

Jindal, Mridul. "A study of the clash of cultures in Jhumpa Lahiri's The Namesake" International Journal of Academic Research and Development, Volume 3, Issue 1, (January 2018) 726-729.

Kaur, Tejinder. "Cultural Dilemmas and Displacements of Immigrants in Jhumpa Lahiri"s The Namesake." Studies in Women Writers in English. Ed. Mohit K. Ray and Rama Kundu.Vol 4. New Delhi: Atlantic, 2005. 266-277.

Lahiri, Jhumpa. The Namesake. 2003, New York: A Mariner Book Hougton Mifflin Company, 2004.

Pal, Adesh, and Tapas Chakraborty. Theorizing and Critiquing Indian Diaspora. New Delhi: Creative Books, 2004

Pratt, M. L. Imperial Eyes: Travel Writing and Transculturation. London: Routledge, 1992.

Siber, Mouloud, and Bouteldja Riche. "Bengali Cultural Identity and 'Multicultural America' in Jhumpa Lahiri's The Namesake (2003): A Cultural Anthropologist Approach, Anglisticum Journal (IJLLIS), Volume: 2, Issue: 3 (June- 2013): 275-281.

"www.writerswrite.com/books/interview-with-jhumpa-lahiri" Readers Read. Writers Write Inc, Nov. 2003.Web. 26 April 2018.

CHAPTER XIV

MARXIST READING OF THE DOLL'S HOUSE BY KATHERINE MANSFIELD AND THE STOLEN PARTY BY LILIANA HEKER

Shaik Anam Abdul Qadar

ABSTRACT

This research paper examines the Class struggle, social-economic conflict and class consciousness through Marxist reading. The conflict theory deals with the conflict between social classes, tension emerging between groups, lack of resources and power. According to Marx the social classes are the Bourgeoisie (upper class) and the proletariat (lower class) by using this approach researcher tries to examine the effect of industrialization and capitalism and the rise of classes and conflict between these classes, it also talks about how the Bourgeoisie and the proletariat status and way of living affect society and the minds of the future generation. The researcher examines short stories of two different authors namely 'The Doll's House' (1922) by Katherine Mansfield and 'The Stolen Party' (1994) by Liliana Heker through the lenses of class conflict and class struggle. These stories have some similarities and differences which can be analyzed through the characters and their behaviours.

Keywords: Bourgeoisie, proletariat, Marxism, class consciousness, struggle, conflict, social-economic

INTRODUCTION

Karl Marx and Friedrich Engels in their book Manifesto of the Communist Party lay out the theory of class struggle and revolution. Class conflict also refers to class welfare and class struggle. Because of the rise of capitalism, the bourgeoisie started to use their influence to exploit the proletariat. In the stories *The Doll's houses* and *The Stolen Party*, some of the characters represent the bourgeoisie and some proletariat. These texts will be explored through the social-economic struggle and class conflict of the society. The analysis of the stories could be drawn on the basis of the attitude of the society towards lower class people. Karl Marx pointed out how the bourgeoisie has always denied basic rights to the proletariat.

The emergence of classes during the Industrial Revolution:

The industrial revolution began in England in the late 18th and early 19th century from about 1760 to 1840. "Historians have identified several causes for the Industrial Revolution, including the emergence of capitalism, European imperialism, efforts to mine coal, and the effects of the Agricultural Revolution" ("Causes of the Industrial Revolution", Historycrunch.com L5). The industrial revolutions paid for Britain's social class into different stages and cause the emergence of new classes. Due to the industrial revolution, there were many problems rising between workers and the government.

People started thinking about their own business rather than working for the government which increases capitalism. The rise of the middle class was one of the results of the industrial revolution. Because of the industrial revolution, there was division in social classes in England which include The Upper Classes, Middle Classes and Working Classes. The characterization of the working class was as a lack of property, food and dependence of wages associated with restricted access to higher education, low living standards and not having a right to take part in important decision making. The working-class people were struggling with their need to fulfil in life, labouring to feed their family because of that the struggling class had to agree on with their owner becoming a puppet in their hands. "In 1840 the graphic artist George Cruikshank produced a caricature entitled 'The British Beehive' which showed English society divided up by class and occupation... By using the image of the Beehive, with its rigidly organized layers, Cruikshank was celebrating the class divisions at work in British society and also depicting them as natural and unchanging" (Hughes, The British

Library Exp9 L22).

The middle class initially appeared in Europe in the late middle age and was also referred to as Bourgeoisie. "By bourgeoisie is meant the class of modern capitalists, owners of the means of social production and employers of wage labour" (Marx and Engels 14). The middle class consisted of newly trained experts in industrial technologies with other professions like engineer, doctor, teacher, clerk, lawyer and other white-collar workers. The middle class was also bifurcated as a higher level and lower level. People from the lower level worked for those in the higher level. The upper-middle-class includes country gentlemen, landlords and factory owner. The working class consist of unskilled labour, labourers who work in the factory, shopkeepers, sweeper, merchants and civil servants and are also known as the proletariat. "By proletariat, the class of modern wage labourers who, having no means of production of their own, are reduced to selling their labour-power in order to live" (Marx and Engels 14).

Capitalism and Conflict:

In the Marxist perspective, capitalism was the conflict between the bourgeoisie and proletariat. Marx and Engle described that capitalism was indefensible and the capitalist society at that time was replaced by the socialist. "From the perspective developed by Karl Marx, capitalism is organized around the concept of CAPITOL implying the ownership and control of the means of production by those who employ workers to produce goods and services in exchange for wages" (Mondal exp4 L13). The most important feature of capitalism is the motive to escalate additional yield, including unfair treatment of the workers and injustice between rich and poor. The expiration of the feudal system pushed bonded people who work under landlords away from the countryside to urban sides, it helps to upsurge capitalism. A major criticism with regards to capitalism is it promotes the concept of the rich becoming richer and the poor becoming poorer.

Class struggle and conflict theory:

The word 'Class' is derived from the Latin term 'Classic' which means a division of the people and fleet. Marx's understanding of the class was Earning profit (Haves) and Earning wages (Have not). There is a class in itself and also a class for itself. . Marx acknowledged class as a unique feature of society. In his book "Manifesto of the Communist Party 1848" Marx discussed class struggle and class conflict. In the opinion of Marx and Friedrich most of history, there have been struggle between classes but Marx explains it as only a fragmented form. "that economic production, and the structure of society of every historical epoch necessarily arising therefrom, constitute the foundation for the political and intellectual history of that epoch; that consequently (ever since the dissolution of the primaeval communal ownership of land) all history has been a history of class struggles, of struggles between exploited and exploiting, between dominated and dominating classes at various stages of social evolution; that this struggle, however, has now reached a stage where the exploited and oppressed class (the proletariat) can no longer emancipate itself from the class which exploits and oppresses it (the bourgeoisie), without at the same time forever freeing the whole of society from exploitation, oppression, class struggles – this basic thought belongs solely and exclusively to Marx" (Marx and Engels 6).

The class struggle occurs due to the bourgeoisie making the proletariat labouring under them for their own benefit. The conflict theory explains that the tension emerged between groups only when the resources, power and status cannot be distributed equally. According to Karl Marx, "the history of these class struggles forms a series of evolutions in which, nowadays, a stage has been reached where the exploited and oppressed class – the proletariat – cannot attain its emancipation from the sway of the exploiting and the ruling class – the bourgeoisie – without, at the same time, and once and for all, emancipating society at large from all exploitation, oppression, class distinction, and class struggles (Marx and Engels 8)."

"As suggested by Karl Marx, conflict theory claims society is in a state of perpetual conflict because of competition for limited resources" (Koop, ZME Science Exp31 L11). For having a better look at war, violence, revolutions, forms of injustice and discrimination, conflict theory can be an adequate source. It explains how the disparity in society is all-natural giving rise to various issues.

The Class conflict is the uncertainty in society means there was an inevitable struggle between the rich and the poor. The working class became conscious of their rights being exploited by the Bourgeoisie leading to the start of class conflict. Max Weber did not fully acknowledge Karl Marx's principal idea of conflict; he believed that along with economic inequalities there also exist inequalities of social structure and political power, contributing to the conflict. The effect of class conflict has a different effect on people depending upon their race, gender and education, food, employment, housing. In the opinion of Karl Marx "A house may be large or small; as long as the neighbouring houses are likewise small, it satisfies all social requirement for a residence. But let there arise next to the little house a palace, and the little house shrinks to a hut" (qtd. in Crossman, ThoughtCo Exp 13 L 18). As long as an individual is living in a class similar to him, it is observed that all the social requirements bring him satisfaction. But as soon there is an up gradation in the class surrounding him, there is social consciousness and individual starts comparing their status with others that cause conflict in society.

Class struggle in literary work:

Marxist theory can also be applied to literature by examining literary work through the lances of the social, economic and political components such as the class struggle, oppression and class division. In the 18th and 19th centuries there were many writers who penned about different social, political and economic struggles such as Charles Dickens in his novel 'David Copperfield' criticizes the struggle between classes and the view of society toward wealth and class representation of person's value. Problem plays were devolved during this era, projects the social illness in a realistic manner. They were social activists who fought to put forth the realities of class struggle and capital abuses. Some of the writers who wrote short stories that involve class struggle, division of power and characters' feelings of class distinction are Anton Chekhov, Chinua Achebe, Liliana Heker and Katherine Mansfield. Anton Chekhov in his short story 'Fat and Thin' tried to explain how power and money change the human way of behaving, as Marx once said, conflict arises because of low-class people becoming conscious about their status and power in society. It is easy to conclude that any literary work deals with the problem regarding high or low class or conflict between rich and poor and the bad behaviour, negative attitude of the society towards poor can lead to class conflict or class struggle.

Depiction of classes and their conflicts in *The Doll's House* by Katherine Mansfield.

The story is set in the late 1800s in New Zealand, at that time society was divided along a stiff class line. A 1922 short story, *The Doll's House* is written in the third person point of view, first published in The Nation and Atheneum. Writers often use this point of view to shed light on examining the broad social issue. The story is about a group of sisters who have received a gift from old Mrs. Hay that is a doll's house. The children are super excited to see the doll's house because of its beauty, size and richness. The gift itself is the symbol of the social-economic status of the Burnells. Burnell's sisters wanted to make a show of their gift to other children so they allowed two girls at a time to come to their courtyard to see the doll's house but not allowed the Kelleys sisters Else and Lil because of their lower background as they know her boundaries.

Mansfield wisely presents the society's nature towards the poor through the place where the all-social groups of children study together in school. "The school the Burnell children went to was not all the kind of place their parents would have chosen if there had been any choice" (Mansfield 2). It was not their choice but it was the only school they have in the area. Mansfield portrays that Kelveys are ill-treated in the school; they were miss treated and discriminated against by the teacher and classmates.

The character of the Kezia is presented as a hope to the readers that maybe our future is free from the class difference because of Kezia's good attitude towards the lower-class people and also she didn't bother about class status and prejudice. Kezia offers the Kelveys sister to see their doll's house Lil said to Kezia that "Your ma told our ma you weren't to speak to us" (Mansfield 5). Kezia doesn't care and shows a Doll's house to them. Aunt Beryl scolds little Kezia because she doesn't care about the class Kelveys belong to but her aunt shooed the kelvey sisters out. The story brings up the question that was the capitalist society was right for the childlike Kezia?

In this story, author Katherine Mansfield depicted the strong supremacy between the upper and the lower class and also criticized the class system and clearly presents the division of the two classes. This story revolves around the children of the two different classes. The Burnells sisters represent the bourgeoisie and Kelveys as the proletariat. This story describes how the class-conscious lead to economic and social conflict. Also projects the condition of the working-class people and their lack of resources. The writer humorously penned the description of the Kelveys dress. Because of their upper-class background, Burnells did not suffer from their survival but for her lower-class background, Kelveys suffered highly for their basic needs. The society illustrated in the text grabbed all the chances and opportunities from proletariats which resulted in endless suffering particularly when it comes to Kelveys.

At a very early age, the children were discouraged by society and their class conscious parents that they can't be friends with the poor. It is the parents and the society who fed the minds of the innocent child negativity towards class differences which resulted in the form of class consciousness. The ill behaviour of the children was the reason for the class consciousness. Mansfield portrayed

Lil's character as silent and weak and with no strength to fight back. Another character of this story, Aunt Beryl, a cold-hearted woman is an example of class consciousness. Shooing away the Kelveys sisters was a proud moment for her. This showcases the harsh behaviour of the upper class towards the lower ones. In a judgmental society, the lower-class holds no place and are often bullied by the elites. Isabella, too, represents their typical behaviour; a bossy little girl who always wants to control others. The upper class always wanted to have first-hand control over everything, especially the lower class.

In a society, where different classes exist, there is bound to be a conflict between those classes varying from social to economic conflicts. Katherine Mansfield in the story *The Doll's House* has excellently portrayed the typical lifestyle of the bourgeoisie and proletariats in the capitalist society and the harsh reality of that era regarding class struggle.

Representation of class and its conflict in the story 'The Stolen Party by Liliana Heker.

The story 'The Stolen Party' is about a young girl who attends her friend's birthday party whose family employs her mother as their housemaid. Through this story, Heker explores social class differences. The story begins with a girl named Rosaura, who was excited to attend her friend, Luciana's birthday party. "I'll die if I don't go..." (Heker 1) But her mother was not satisfied with the invitation because she thought the family was rich and they don't belong to such a high-class party "It's rich people's party" (Heker 1) and Rosaura was only a daughter of their maid but Rosaura believed they were friends. Her mother's opinion about their relationship saddens Rosaura and she argued that her mother doesn't know about their friendship. "Shut up! You know anything about being friends!" (Heker 1) They use to do their homework together, drink tea in the kitchen share secretes and have a good time together, which made Rosaura to believe that Luciana was her good friend. At the party, Rosaura helped Luciana's mother by serving others and passing out the cake because she was an expert in handling household chores. She felt a sense of power over others. Everyone was asking for her at the party which made her happy and she felt like a very important person at the party. Even the magician praised her as "my little countess" (Heker 4). Which made her feel good and she had a wonderful time at the party. Rosaura's mother came to pick her up from the party and Rosaura immediately started babbling about the party and the magician with the anger towards her mother slipping away.

When everyone was leaving, Senora Ines gave return gifts to all the children. Rosaura, too, was eagerly waiting for her gift but instead, she was handed two bills. And she was shocked that in the end, her mother was right. "Rosaura felt her arms stiffen, stick close to her body..." (Heker 5). In the end, she has realized that she was not a guest but a servant. Liliana Heker wisely presented the social class through the character of Rosaura and her mother as a lower class and Luciana and the other as upper class. Society has created a structure of social class that brings imbalances between individuals as they are divided on the basis of their economic, political and financial status. The idea of communism can be seen throughout the story. Rosaura's character was very cheery and symbolizes hope. However, her mother, Herminia's character was exactly the opposite. Herminia was aware of the social class in society and its consequences. She struggles to explain the same to her daughter who was living in a utopian world where there is no evil, an ideal world without any discrimination.

The basic ideology of communism is seen through Rosaura by her good and kind-hearted character who always looked others at par with her without any discrimination. Their opposite characters showcase class consciousness in society. Herminia was class conscious, she was aware of the discrimination happening in the society but her daughter was ignorant and unaware of the division and conflicts in the society. In the capitalist society, the bourgeoisie exploits the proletariat taking their undue advantage. Proletariats are always at a disadvantage as the bourgeoisie lives off the surplus-value of their labour. Similarly, in the story, Senora Ines took unfair advantage of Rosaura for her own benefit. Rosaura was also bullied by Luciana's cousin which makes the wide gap between the upper and lower classes visible. This also illustrates the inequalities that existed in the society which is well-established on the basis of human nature.

The conflict between Bourgeoisies and the proletarians in the story was projected through the magician and the monkey. The magician can be referred to as an owner and the monkey as labour, who took charge of it; on the other hand, Rosaura was exploited by the hands of Senora Ines so-called upper-class people. Monkey was also symbolised Rosaura; the monkey was there at the party odd one character so was Rosaura, because of her social class she does not fit into rich people's parties. Rosaura's character was noticeable that children are innocent to the world or society which got divided into social classes and has conflict or struggles within them. At the end of the party when everyone has received their gift, Rosaura was also assuming that she will be receiving the gift from Senora Ines but reality hit her hard. It was enclosed at the end of the story to Rosaura that there exist such classes like upper class and lower class or concepts like rich or poor which shattered her hope. She was struggling to identify her place or class in society. The story 'The Stolen Party by Liliana Heker remarkably depicted the class struggle and the consciousness of the proletarians through the character of mother and daughter. Hecker used the innocent child and her utopian world to bring forth the cruel reality of the society to the readers that there was no utopian or an ideal world, in reality, people have to struggle for their preferable existence. This class conflict was wisely disclosed at the end of the story by Heker.

Similarities and differences in both stories 'The Doll's House' by Katharine Mansfield and 'The Stolen Party' by Liliana Heker

The stories 'The Doll's House' by Katherine Mansfield and 'The Stolen Party' by Liliana Heker well-characterize the class struggle and class conflict and have some similarities as well as differences. Through this one can get an apparent idea of how the society was structured and were divided into different classes and have disagreement between them. Both the stories have children as a common medium to convey ideas. Both the story has some kind of upper class (the Bourgeoisies) and lower class (the Proletariats) characters. With the help of these social classes authors intellectually exhibited the class struggle and class conflict. Both the writer has used the third person point of view to shed light on the broader issue of that time.

Children were the prominent character throughout both stories. In the story 'The Doll's house' Kelveys were ill-treated by rich people such as Aunt Beryl, Burnells and classmates. Mansfield introduces Kelveys sisters as poor who did not have much resources and unstable social and economic condition, they were teased by the other girls in the school because of their poor background, and they never fight back or argued with them. Lil just give them a shameful and silly smile and walk away with the situation; she does not have courage to stand for herself. Lil's personality was pitiful, scared and she rarely speak, she was scared by the upper-class people. When Burnells little sister Kezia invite Kelveys to see their doll's house, at first Lil hesitate to go there because she was aware of her class and her status in the society, she also knew that if she goes there, it would not be accepted by rich peoples. As she belongs to the class which was treated badly and not accepted in the society. In her opinion she does not have that authority to cross the line between them and enter in the house of Burnells, the line of the class which brings her back simultaneously. Her little sister Else was just the opposite of her; she encouraged her sister to going inside the house. When both finally see the Burnells' doll's house Else catch sight of the small and little lamp which symbolizes hope. Else and wealthier Kezia was the one, who at first glance find the lamp beautiful and shiny. Through the lamp, they both were filled by the hope, hope for the classless society, and hope for the society who will not create discrimination amongst people in future on the bases of status.

On the other hand, in the story *The Stolen Party* Rosaura's character was imaginative, sensitive, and full of positivity and hope.

For her, financial status doesn't matter; she was an inexperienced child and excited to attend rich people's party with full enthusiasm without knowing its consequence. Both the stories well outline the Bourgeoisies power or control and the Proletarians suffering. Each character have unique characteristic which defined different classes in general.

In *The Stolen Party*, the upper-class family of Luciana was kind enough to treat their maid with respect. Luciana was allowed to spend time with Rosaura; daughter of the lower-class maid. However, in the Dolls House, The Burnells daughters were not allowed to interact with the Kelveys Daughters as they belonged to lower class. This shows the difference in their behavior towards other class. At the end of *The Stolen Party*, despite having a kind attitude towards Rosaura and her mother, Senora still viewed them as those from lower-class. She treated them as their maid and her behavior was restricted to that of a maid and her servant. This implies that irrespective of good or bad attitude toward lower-class people, they are still looked down upon and face lot of trouble to find a respectable place in the society.

Conclus

It is easy to conclude that both stories *The Stolen Party* by Liliana Heker and *The Doll's House* by Katherine Mansfield deal with conflict between social classes and Social economic struggle. In the opinion of Marx, society is divided into two social groups i.e., Bourgeoisie and proletariat. One who owns the production and proletariats are the worker. The conflict theory describes well the conflict that accorded due to division of power in a society based on economic and social status of the people. *The Doll's House* and *The Stolen Party* both the stories perfectly illustrate the attitude and the behavior of the society towards lower class. These stories also depict the struggle of the lower class to survive in the society. The conflict between these two classes described in a persuading manner in the stories *The Doll's House* and *The Stolen Party*.

The Doll's House by Katherine Mansfield was a remarkable short story through that author Mansfield tried to create awareness among the society about how bourgeoisies always neglected the right of the proletarians and also manipulates the proletarians to earn profit. The bourgeoisie's attitude and the voice can be heard through the characters. The capitalist ideology was represented through the character of Isabela who with help of her status and power tries to control thing around her.

'The Stolen Party' by Liliana Heker on the contrary portrays the character of Rosaura to highlight the proletarian's voice, their expectation from the society. They do want the world of their dream, equality, proper resource etc. The friendship between rich and poor classes cannot fill the gap between them which was excellently presented in the story *The Stolen Part'* through friendship between Rosaura and Luciana. No matter how good rich were towards poor there was something that differentiates them because of that they never cross the line. By analyzing the story *The Doll's House* and *The Stolen Party* with the help of Marxist reading, class struggle and class conflict were easy to understand.

In the words of Engels and Marx "The proletarians have nothing to lose but their chains. They have a world to win" (Engels)s

Primary Text

Heker, Liliana. "The Stolen Party." Microsoft Word - Short Story- The Stolen Party.doc, 2021, www.sturgeonenglish.com/uploads/1/3/6/0/13602064/short_story-_the_stolen_party.pdf. Mansfield, Katherine.

"The Doll's House." Katherine Mansfield society, 2021, www.katherinemansfieldsociety.org/assets/KM-Stories/THE-DOLLS-HOUSE.pdf.Marx, Karl, and Frederick Engels.

"Manifesto of the Communist Party by Karl Marx and Frederick Engels February 1848." Manifesto of the Communist Party, 1848, www.marxists.org/archive/marx/works/download/pdf/Manifesto.pdf.

Citation

Mondal, puja. "Capitalism: Essay on Capitalism (Market Economy)." Your Article Library, 25 Mar. 2014, Capitalism: Essay on Capitalism (Market Economy) (yourarticlelibrary.com)

History Crunch, Writers. “CAUSES OF THE INDUSTRIAL REVOLUTION.” Historycrunch.com, 15 June 2017, Causes of the Industrial Revolution - History Crunch - History Articles, Summaries, Biographies, Resources and More

Hughes, Kathryn. “The Middle Classes: Etiquette and Upward Mobility.” The British Library, The British Library, 13 Feb. 2014, The middle classes: etiquette and upward mobility - The British Library (bl.uk)

Koop, Fermin. “What Is Conflict Theory? Looking at Marx’s Main Concepts.” ZME Science, 28 Jan. 2021, www.zmescience.com/other/feature-post/what-is-conflict-theory-19092019/.

Crossman, Ashley. “What Is Conflict Theory?” ThoughtCo, 3 July 2019, www.thoughtco.com/conflict-theory-3026622

CHAPTER XV

CITY LIFE, A PROGRESSIVE CHANGE FOR SURVIVAL – A NARROW STUDY ON THE CHARACTER OF HARI IN ANITA DESAI'S NOVEL, THE VILLAGE BY THE SEA

Heena Ansari

ABSTRACT

In this research article, *City life a progressive change for survival* the research looks upon the importance of urbanity in today's era. This research focuses on why in the contemporary era, urbanization has become the world's need for survival. Around the world, villages are transitioning towards urbanity. Cities have become a necessity for human growth, development and sustainability. This research laid out urbanism's importance by comparing Christopher Charles Berninger's *Principles of Intelligent Urbanism* with the character of Hari a boy from village Thul, India in Anita Desai's novel, *The Village by the Sea.* The role played by the city of Bombay in Hari's life through Anita Desai's narration in the novel is the main focus of this article. Berninger's principles of Intelligent Urbanism explain how urban life is a modern solution for human survival and to their various contemporary issues.

Objective

To understand any theory it is certainly advisable to have known its origin and originator. Christopher Charles Benninger is a highly successful American-Indian architect and well–planner who is based in the city of Pune, India. His professionalism and success can be marked by the projects he has designed. Naming few of his well–established designed projects are the Royal Supreme Court situated in Bhutan, the College of Engineering in Pune and the Indian Institute of technology-based in Hyderabad.

However, in regard to the focused theory of this research article, the most notable work of Christopher Charles Beninger is of 1986, when he was included by the Asian Development Bank to write their position paper on the topic of Urban Development. This paper was considered to successfully put forth arguments of the case about extending financial support to the urban development sector.

Theory

Christopher Charles Benninger's remarkable architectural works focusing on urban designing, city management and town planning ultimately resulted in drafting his *Principles of intelligent urbanism* (PIU). These principles seemed to have guided his planning of the new capital of Bhutan. To elaborate further understanding, the *Principles of intelligent urbanism* (PIU) consists of a theory of urban planning and construction that is composed of ten set axioms. These ten axioms give the reader a guide to formulatc and cxccutc city planning and urban dcsign. The ten axioms of urban planning aim at reconciling and integrating the various diverse concerns regarding urban planning and management.

To elaborate further on the ten axioms, principle one is the *Balance with Nature.* This principle aims to reach a level of human habitation intensity where the consumption of resources is replaced through the refilling natural cycles of the seasons. This helps in creating environmental equilibrium. The second principle is the *Balance with Tradition.* This principle planned to amalgamate interventions with existing cultural assets, to respect traditional practices and precedents of style (Spreiregen, 1965). This principle aims to value the historical and cultural heritage and the importance of a particular place. This principle states that urbanization should be emphasized within the balance of tradition which means to promote and conserve elements and generic components of the urban patterns.

The third principle is *Appropriate Technology.* Appropriate technology aims to implement building materials, construction techniques, systems of infrastructure and project management that are in sync with local contexts such as situation, setting and circumstances. These ultimately results in abundant craftspeople, labour-intensive methods, surplus savings and capital intensive methods. Technology has become the potential solution to all problems. This has to lead to an appropriate balance between technology and other resources.

The fourth principle is *Conviviality.* Conviviality aims to promote social interaction by public domains, following a hierarchy of places, planned for personal solace, companionship, romance, domesticity, along with neighbourliness, community and civic life (Jacobs, 1993). This principle leads to the creation of vibrant societies that are interactive, socially active and offers their people uncountable opportunities for gathering and interacting with one another, and being space-specific is achieved through design.

The fifth principle is *Efficiency.* This principle is quite important to maintain a balance between the use of resources that includes energy, time and fiscal resources, and simultaneously achieving comfort, safety, security, access, time, productivity and cleanliness. This principle aims to lead to optimum sharing of public land, roads, facilities, services and infrastructure also to reduce household expenses, increasing affording capacity, production and access and civic viability.

The sixth principle is *Human Scale.* The PIU aim at ground level, walkable and people-oriented urban structures that are based on anthropometric measures. This principle aims at the removal of artificial barriers and promotes one-to-one contact, providing friendly engaging places, walkways for pedestrians and public interactive places to meet freely.

The seventh principle is the *Opportunity Matrix.* This principle along with various available opportunities encourages increased availability of shelter, health care, human resources development along with safety and hygiene conditions. PIU's goal towards urban plan hand in hand with physical, social and economic plan. This principle sees the city as a place of processes and an opportunity system.

The eighth principle is *Regional Integration*. The PIU views the city as an organic part from a larger environment, socio-economic and cultural-geographic system that seems essential for sustenance and viewing the development of the city and its hinterland as a single holistic planning process.

The ninth principle is *Balanced Movement*. As Intelligent Urbanism encourages integrated transport systems that maintain a balance of modal splits amongst movement through walking, cycling, driving and rail or bus mass rapid transit. This principle although considered an automobile system, it, however, does not make it essential by design.

The tenth and last principle of Intelligent Urbanism is *"Institutional Integrity"*. This principle focuses on good practices that are realized through accountability, transparency, competence and participation of local governance that are found by correct databases, due entitlements, civic responsibility and their duties.

The novel *"A Village by the Sea"* is written by the author Anita Desai and was published in the year 1982. The novel highlights the story of a struggling family based in the Thul village of India and mentions a village situated near the sea. The changes that Hari goes through and the change in the setting of the novel are what the article primarily focuses on. As to how Hari migrated to Bombay to find a better living and how could the village Thul, if only the villagers accepted urbanity warm-heartedly have brought a progressive change in him and his family's lives at the end of the novel. The role that Bombay played in Hari's life was the major turning point in the character's life in the novel.

At the very beginning of the novel, the reader saw Hari working on the fields. He had given up on his study because of poverty and struggling family life and earning a living for his siblings. The main reasons to highlight Hari and his family conditions can also be less availability of opportunities. The PIU principle of the *Opportunity Matrix* fits here very well to explain the contemporary necessity of urbanism. As compared to village-like Thul, the urban city can change human social and economic conditions very effectively due to the availability of numerous living opportunities. The city is a running engine of economic growth that enhances individual knowledge, skills and abilities. This is possible of access to modern organizations, services and facilities that create human resources development. As per PIU, Intelligent Urbanism encouraged equal distribution of opportunities that lacks in a village environment and fuels the growth of humans according to individuals' capabilities and hard work.

The idea of building up a factory in the village of Thul was seen as a new life by many villagers in the novel, "The Village by the Sea" who had no occupation, skills and occupation, especially by the youngsters of the village. The factory will create jobs opportunities definitely, but Hari doubts that as an uneducated and less skilful person get a job with the factory. The PIU principle of Appropriate Technology fits in well here supporting urbanity. This principle aims at the implementation of building materials, construction techniques, set up of infrastructure and project management that are set up in sync with local contexts such a situation, its setting and circumstances. A factory will not only bring in jobs but make villagers move out of their small conserved environment and learn numerous skills and confront their own abilities and capacities. A factory will be a life-changing event in many villagers' life and a door towards urbanism.

In the novel, the reader sees Hari struggling with jobs. He tries really hard to earn money but never earns enough for his family, because of which the family times sleeps with a half-filled stomach. The cause to note behind this is inefficiency and uneven distribution of resources. The PIU principle of Efficiency is relevant here encouraging urbanism. A village can up bring the life of village if it aims to maintain balance in the use of resources and productivity. With the right resources and subordinating technology, resources can be used in reaching their full capacity and become beneficial to a large number of people. This principle aims for efficient residential development, socio-economic facilities, public services and urban infrastructure at the least cost and thus paves the way to social, economic and personal development.

In the novel, Biju's new boat was another event through which the reader got an insight into modernity and urbanity. In order to increase earnings and expand occupation, Biju a villager in the Thul village was creating a better-advanced boat which will be the biggest boat in the Thul village. At this point in the novel, "The Village by the Sea" the reader gets an understanding that change is the core of living. As human life progresses there is a need for its surrounding to progress too and adopt new changes for living. Human needs increase with time and growth because of which they need various urban resources for sustainability. All the PIU principles are very relevant here like Appropriate Technology, Efficiency, Opportunity Matrix, balanced movement, balance with nature, balance with tradition and Institutional Integrity. How Hari realized the need to make a choice out of his primary zone and just like Biju see the importance of future urbanism.

In the novel *The Village by the Sea*, when a strange informed Biju, Hari and villagers who were standing around to see Biju's boat being constructed that the construction of a factory in Thul will lead them to sell their farmlands to the government. The PIU principle of *Balance with Nature* is relevant here. In the novel, the villagers were scared that their farmlands will be taken away making them an outsider in their own place. Urbanism encourages urban ecological balance and aims to distinguish between utilizing resources and its exploitation. Every modern invention environmental assessments are encouraged so to safeguard fragile zones, ecosystems and habitats by techniques of conservation, density control, important here land us planning and one space design.

In the novel, *The Village by the Sea* we see the helplessness in Hari because he was unable to find a solution for his sick bedridden mother. The PIU principle of *Efficiency* encourages resolving such issues. The availability of balanced resources is the solution to a human helpless situation like these in villages. Intelligent urbanism aims at optimum availability and distribution of resources and facilities in the city. These facilities include public land, roads, health care facilities, services and proper infrastructure to fuel the continuity of these facilities and services. This principle not only facilitates resources but also aims to reduce household expenses, increasing human capacity to afford these services, their production and access with civic viability.

In the course of the novel, *A Village by the Sea* when the villagers started to oppose the factory set up in Thul, Adarkar came in support of the villagers. The PIU principles axioms of *Balance with Nature, Appropriate Technology, Opportunity Matrix* and *Regional Integration* is the solution here to change villagers' thoughts about the construction of the new factory. Intelligent urbanism keeps in mind that the nature natural cycle is not hindered, the use of technology will lead to advancement in the region and in social and economic growth and development, the factory will definitely pave way for new occupations and employments and not just fishing and farming that the villagers did for a living and will also aim at regional integration paving way for exchange of ideas and communications.

In the novel, *The Village by the Sea*, Hari's journey began when he was searching de Silvas's home address. He taught that no way to survive in Bombay was to have a job and so he was looking out for de Silvas who in the Thul village promised him to offer a job if ever he came to Bombay. As Intelligent Urbanism encourage the creation of the city as an *Opportunity Matrix*. Any person in the city can find his interest and earn a living. At times even being illiterate is not an obstacle. The PIU principle of *Regional Integration* is relevant to Hari's condition of finding a job. This principle highlighted the occurrence of employees and students commuting to the city every day from places known to be catchment areas. The commuters came to the city for various reasons but to mention to have urban facilities and services. In the novel, Hari too is a commuter in search of the economy in the city of Bombay.

Hari understood the need for change and urbanism when in the novel, *The Village by Sea* Mr. Panwallah said, "and if you want to survive, you will have to change too...So Hari the fisherman, Hari the farmer will have to become Hari the poultry farmer or Hari the watch mender!" (88).

At the end of the novel, Hari by working hard day and night in the restaurant and repairing watches in the big city of Bombay went back to his village Thul, during Diwali. This time he didn't have to look out for a boat or help to travel; Mr. Panwallah and Jagu brought him a bus ticket jointly. When he went back to his home in Thul, his siblings Lila, Bela and Kamal were delighted. They informed him of all the happenings that took place when he was not around, especially his mother's health recovery in Alibaug. After a very long time, the Hari family was celebrated Diwali together and happiness was double because his mother was feeling well and his father gave up his habit of drinking alcohol. Finally, in the end, Hari was a capable being with better thoughts and mindsets towards acceptance of urbanism because now he himself has experienced it in the city of Bombay.

CONCLUSION

To conclude, in the novel, *The Village by the Sea* Anita Desai brought a drastic change in Hari's character through his transition to the city of Bombay. Christopher Charles Beninger's 'Principles of Intelligent Urbanism supports the thesis statement that "City life a progressive change for survival". A village can never be the only environment a human can survive in but a constant change is needed from time to time towards urbanism. Humans are progressive living beings and their increasing needs are to be fulfilled by modern technologies and techniques. As generation changes, it's in human nature that he finds more upgraded solutions to problems or anything around him. No life can live in denial of urbanism.

Works Cited

Desai, Anita. The Village by the Sea. Penguin Books, 2015. 16th May 2021.

Gordon, Mervin. "Research Quotes." Forbes, Forbes Magazine, www.forbes.com/quotes/theme/research/. 3rd June 2021.

Spreiregen, Paul D. Urban Design the Architecture of Towns and Cities. McGraw-Hill, 1965. 4th June 2021.

McHarg, I. L. Design with Nature. John Wiley, 1995. 5th June 2021.

Beninger, Christopher Charles. "Principles of Intelligent Urbanism." Wikipedia, Wikimedia Foundation, 20 Apr. 2021, en.m.wikipedia.org/wiki/Principles_of_intelligent_urbanism#Axioms. 5th June 2021.

Leneurbanity. "10 Principles of Intelligent Urbanism in City Planning and Urban Design." Eud, 10 Apr. 2015, eud.leneurbanity.com/10-principles-of-intelligent-urbanism-in-city-planning-and-urban-design/. 10th June 2021.

Bates, Charlotte. "Conviviality, Disability and Design in the City - Charlotte Bates, 2018." SAGE Journals, journals.sagepub.com/doi/10.1177/0038026118771291.

Study Moose. "Anita Desai's The Village by the Sea Free Essay Example." StudyMoose, 5 June 2020, studymoose.com/anita-desais-the-village-by-the-sea-essay. 10th June 2021.

Desai, Anita, et al. "The Village By the Sea Themes." GradeSaver, www.gradesaver.com/the-village-by-the-sea/study-guide/themes. 11th June 2021.

Anis, Zulaikha. "Novel Analysis: The Village by the Sea (Anita Desai)." Academia.edu, www.academia.edu/3669199/Novel_Analysis_The_Village_by_the_Sea_Anita_Desai_. 11th June 2021.

Yang, Chua Song. Village By The Sea - Character Analysis, 22 May 2009, 2p203chuasongyang.blogspot.com/2009/05/while-you-all-might-be-interested-of-my.html?m=1. 12th June 2021.

Sammi. The Village by the Sea - Character Analysis, 1 Jan. 1970, samiigsblog.blogspot.com/2010/07/village-by-sea-character-analysis.html?m=1. 12th June 2021.

CHAPTER XVI

TOXIC BEHAVIOUR SUCH AS STALKING, PHYSICAL ABUSE, MENTAL TORTURE BEING GLORIFIED AS TRUE LOVE IN BOLLYWOOD MOVIES

Sara Pawaskar

ABSTRACT

Bollywood or Indian cinema has been normalizing and glorifying toxic behaviours such as abuse, mental torture, stalking, blackmail in the name of love and romance. The research tries to highlight such misogynistic traits in the protagonists of Bollywood movies being normalized in the name of love and romance. Analyzing movies like Tere Naam released in 2003 and Kabir Singh released in 2019. Also, analyzing another movie from the 1990s, Daraar (1996) highlights the abusive marriage of a couple under the stance of love. The aim is to look at how Bollywood has been normalizing such behaviour for ages and still continues to do so in the name of entertainment. These movies influence the social and cultural thinking of the audiences. The problematic cinema sends the wrong message to the viewers. Such movies filled with toxic elements being normalized have adverse effects on the behaviour of the youth. The attempt of this research is to assemble and analyze three different movies belonging to different eras, consisting of abusive behaviour, misogyny and suppression of women in the name of love and romance.

Keywords: Bollywood, Toxic behaviour, misogyny and patriarchy.

INTRODUCTION

India has a population of over 130 million people, the majority of whom have access to, a television. And where there's a screen, there'll be Bollywood movies, and those who can afford a movie ticket can choose from a variety of movie theatres and multiplexes. According to a HIS business survey, the Indian film industry is ranked third in the world, with a $1.9 billion marketing budget among the top 20 foreign box office markets. Furthermore, Indians are the top movie ticket purchasers, with annual sales of 2.7 billion dollars. An individual who has been exposed to Bollywood films since he was unable to talk properly would naturally learn about many important aspects of life from them, including his ideas about love, romance, and relationships. Unfortunately, Bollywood movies cannot be said to be the best instructors when it comes to love and relationships. Bollywood movies glorify and normalize toxic relationships and these movies do great on the box office but knowingly or unknowingly, these movies also affect the thinking of the youth.

The dialogues like "Everything is fair in love and war" are applauded by the viewers and in the name of romance, abusive behaviours, stalking and domination is being normalized. Tracing back to the songs and movies released in the 1990s, stalking was always the first step to approach the female protagonist, later giving it a romantic angle. Not only in the 90s but even the recent movies like Ranjhana, Badrinath ki Dulhaniya and Wanted. The viewers sympathize with the protagonists of such films and completely ignore the fact that stalking is a criminal offence. What may appear to some as stalking is considered "normal behaviour" in Indian cinema, as numerous films promote the idea that if a guy pursues a woman long enough, she will finally fall in love with him. For example, the films like Tere Naam and Kabir Singh portrayed that if a man keeps trying to persuade a woman, she will finally fall for him. He can stalk her, abduct her, dominate her and may possess all kinds of toxicity yet the women in the movie would fall in love with him just because he "loves" her too.

The songs like "*tu haan kar, yana kar, tu hai meri kira*n" and "*hoton pe naa, Dil mei Haan hoenga*" seem to take away the right of a person to refuse if they're not interested. But refusing or saying 'no' to someone is a concept that Bollywood missed and normalized torture, stalking and harassment until the other person surrenders to the so-called 'love'. Derné explains that while it is typically the villains in films who attempt rape, "there is often substantial force even in the consenting relationships of the hero and heroine. By presenting force as leading to legitimate love, films equate love and force." (Derné, 2000, p. 152). Films such as the 1990 blockbuster Dil (Kumar &Thakeria) suggests that "a man's violent harassment will make a woman love him, and men in film theatres sometimes act as if they believe that message." (Derné, 156)

The dangers of eve-teasing and item songs collide in "*Chumma Chumma De De*" — "Give Me a Kiss," in which a woman dressed in an ostentatious red gown and wearing bright red lipstick dances onstage in front of a large crowd of men. The song features a call-and-response between the woman and the men, with the woman saying, "Do not kiss me!" and the men responding, "Give me a kiss!"

According to Oxfam India, 95 percent of young girls surveyed said that boys used these derogatory songs as "tools for sexual abuse" when they walked by. Bollywood has consistently objectified women in the movies and the item songs that showcase women as the 'eye-candy' to the audience. "Objectification involves the lowering of a person, a being with humanity, to the status of an object," wrote philosopher Immanuel Kant (1797). Objectification Theory" was created by Fredrickson and Roberts (1970), who proposed that women are sexually objectified and treated as a commodity to be valued for its usage by the male gender and the media. Women have also been presented as sex objects by wearing revealing or provocative apparel and exhibiting an excessive amount of skin, according to studies (King, Laake, & Bernard, 2006; Seidman, 1992; Smith, 2005). For Example, it was Salman Khan's dialogue "*Pyaar se de rahe hain rakh lo, varna thappad maar ke bhi de sakte hain*" in Dabangg certainly glorified domestic violence but with the background music, it was portrayed as a romantic scene.

Dwyer in Hindi Romantic Cinema (1998) discusses how Yash Chopra has created a different brand of Romantic Cinema, which has a unique visual aesthetic manifested through location and the way he presents his stars. Shots of misty valleys, snow-capped mountains, lakes and rivers, women in chiffon and field of flowers. According to the writer, Yash Chopra is synonymous with the genre of romantic Hindi movies. Yash Chopra's heroes and heroines fall in love often sometimes more than once, and even share sexual relations with more than one partner. However, one must be committed to the bourgeois nuclear family, one must be faithful to one's spouse and let go of the past, live in the present.

The concept of romance in Bollywood revolves around men's insistence on attention, regardless of women's consent. In fact, men's urging to the point of harassment is regarded as an element of romance and displays of affection. The worst part about these scenes is that the woman is shown to enjoy the ritual and reciprocate her feelings once the man has finished his machismo display. (Tariq, 2017)

TERE NAAM

Tere Naam is one of the romantic Bollywood movies that normalized stalking, abducting the woman until she finally confesses the love for the hero. Directed by Satish Kaushik, Tere Naam is known to be one of the super-hit Romantic films. Radhe Mohan, the character played by Salman Khan of a rowdy, unemployed, violent, aggressive man who would go insane if things did not go according to his will. He falls in love with the female lead in the movie. He helps her two to three times and then confesses his love for her. The female lead is afraid of him but she gathers courage and refuses his proposal because she doesn't love him. But later in the movie, he abducts her and then she eventually falls in love with him. There are also instances of the male lead ragging and harassing the female lead asking her to call him "sir" and stopping her whenever he feels like it. The female lead is suppressed and dominated by the male lead. Even though she takes a stand for herself, he tries to persuade her by abducting her. In one scene, Radhe is also seen threatening the female lead, Nirjara that if she did not accept his proposal, he might beat up her dad.

The examples of toxic masculinity can be seen in this movie that glorify the "angry young man" behaviour of the male lead. This type of masculinity is harmful to society and encourages regressive behaviour. It has a psychological influence on men as well, as they try to maintain their image, which leads to domestic violence, rapes, including marital rape, and other dominating tendencies. Terry Kupers defined toxic masculinity as "the constellation of socially regressive male traits that serve to foster domination, the devaluation of women, homophobia, and wanton violence. (Salter, 2019) The problem becomes even worse when such behaviours are taken as role models and accepted without question by opinion-makers and, more recently, popular media such as films, which are frequently representations of Indian society. Masculinity is depicted in movies as expressing the "traditional" man's desire to objectify women, be driven by sex, be emotionally repressed, self-reliant, and eschew all aspects of femininity. Instead of seeing a man cry, watch them "become aggressive or show an extraordinarily tough exterior" on video. (2018, "Masculinity in Films").

From the perspective of the cinema, we may consider as particularly useful the concept of stereotype and the processes associated with it, which Hall brings from his predecessors, Richard Dyer and Homi Bhabha, among others:

Stereotypes get hold of the few 'simple, vivid, memorable, easily grasped and widely recognized' characteristics about a person, reduce everything about the person to those traits, exaggerate and simplify them, and fix them without change or development to eternity. [...] So, the first point is– stereotyping reduces, essentializes, naturalizes and fixes 'difference'. Secondly, stereotyping deploys a strategy of 'splitting'. It divides the normal acceptable from the abnormal and the unacceptable. It then excludes or expels everything which does not fit, which is different. [...] So, another feature of stereotyping is its practice of 'closure' and exclusion. [...] Stereotyping, in other words, is part of the maintenance of social and symbolic order. [...] The third point is that stereotyping tends to occur where there are grossing-qualities of power. (Hall, 1997: 258)

The concept of stereotype proposed by Hall brought obvious implications for film studies, especially regarding character analysis, criticism of negative characterization of marginalized groups of society, review of film history from new parameters and even calling attention to the social function of stereotypes in some specific cases.

KABIR SINGH

For example, the movie Kabir Singh, normalized stereotypical patriarchy and toxic masculinity. It was like a modern-day Devdas, but with anger issues. Kabir Singh is a remake of Arjun Reddy, a Telugu film directed by the same filmmaker, Sandeep Reddy Vanga, which was a box office smash. The hero's first scene establishes him as a masochist male addict. He smokes, drinks, and has sex at will, with or without an agreement, such as when the girl with whom he is trying to have sex asks him to leave. At gunpoint, he demands that she strip. He has a drink before a major procedure that his nurse is preparing for him. He named his bitch Preeti after his sweetheart, whom he loves more than any other human being. He is in Medical College and playing football for his college, where the teams collide, using gender-related swear words and vulgar gestures, all justified by the fact that football is a brutal sport. When the Dean of the College begs him to control his anger if he wants to be a decent doctor, Kabir refuses to apologize, claiming that he is who he is, and instead chooses to drop out of college. It's love at first sight, and the girl is eternally his possession. As a result of his declaration to the campus, "Meri band hai" or Kabir's interest, everyone is warned to keep off-limits because there are lots of other girls. He chooses a plump-looking female for her, claiming that healthy girls are more faithful. Instead of allowing her to attend classes, he personally coaches her. He has taken on the role of her local guardian.

They, continue to meet and become physically involved even when he moves on to pursue his Master's degree, travelling back and forth until they are discovered romancing on the terrace of her own home by her father. He boldly says, "This isn't a collegiate romance." He tries but fails to persuade her parents, so he gives her an ultimatum by hitting her on the street while she clings to him and begs for philosophical contemplation. On the eve of his elder brother's wedding, he locks himself up at home with a cocktail of morphine and alcohol. Preeti is married off when he is unconscious. When he learns of it, he gets up and makes a disturbance at her house, refusing to accept her marriage and is tossed out by her father and relatives, as well as his own family. Even when his friends try to persuade him to move on, he continues to live a bohemian, dissipated existence of beer, drugs, and sex over the next few months. In Hindi cinema, the typical route out of a painful scenario or loss of love for males is drinking and sex, while for ladies it is torn. He makes a frank sexual proposal to his patient, who is a film actress who stomps off at the mention of love. Later, he becomes embroiled in a medical scandal when he conducts a vital surgery while drunk and intoxicated, and his medical licence is revoked for five years. He is evicted by his landlord and returns home to attend the burial of his grandma. He sees a hugely pregnant Preeti in a park and chooses to take her away with him, even if the child is not his, only to discover that the kid is indeed his. She states that she left her husband three days after the wedding and that she did not allow the other man to touch her. And then, they sort their misunderstandings and get married to live happily ever after.

There is a scene in the movie where Kabir says *"Kaun hai tu? Campus mei kaun jaanta hai tujhe! Kabir Rajdheer ki bandi hai tu, that's it"* which means that you are no one but my girl and that's why people know you. This dialogue talks about how the women are presented as passive object and are only being addressed in the movie in reference to the man. Kabir is preoccupied with her, demonstrating that she is nothing without him. This is a pivotal moment in the film; following this exchange, he hits her and storms out in rage.

Promiscuity is a way for men to cope with rejection in love, whereas for women it is a way to cope with rejection. Preeti has been conditioned to remain faithful. He refers to her as *meri bandi*, rather than my love. Objectifying her in the most heinous way possible. "Real/Indian men protect women regardless of their stupidity; real/Indian women recognize the wrong of their ways and change their behaviour to meet approved patriarchal dictates" (Banaji, 192). This appears to be partially true of Kabir Singh, but more subtly. According to Neelam Mishra, a Delhi-based Psychologist, they can.

The basic phenomena of human psychology say that people choose and follow whatever makes their image come across as 'powerful'. In such movies (like Kabir Singh) where so much aggression, misconduct, mis-behaviour is shown, sometimes people take it as a correct step and follow it. They consider it correct as their immediate need is being gratified. Secondly, it also depends upon the fan following of the actor, as people follow their idol without realizing or rationalizing that they are playing a character in a movie. (193)

The latest among these is the case of UP's Ashwini Kashyap, who was an avid Tik-Tok user. He, often known as Johnny Dada, would post images of actor Shahid Kapoor from his film Kabir Singh. In one of his Tik-Tok videos, he also repeated the dialogue from the film: "Jo mera nahi ho sakta, use kisi aur ke hone ka mauka nahi doonga (Who is not mine, will not be someone else's either)." Kashyap murdered Nitika Sharma, a Dubai-based flight attendant he was obsessed with and who was to get married in December to someone else. (Hindustan times)

Sandeep Reddy Vanga, the director of Kabir Singh, stated in an interview (Film Companion, 2019) that the public and reviewers who disapproved of Kabir slapping Preeti were never truly in love. Such bodily demonstrations of emotions, in his opinion, are typical in love relationships Women have always been one-dimensional figures in Bollywood, either nice or evil, white or black. There are no ambiguities. This dichotomy was encouraged by popular films that differentiated between the heroine and the vamp, the wife and the other woman. In, films heavily influenced by religion and mythology, women characters were viewed as the embodiment of morality and morals, people who could do no wrong. Following independence, the image of women as "Sita" was extensively used in films. Indian cinema successfully established patriarchal ideals through ideals of loyalty and obedience to the husband. Women were portrayed as docile, obedient wives in films such as "Dahej" (1950), "Gauri" (1968), "Devi" (1970), "Biwi ho to Aisi" (1988), and "Pati Parmeshwar" (1988). Though patriarchal behaviour was criticized in these films, it was implicitly patronized in the sense that the victim wife refuses to leave her husband's house despite severe physical and emotional abuse on the grounds that she will only leave when she dies.

DARAAR

Bollywood movie Daraar highlights the misogynist, patriarchal side of the society through the main lead Vikram, acted by Arbaaz Khan. He is portrayed as an overprotective husband who gets violent and uses his power to dominate his wife, Priya acted by Juhi Chawla. He abuses her, terrorizes her in the name of love. But, in contrast to the other two movies, Tere naam and Kabir Singh, this movie doesn't normalize the toxic behaviour of the male lead. Priya leaves Vikram and falls in love with Raj (Rishi Kapoor), the man who is given a choice whether to accept Priya after knowing her past or not. However, even in this movie, the women are portrayed as if they're dependents on another man. When Vikram gets to know that Priya is alive and is getting married to Raj, he tries to kill both of them. Towards the end, when Priya tries to save Vikram, despite his ill behaviour towards her, he pushes her away saying "you're free". This movie also focuses on domestic violence and abuse, in the name of marriage. Sexual depictions in Indian Films are particularly salient to Indian viewers because sexuality is rarely discussed outside of the cinematic context (Derné, 1999). This content is problematic; an analysis of nine feature Hindi films from the late 1990s revealed that 60% of sexual scenes contained sexual violence. The victim was generally the "heroine," and the perpetrator, the film's "hero" (Ramasubramanian& Oliver, 2003).

An Indian man recently stalked two girls in Australia and escaped punishment saying that he was influenced by the Bollywood movies. His lawyer claimed that "stalking is quite normal for Indian men". Violence against women in Indian cinema is not limited to the films that belong to the action or rape genre, rather it begins in a subtle way in many of the sweet and seemingly harmless love stories for which Bollywood is known. The majority of the 309 acid assaults documented across the country in 2014 were against women, and many of them are thought to be the result of failed or spurned relationships. Cinema's protagonists engage in covert stalking and psychopathic behaviour, and it's strange that people condemn such behaviour on the streets while applauding it in movies. Stuart Hall, a prominent sociologist, cultural theorist, and political activist, described popular media representation in several of his important scholarly publications. One of his most popular representation theories claims that representation is a process in which specific meanings are formed, transferred, and further reproduced between members of society through the use of signs and language.

CONCLUSION

Cinema appears to be both entertaining and educational. When parents set a poor example or a person has had a negative relationship, they feel vulnerable and turn to movies as a kind of wish fulfilment. If romance was more publicly acknowledged in society, there is a better chance that young people would choose real-life role models. According to certain studies, most romantic motifs in movies are believed by young people. The concept of 'soulmates,' or the notion that someone "perfect" is waiting in the wings for everyone, or that one needs another person to "complete" them, can be deceptive. This is typically the reason why people either never end up in toxic relationships or regularly shift partners in the hopes of finding the "ideal" mate. Disappointment and depression follow as a result of this. Many people are unaware that the ideal relationship does not exist and that the media deliberately promotes the concept of the perfect partnership. The second most popular cliché is “genuine love.” Life isn’t always fair, and individuals who want for true love and feel that love can make the world a better place often end up disappointed. Many people believe in serendipity/happy coincidences, which is surprising. Dramatic moments of serendipity, such as “bumping into a handsome stranger in a store” or “hitting instant connection with a lovely co-passenger,” are frequently shown in films, concluding in a fairy-tale finale. However, the chances of such events occurring naturally in life are quite rare. The foundation of any successful relationship, according to research, are similar interests and friendship. Belief in concepts like “love is the remedy for everything,” “love will eventually find a way,” and “unrequited love is lovely” could be life-threatening. A person may spend their entire life waiting for the elusive ‘love’ to appear, only to miss out on other chances.

This dominant masculinity must be dismantled. This can only be accomplished by portraying masculinity in a different light, one that includes a polite acceptance of rejection. Even the recent disputes over the film Kabir Singh show how mainstream media and popular culture can have such an impact on young minds that they stop considering different types of masculinity. People believe their masculinity is being attacked because of the contradictions in these popular Bollywood films, which makes them defend patriarchal institutions even more. Though, as adults, the youth should be able to distinguish between overromanticized love and healthy reality relationships, these tantalizing and enticing cinematic images do influence their behaviour and romantic expectations.

Society will not change for the better as long as popular culture continues to glorify stalking and harassment of women. Popular culture representation can be both dangerous and influential. The presentation of non-harmful activities, on the other hand, can have a positive impact. It is necessary to canonize the concepts of mutual respect and acceptance of dismissal. Because Bollywood is a popular source of entertainment, there is a lot of potential for influencing society through visuals that convey important information.

WORKS CITED

Bussey, K., & Bandura, A. (1999). Social cognitive theory of gender development and Psychological Review, 206(1), 676–713. DOI: 10.1037/0033-295x.106.4.676

Daraar Movie: https://youtu.be/fC8bmK6EtSE

Derné, S. (2000). Movies, masculinity, and modernity: An ethnography of men's filmgoing in India (Vol. 129, Contributions in sociology). Westport, Conn: Greenwood Press.

Derné, S. (1999). Making sex violent: Love as a force in recent Hindi films. Violence Against Women, 5(5),

548–575. Retrieved from http://dx.doi.org/10.1177/10778019922181365

Does Bollywood Promote Crimes Against Women?

Divya Arya, Kabir Singh: Bollywood's misogyny problem is not new,(2019), retrieved from https://www.bbc.com/news/world-asia-india-48754412

Dwyer, Racheal.(1998). The Hindi Romantic Cinema. Journal of South Asian Studies.21:1.Retrieved from: http://www.tandfonline.com/loi/csas20

Dwyer, Rachel (2000). The erotics of the wet sari in Hindi films, South Asia: Journal of South Asian Studies, 23:2, 143-160, DOI: 10.1080/00856400008723418

Fredrickson, B. L., & Roberts, T. A. (1997). Objectification theory. Psychology of Women Quarterly, 21,

173–206. Retrieved from http://dx.doi.org/10.1111/j.1471-6402.1997.tb00108.x

Kabir Singh Movie: https://youtu.be/4D2woHMtStY

Manohar, U., & Kline, S. L. (2014). Sexual assault portrayals in Hindi cinema. Sex Roles, 71(5– 8), 233–

245. Retrieved from http://dx.doi.org/10.1007/s11199-014-0404-6

Misogynistic cinema responsible for violence against women: https://www.dtnext.in/News/TamilNadu/2017/05/04184909/1032936/Misogynistic-cinema-elevates-violence-against-women-

.vpf

Role of Women in Indian Cinema. Retrieved March 5, 2012 from http://oorvazifilmeducation.wordpress.com/2010/10/08/interview-with-shoma-chatterji-role-of-women-in-indian-cinema/

Shruti Das (2019), Can movies motivate crimes in real life: https://www.newslaundry.com/2019/10/26/can-movies-motivate-crimes-in-real-life

Stuart Hall, Cultural Identity and Cinematic Representation.

Tariq, B. (2017, May 20). The Depiction of Women in Indian Cinema, (2018), retrieved from https://www.ukessays.com/essays/india/depiction-of-women-in-indian.php

Thussu, D. K. (2008). The globalization of "Bollywood": The hype and the hope. In A. Punathambekar & P.K. Anandam (Eds.), Global Bollywood (pp. 97–116). New York, NY: NYU Press.

Tere Naam Movie: https://youtu.be/lpURFyFQMa4

CHAPTER XVII

THE GOTHIC, GROTESQUE AND GHOSTS IN GHOST STORIES FROM THE RAJ

Sara Mahimi

ABSTRACT

"Ghosts Don't Require Passports.

They can turn up Without Papers in the Most Unexpected Places!"(Bond, Ruskin, 2)

Gothic literature deals with the tales of horror and supernatural often enticing the readers with its description of the unnatural. Death, decay, elements of mystery and suspense, curses, etc. are the main features of gothic literature. The book presents a picture of 'haunted India' as seen through the eyes of British writers, officials and travellers during the 19th and 20th centuries. Written in the first-person narration, the tales can be said to be first-hand experiences though no evidence is found about the authenticity of these incidents. Environment forms a major factor in gothic literature; without it, the genre is mostly incomplete. Both flora and fauna along with the weather conditions are highly utilized in the gothic style of writing to add effect. The purpose of this paper is to analyze the short stories by different authors, compiled and edited by Ruskin Bond in *Ghost Stories From The Raj*, in terms of gothic perspective. This paper also brings to light the role of the environment in gothic literature by analyzing the stories in the mentioned book. The method used can be said to be descriptive and analytical as well.

Keywords: Gothic, terror, macabre, colonialism and environment.

Introduction to Gothic Literature

Gothic novels originated from Gothic architecture. The birth of the Gothic genre can be traced back to the Renaissance when the Europeans rediscovered Greco-Roman culture during the

Renaissance and began to regard a particular type of architecture, which was built during the Middle Ages as 'Gothic', not because of any connection with the Goths, but because these buildings were considered as barbaric and definitely not in that Classical style that they so admired. 'Gothic' came to be described as a certain type of novel, which had its settings in Gothic style architecture, mainly castles, mansions and abbeys. Thus, the term 'Gothic' has been extended to a type of fiction that develops an atmosphere of gloom and terror unlike the exotic settings of the earlier romances and represents events that are melodramatically violent and aberrant psychological states. The gothic characters are caught up in a complicated world where all values - social, political and religious are in doubt. The gothic hero, either involuntarily or voluntarily, is usually isolated. For example, in Frankenstein, Victor is isolated. The villain is an epitome of evil, either by some implicit malevolence or by his/her own fall from grace. Vijay Mishra states that the Gothic novel is a "presentation of the unpresentable" (Mishra,1).

The original work which ushered in the Gothic era was Horace Walpole's The Castle of Otranto: A Gothic Story. The locale was often a gloomy castle furnished with dungeons, subterranean passages and sliding panels or places like old ruined houses with secret cellars. The typical story focused upon the suffering imposed upon an innocent heroine by a cruel and lustful villain. The principal aim of such novels was to create chilling terrors. Valdine Clemens points out that "the Gothic tale is generally most effective when it is more effective" (Clemens, 1).

Mary Shelly's Frankenstein has mysterious circumstances in which Victor created the monster: The cloudy weather in which Victor gathers the body parts and the use of little known modern technologies for unnatural purposes. The stories in the gothic genre are mostly set in places unbeknownst to the readers - eg. the chase in Frankenstein through the unexplored Arctic regions. The characters in the Gothic novel seem to bridge the mortal and supernatural world. For instance, Dracula lives as both a human being and as the supernatural entity moving easily between both worlds. The Twilight Series by Stephanie Meyer also projects vampires as normal human beings. The literary critic David Morris believes that the "Gothic novel addresses the horrific, hidden ideas and emotions within individuals and provides an outlet for them"(Morris, 1).

Examples of Gothic novels include William Beckford's Vathek, Ann Radcliffe's The Mysteries of Udolpho, Charles Maturin's use of the supernatural in Melmoth the Wanderer, Mary Shelly's Frankenstein, Emily Bronte's Wuthering Heights, Charlotte Bronte's Jane Eyre, Matthew Gregory Lewis' The Monk. Other authors and their works include Irish Murdoch's The Unicorn, Daphne du Maurier's Rebecca, Tales of Horror by German E.T.A Hoffman, Tales of Edgar Allan Poe, etc.

Introduction to the Editor and Authors

Ruskin Bond, born on 19 May 1934, is an Indian author of British descent. He has been writing for over sixty years ever and has over one hundred and twenty titles to his name including novels, short stories, essays, books for children, etc. His first novel is *The Room on the Roof*. Most of his works are a contribution to children's literature. Bond's interest in the supernatural led him to write titles such as *Ghost Stories from the Raj, A Season of Ghosts, A Face in the Dark, The Blue Umbrella*. He has many prestigious awards to his name. In his essay, he explained his Indian identity, "*Race did not make me one. But history did. And in the long run, it's history that counts*" (Bond,3). Writers include Alice Perrin, C.A. Kincaid, Sir Henry Sleeman and Joseph Rudyard Kipling, who were all prolific writers of British nationality.

A Short Glimpse of Short Stories

"The power of the older gothic is to use the supernatural as an image for real and carefully depicted social fears."(Punter, David, 4). *The Wondrous Narrative of John Cambell* involves Cambell and other British officers who had learnt of the treasure obtained by Asaf Khan by looting and plundering Hindu places of worship. The officers dig the house for the treasure which is guarded by devils and spirits. Whenever the devils appear the officers protect themselves by reading the Bible. After obtaining the treasure, the devils don't let the officers live in peace and keep tormenting them until they die. *The Old Graveyard at Sirur* begins with a description of Sirur's cemetery with the tomb of Colonel Hutchings at the very centre. Indian soldiers used to salute the tomb. Several years ago, a fifteen-year-old widow was forced to commit Sati and Hutchings saved her and married her. The girl's family honour had been hurt and they killed Hutchings to take revenge. The wife consumed opium and died. She was buried beside her husband. Ever since Hutchings can be seen sitting on the tomb along with his wife at times. The narrator goes to the graveyard on a full moon night and sure enough, there was the Colonel with his wife alongside.

In *A Tale of the Malabar Jungles*, Anderson demonstrates to Peter some supernatural powers that he had acquired; he can make an object move just by looking at it. But he is not perfect in art, as he is yet to learn to keep the objects last for long. The next day, when they are returning after hunting, a rogue elephant appears. Anderson uses his powers to turn his walking stick into a rifle and shoot the elephant. Unfortunately, the dying elephant falls on Anderson and he too dies. Peter finds a bullet in the elephant's head which Anderson had shot, though the rifle had turned back into the walking stick the bullet was still there. At last, Anderson did master the art of making the objects of his creation last. In the narrative *Caulfield's Crime*, Caulfield goes to the countryside for hunting a fakir comes to ask for alms but Caulfield throws a stone at him.

From then on, whenever Caulfield is about to shoot, the fakir upsets the target. In a fit of rage, Caulfield shoots the fakir and hides the body to dispose of it later. When he returned to the spot to dispose of the body, a jackal having only one ear was devouring the body. He buries the body. However, from then on Caulfield begins to hear the howling of a jackal around his house and is convinced that the spirit of the fakir has possessed the jackal and dies of fear one day. After seeing the last of Caulfield, the friend takes leave and sees a jackal with one ear missing going inside the house Caulfield.

But when the house is combed there is no jackal to be found!

Analysis of the stories from a Gothic perspective.

"The events in the gothic novel tend to have supernatural origins."(Guste, 29). In Caulfield's Crime, Perrin has made use of a jackal which is a cunning and ferocious animal. It was believed in colonial India that the jackal's cry is of ill omen and if a jackal cries near a sick person's house, it is a sure presage of death. Caulfield and his friend both notice that the jackal's face is similar to the fakir. Reincarnation since olden times has been a subject of interest for many. The supposed reincarnation of the fakir is another important gothic aspect. By reincarnating into a jackal, the fakir is able to take revenge. Streams are associated with gothic as they are believed to be having water spirits or ghosts of those who had died by drowning in them. The sinister description of the jacket devouring the body and refusing to go away is also hideous. The grave in which Caulfield buries the fakir was filled with stones from an ancient temple. These places of worship were often regarded as having guardian spirits to them.

"There is something at work in my soul which I do not understand." (Shelly, Mary, 5). A Tale of the Malabar Junglesinvolves Anderson, who stays at an isolated mansion in the midst of the dense forest. His seclusion from the rest of the world raises eyebrows. Settings such as a huge house furnished with middle eastern decors, artefacts and other items, in the middle of the forest are typically employed in a gothic tale. The middle eastern setting of the house adds essence to the gothic tale. The tribals have been a subject of interest for many tribal anthropologists. They have their own soothsayers who have miraculous powers to heal an ill person, to predict an ill omen and to foresee other such things. Many of the tribe's secrets to date are unknown as the tribals are supposed to keep the knowledge hidden and not share it with those who are alien to them. As Anderson mentions in the story, "the jungle tribe of this part are one of the most primitive races in the world and yet have control over powers of which the rest of the world knows nothing." (Dennys,71).

Not all mysteries are gothic, however, mysteries combined with supernatural occurrences or powers can be said to be gothic.

For example, in Achebe Chinua's *Things Fall Apart*, the tribes possess supernatural powers and can summon spirits. In the story, too, the tribes have such remarkable powers which Anderson learns. He has learnt to make objects which others think appear out of thin air. He has also learnt to make objects float in the air with his eyes and concentration. When the rogue elephant appears, Anderson changes his walking stick into a rifle and shoots the elephant. It is also mysterious that if a person is shooting an animal, he would stand a few feet away to shoot it and not beside it, especially if the animal is wild or not in its senses. When Anderson shoots the elephant, it falls on him and he dies too. It might be possible that Anderson died due to the powers that he had learnt. The graveyard is the main setting for *The Old Graveyard at Sirur*. Graveyards arc always looked upon as haunted be it any place in the world.

There is a popular saying that graveyards are a house for many nasty spirits. Therefore, in gothic literature, they form an important part as the setting. In the story, too, it is mentioned that Colonel Hutchings is seen sitting on his tomb along with his wife. The thought itself gives goosebumps. Major Shinde tells the story of a young widow who was forced to commit Sati. The girl refused to jump into the funeral pyre and started screaming with fright. In order to control the situation, her mother and sister forced her to consume opium and one of her brothers wished to stun her with the burning logs. The act of making a young girl jump into burning flames, offering her opium to numb her senses and wishing to beat her with burning logs is itself barbaric. Gothic literature encompasses barbaric things. Hutchings was killed brutally by the Shindes and the young wife consumed opium and took her own life. It is often said that the people who commit suicide or are murdered are stuck between heaven and earth and their spirits roam about in search of a mortal body. The cold, chilly weather on a full moon night was perfect to capture two ghosts in a still, silent graveyard with its silence being disturbed occasionally by the cry of some nocturnal creatures.

The tale, *The Wondrous Narrative of John Cambell* is about hidden treasure, which was obtained by the Mughal general by plundering religious places that were adorned with valuable antiques and jewellery. Legend has it that these valuables were cursed so that they don't fall into wrong hands and if such a situation arises, then whoever had stolen the jewels was either met with some calamity or death. It was also believed that these valuables had guardian spirits who were made guardians to the jewels by special mantras and yagna. In the Muslim community, these vast treasures are supposed to be guarded by djinns, who are pacified only after taking a human life. When the British officers are faced with the spirits they recite the Bible. These spirits can be the servants of the person to whom those treasures belong as it was a popular practice that a rich man in order to secure his wealth would kill his servants and bury them with the treasure so that they can keep an eye and ensure it goes to the rightful owner. This is similar to the legends of sea pirates who die on their expeditions or in some conflict, but their souls guard their treasure. Gothic literature is supposed to be made up of all these elements - djinns, spirits, cursed treasures, ghosts, etc. Initially, the British officials were tired of digging as there seemed to be no treasure, as a consequence, magicians were called in who gave the exact location of the treasures. Magic, supernatural, curses are all used in gothic literature. When the devils appeared, the officials recited the Bible and kept Lord Khan in between as the spirits demanded his life as he had given up the secret to where the treasure is. The spirits kept tormenting the officials and took leave only after they breathed their last.

Colonialism

"Much of the American Literature is concerned with conquering the hostile wilderness and 'winning the west'."(Velie, Alan,3) The British ruled India for more than a century, imposing their atrocious rule first through the company and then through the governors. The ghost stories analysed belong to the British era and have been written from the first-person point of view by the British officials or their kins who narrate their ghostly and frightening experiences in colonised India. When Caulfield kills the mendicant, he is afraid because killing a native and that too, a saint; which was seen as a heinous act by the locals. This act also portrays and reflects the attitude of the English towards the Indians. These events between the imperial and the native took a gothic turn, Caulfield dies out of fear that the mendicant he killed has come in the form of the jackal to take revenge. Colonised India was not as developed as India we see today. People strictly followed beliefs, superstitions, customs and traditions, etc. While no scientific evidence supports these beliefs, there are still some of them which are beyond science and keep the scientists confused to date. When the advanced British came in contact with such things, they found it hard to believe.

People such as tribes, or babas and fakirs who secluded themselves from the material world for penances, often had unbelievable miraculous powers which cannot be explained and substantiated with proofs from science. Before the development of science, these same powers were used for healing the ill. The gothic genre comprises such mystic and miraculous unexplainable powers. Though some of these powers were learnt and practised by some Englishmen (Anderson in A Tale of Malabar Jungles), the technically advanced British refuted the existence of such supernatural powers. These powers and rituals can be said to be gothic because they are mysterious in nature and often involve unnatural potents. However, what Anderson learnt from the tribes (to make things move in the air through constant focus on them) can be said to be modern-day telekinesis. The British were spellbound by many of these ancient beliefs and mystic powers and learnt them to carry it to their homeland upon which many gothic tales and other materials have been written.

The short story *The Old Graveyard at Sirur* involves the inhuman practice of sati. The thought of a young girl jumping into raging flames is horrifying in itself. The practise of sati was banned by

Lord William Bentick, with the efforts of social reformer Raja Ram Mohan Roy. It was a custom that the wife must die along with her husband, with the interruption of the British this practice was banned and declared as a crime. In *The Wondrous Narrative of John Cambell,* the British had their eyes on the Indian wealth which was well guarded over the years by spirits and devils, which establishes a connection between colonialism and gothic. The British dug in the house to usurp the wealth that originally belonged to the Indians and was guarded by the ghosts of the owners and their servants. The English even after knowing that there are guardian spirits to the immense treasure, unearthed it and invited the torment of the devils upon themselves. The spirits left them only when they had died. The British have robbed most of India's precious wealth in such a manner.

The English were astonished at the vast unexplored forests and the rich resources that they contained. They used the forests both as a means of pleasure and for making money. Initially, the Indians used to hunt animals either for food or for pleasure. However, with the arrival of The British, the Indians became acquainted with the fact that animal parts make quick money in the international markets and there is a huge demand for leather, horns, etc. Thus, the motive of hunting changed from leisure to measure i.e. from passion to money. The British utilised the natural resources both for money and pleasure making them decrease. But nature has its own ways of taking revenge. In many instances, the Englishmen going for a hunt have met with some disaster which is unnatural (for example, Caulfield is killed as he murdered the fakir, Anderson tries to shoot the elephant but the elephant falls on him, etc.). Nature punishes the colonizers by killing them in mysterious circumstances.

Environment

"For a long time, Americans read little Indian Literature, and so we learned almost nothing from the people who 'lost' the West and who considered wilderness not hostile but home."(Velie, Alan,3). The environment is an inseparable part of literature, be it any type of genre or theory in literature, environment to some extent, adds effect or contributes to it. The natural world has been an important subject and a source of inspiration for many prose and poem writers. The time of a gothic novel is mostly night. Authors use violent climatic conditions, such as intense hail, snow, downpours, complete with flashes of lightning and booming thunder to add effect. For example, in Frankenstein, Victor follows the monster amidst the hail and storm. Elements like barren snow-clad mountains, vast stretches of grasslands, wilderness or forests where any mortal has not set foot upon or deserted areas are used in gothic literature. Further on, the fast blowing wind whistling, branches of trees rubbing and crashing against each other, dark and thick foliage or forest against the half-moon hidden behind the clouds forms a perfect background for a tale of fear. The crying of nocturnal creatures sends chills down one's spine. For example, an old untended garden forms the setting of Swinburne's *A Forsaken Garden* adding a gothic touch to it. Animals such as black cats, bats, etc. are associated with many horror stories.

A Tale of the Malabar Jungles contains nature (jungle) in the title itself. The narrator in the story talks about 'slaughtering' animals such as elephants, tigers, bison, bears, panthers and even crocodiles. Anderson learns a few mystic powers from the local tribes who stay in the nearby jungles. The forests are unexplored and house innumerable secrets. The tribal people are secluded from the outside world, they are not aware of the advancement of science and technology. They have their own traditional ways and beliefs. There are some powers of which science still has no answer and is unable to prove and define. These powers rest with the tribes and some of the ancient saints and sages which Anderson learns. The tribes are dependent totally on the forest for their survival and even worship it. Thus, the environment is found at the very base of the story as Anderson has powers that he had learnt from the tribes who are dependent on the forests and worship the forest goddess and other natural elements.

Moreover, the thick silent forest sets the atmosphere for a gothic tale. Anderson kills the elephant who is a part of nature but the elephant falls on him and he dies too. Anderson kills nature (elephant) and in return nature (elephant) kills Anderson. The central character of Caulfield's Crime goes on shooting expeditions to kill ducks and other birds. The dense forest and the wild hunt is perfect for a gothic tale. When Caulfield shouts at the fakir, he takes revenge by disturbing whatever Caulfield aims at. The fakir might also be trying to save the birds from becoming someone's dinner, as people such as the fakir are god-fearing and encourage non-violence. The fakir tries to save the environment and the ecosystem. In short, the Fakir dies due to the environment but he also avenges his death through the environment. The howling of the jackal adds to the eerie atmosphere of the story.

The Old Graveyard at Sirur involves a graveyard as its main setting. There is less danger to the ecosystem in a cemetery because man is bound to his religious beliefs, develops the environment rather than upsetting it. Hutchings had gone hunting for chinkara or a blackbuck. These animals are endangered in today's times. People have hunted them to such an extent that they are now enrolled in the Red Data Book of endangered species. Hutchings was going to kill animals but the Shindes killed him to save their family honour. Nature revolted by killing men through men themselves. The cold weather and full moon night in which the author goes to the graveyard is frightening.

Conclusion

Gothic literature focuses on the elements of mystery, macabre and terror. The gothic genre can be said to be romance and horror twisted together. The mentioned stories are infused with gothic elements which creates an atmosphere of mystery, inviting the feeling of fear from the readers. Whether they are spirits returning for revenge or some ancient treasures with guardian spirits, etc. all create terror and provide a spine chilling experience to the readers. It can be concluded that the environment is a significant part of the genre and is employed mostly as a setting to create the required atmosphere for the events to unfold dramatically. The environment is also significant to create the desired impact on the readers. Unlike other genres, the wilder side of the environment is utilised in the gothic trend. Colonialism can be identified at many places in the stories, as they are written by the British themselves. The stories often highlight the attitude of the British towards the Indians. The stories reveal the arrogant, cruel aspects of the British officials leading to events that can be termed as gothic. The spirits of the dead recognise no frontiers, they are universal beings, attacking the person who has wronged them irrespective of any nationality or other aspects. Thus, gothic literature focuses on the supernatural, the gothic stories are told through the colonialist's views involving the environment as the setting evoking the feeling of dread and fear.

Works Cited

Bond, Ruskin. Ghost Stories from the Raj. New Delhi: Rupa Publications India Pvt. Ltd, 2002.

Ghost Stories From The Raj - Exotic Indian Art.

https://www.exoticindiaart.com/book/details/ghost-stories-from-raj-IDK431/. Accessed 16

October 2021.

Harold, Ruth. "Gothic Animals: Uncanny Otherness and the Animal." Studies in Animal Literature. Palgrave Macmillan. ISBN unknown

https://www.palgrave.com/gp/book/9783030345396. Accessed 16 October 2021.

"The Creeping Unknown: Re-Making Meaning in the Gothic Novel." The Emergence of Irish Gothic Fiction: History, Origins, Theories, by Jarlath Killeen, Edinburgh University Press,

Edinburgh, 2014, pp. 79–105. JSTOR, www.jstor.org/stable/10.3366/j.ctt9qdrh2.6. Accessed 15

October 2021.

The English Bildungsroman | Gothic Fiction | Jane Eyre.

https://www.scribd.com/presentation/90027598/The-English-Bildungsroman. Accessed 16

October 2021.

The Gothic Novel- Food for thought. 8 February 2011.

http://ticer-swim.blogspot.com/2011/02/gothic-novel. Accessed 17 October 2021. "The Indian Gothic." ResearchGate. Nalini Pal. 16 November.

https://www.researchgate.net/publication/310486046_The_Indian_Gothic. Accessed 14 October 2021.

Bio-Note

Sara Mahimi has completed her bachelor's and master's degree in English Literature from R. D. National College affiliated with the prestigious University of Mumbai. Born and brought up in Mumbai, is interested in horror, cultural and historical subjects. The Gothic, Grotesque and Ghosts in Ghost Stories from the Raj is her pioneering research work followed by Portrayal of Women in Kandasamy's Works in which she describes the condition of Dalit women as projected in Meena Kandasamy's poems.

CHAPTER XVIII

EXPLORING MASCULINITIES IN MILLENNIAL BOLLYWOOD MOVIES

Ms. Priyal Jairaj Master

ABSTRACT

The concept of masculinity has been discussed for generations and the common impression would be that an arrogant, stoic or aggressive man is considered as an ideal form of masculinity. Bollywood movies are the forerunner in portraying 'the ideal perfect man' with a macho, posturing, handsome personality which adds pressure on men in the society to behave in a certain manner. With the rapidly changing culture and time, the definition of masculinity has evolved and become broader and accepting, that men have different traits and their personality differs depending upon their mental, physical and social status. Millennial Bollywood cinema has been accepting of the various forms of masculinity and has been working in presenting them on the big screen. The main focus of this paper is to explore the manner in which different forms of Masculinity are portrayed in Millennial Bollywood Movies. This dissertation will analyze two films: Manmarziyaan and Masaan, both showcasing varied forms of masculinity. This research paper will look at applying Connell's theory of masculinity to the selected movies and examine how Masculinity is constructed in Millennial Bollywood Movies.

Keywords: Manmarziyaan, Masaan and Connell's theory of masculinity.

INTRODUCTION

The cinema was born in India in the year 1930 the cinema then was in its first stage and the movie was cinematized in black and white print and does not contain any dialogue they were silent films. The Bollywood movies from the early 70's witnessed the rising of the second phase of Indian cinema. This phase of cinema represented the transition from poverty and helplessness of a man to urbanization and highlighted the working class society. The Cinema has now reached its third phase, this new phase of Indian cinema began in the early 2000s to the cinema of today. The turning point of Indian cinema came with the beginning of the 21st century. The cinema by now has evolved with Time and changing society. This cinema is called the Millennial cinema. This new type of cinema is more modern, it explores the themes such as human race simplicity of domestic life, Concoction of human misery depiction of reality-society and politics, global appeal, visual effect, technologies, space exploration and many more along with this change the roles portrayed in the movies by the men have been Revolutionized.

Bollywood films in the past have portrayed male characters as very strong macho men without a drop of emotion in them. The portrayal of such overtly strong characters still continues in this Millennial age, such movies portray a male character with superhuman qualities who is ready to face every challenge and strong enough to fight single-handedly with hordes of enemies and eliminating them and rescuing the damsel in distress. Men are more often than not portrayed as rugged, violent and active in action films that are produced in Bollywood."Aam Aadmi " is indeed the new hero on the silver screen, with the larger than life image of the hero from the past slowly fading away. The actor turned into a charismatic hero and moved ahead to be an angry young man and further into the villain, the cool dude and of lately a realistic male figure. It is a crucial change in trend and it has been taking place over the recent past. The heroes in Bollywood films now have a different perspective and are in the mood to be Human. He is an important ingredient of the movie but not superior to any other character in the movie script. It is crystal clear that the real actor is the new rising superstar. Bollywood seems to be bringing up and portraying the uncommon topic from the house of 'commons' to move ahead from here. The film industry has entered into its age of disruptors. The new unconventional hero is here to stay in

Bollywood.

The theory that will help to justify this research is Connell's theory of Masculinity - Relations among Masculinities: Hegemony, Subordination, Complicity, and Marginalization. R.W Connell has introduced this concept in the text 'Masculinities' (2005). She has explained the theory with the help of the hierarchy of Masculinities, she has arranged four types of masculinity in such an order that each type is connected to one another. This hierarchy includes four categories of masculinity: Hegemonic, Complicit, Marginalized and subordinate.

The two films that are under the scanner for this dissertation are Manmarziyaan and Masaan. Anurag Kashyap's 'Manmarziyaan' (2018) is a love story that exhibits the grey side of relationships and romance. The movie is a seemingly conventional story of a love triangle that gets original with its treatment and portrayal of love. The new-age love story with chatting on social media and finding love by swiping right on dating apps and also with the touch of old-school love saga. Manmarziyaan looks at love with new lenses. Neeraj Ghaywan's Masaan (2015) is a tale of love and shattered dreams from the banks of the holy river Ganga. Masaan means crematorium, a desolate place. The story follows two heartbreaking tales. Both the tales faced brutal inevitable instances which leave them numb. Masaan is a beautiful film with the message of true love and affection.

APPLICATION OF THE THEORY TO THE MOVIES

Applying Connell's Theory of Masculinity to the Movie Manmarziyaan:

The Film Manmarziyaan is a modern-day romantic drama, it breaks a number of stereotypes, and its fast-paced drama is directed by Anurag Kashyap. The film reinforces the gender stereotype. Manmarziyaan also represents the 'Practical' side of relationships. The movie is a tale of a love triangle. It begins with Vicky (Vicky Kaushal) jumping across the terraces of neighbouring houses to meet his girlfriend Rumi (Tapsee Pannu). They both are immature yet innocent, for both of them the mixture of sex and love serves a high. This couple is a puppet in the hands of time and circumstances. Vicky is a young fun-loving boy who is highly inspired by western hip-hop music. He works as a DJ, he is popularly known as DJ Sandz among his friends. Vicky's personality is similar to the description by Connell's theory based on Hegemonic masculinity that is used to justify man's behaviour as well as his use of violence.

Hegemonic masculinity is practised under a social structure that dominates over other types of masculinity in a given period or culture. Hegemonic masculinity is practised worldwide but is also criticized. As stated by R.W Connell, "Hegemonic masculinity can be defined as the configuration of gender practise which embodies the currently accepted answer to the problem of the legitimacy of patriarchy, which guarantees (or is taken to guarantee) the dominant position of men and the subordination of women". (Connell 77). Vicky and Rumi are lovebirds; they are careless, free and wild. They are caught in Rumi's room by her family. The family then asks Rumi to marry Vicky or else with a man they choose for her. Rumi commits to them that Vicky along with his father will visit them and ask her hand in marriage. She informs Vicky about her situation and that's when he says that he is not ready to take up the responsibility of marriage. Vicky does not take steps toward showing his commitment to the relationship, instead blackmails her that he will cut his wrist if she marries someone else. This type of masculine behaviour subsumes other men's or women's by force, coercion and even ostracization. Later, he agrees to come along with his family to Rumi's place with a marriage proposal, Rumi has faith in him that he will come but, he is commitment-phobic and does not arrive.

Vicky loves her enormously and is reluctant to comply with her demands, it is too sudden for him and he is too selfish. He places his comfort and perhaps his constant desire to exist outside a societal structure above his love for her, he is impetuous and hedonistic, and for him, his life priority is assigned to himself and is unwilling to sacrifice for his love. As Vicky does not turn up; Rumi, according to her commitment to her family, agrees to marry the first suitor that comes her way. Rumi's love for Vicky made her give him another chance and the two planned to elope, By travelling for a few hours on the road, Rumi thinks about their future and understands that they lack perspective and she confronts Vicky about their future plan. He says that he's eloping with her because she asked him to. Frustrated, Rumi returns to her home. On the day of Rumi's 'Mehndi' ceremony, Vicky stands for the whole day outside her house and finally tells her to run away with him, while he was packing his bag his father gave him a reality check, he tells him about the decision that he took in his past life but did not stick to one and kept changing his mind constantly, his lack of seriousness and is not consistent with his work. He stops Vicky from eloping with Rumi and ruining her future.

As Vicky did not show up, Rumi is left with no choice and gets married to Robbic. Vicky constantly tries to get her back, knowing the fact that she is married but he also knows that she still loves him. Rumi was confused about her life choices and was not happy in her marriage and still has feelings for Vicky, she tries to get in touch with him. This is the only factor that is responsible for Rumi's divorce. For a man, in 'Public' there is a great pressure on him to appear confident and to display his Masculinity in an effective way, and there is a fear of being humiliated for appearing weak or for having feminine traits. Now that Rumi is separated, Vicky takes this opportunity to prove himself that he has changed and portrays himself as an Accountable man. But Rumi realizes that he is doing this for the sake of proving himself to society and she knows that he is still not ready to take responsibility for the marriage and rejects his proposal of marriage.

Along comes Robbie (Abhishek Bachchan), the first suitor arranged by her family through the local matchmaking agency. He is an NRI from London; he is a mature, polite banker who is in search of a bride in Amritsar. Robbie falls for Rumi the minute he sees her smiling photograph shown by the matchmaker. He is attracted to her, so much that he doesn't want to see any other girls for an arranged match. When Robbie's Mom asks him to let her select his life partner, Robbie says, "Aap na meri shaadi naal apni bahu ki fantasy puri na karo". ("Manmarziyaan" 00:29:13- 00:29:16) (Don't try to find me a wife that fits in your criteria) He then says that he does not want a nurse or an escort, but a life partner. He traces Rumi on facebook and discovers Rumi and Vicky's affair through her Facebook account. During his first meeting with Rumi he knows that she is distracted and not thinking about him, later when he is confronted by Vicky in the club that night, Vicky threatens Robbie to not see Rumi's photograph, but Robbie does not step back, he has fallen for Rumi and isn't going to give up without a fight. Robbie shows every imaginable characteristic of a perfect 'Husband Material'; he is instantly liked by Rumi's family and is even distorted by her. Robbie's personality is similar to Complicit Masculinity discussed by Connell in her theory on masculinity.

According to R.W Connell, "A great many men who draw the patriarchal dividend also respect their wives and mothers, are never violent towards women, do their accustomed share of the housework, bring home the family wage, and can easily convince themselves that feminists must be bra-burning extremists".(Connell, 79). These are the characteristics of Complicit Masculinity mentioned by Connell in the theory. Robbie's character is like a third wheel in the love triangle. The night before her wedding with Robbie, Rumi changes her mind and meets Robbie at midnight and says that she won't be marrying him tomorrow. Robbie calls up the marriage matchmaker and inquires about Vicky's profession and gets to know that he is a Disc jockey and is not financially stable, he says to the matchmaker "Aisa ladka Rumi ko kaisa ghar dega, pyaar se na toh pet bharega na kiraya". ("Manmarziyaan" 1:11:15-1:11:36) (How can this type of boy provide Rumi with a secured future, through love one cannot feed or pay rent).

Robbie tells the matchmaker to talk to Vicky's parents about Vicky's behaviour and explain to them that Vicky will not be able to feed Rumi even if he marries her. This is indicative of the mindset of the society at large, which lays emphasis on the need for a man to fill the space as the provider and breadwinner for the family. This is the framework regarding the role of the man in contemporary society. As Vicky did not turn up, and finally Rumi realizes that there is no way out and she has to get married to Robbie. Amidst all the confusion, Robbie marries Rumi and he patiently waits for her to look at him once. Rumi on the other hand is heartbroken, filled with anger and has no perspective. She walks herself into this marriage on a whim and is clueless about what her life is going to be like. Robbie understands her and never questions her about her behaviour and past life; he never stops her from doing anything. He with his calm and matured mind tries to unflinchingly support Rumi. He gives her space and even tries to make her understand that he will always support her with her decision and tell her to think about their Marriage and about her never-ending love for Vicky.

Robbie gets to know about his wife's extramarital affair, he does not shun her or treat her as a culprit, but he tries hard to make his marriage sustain. After seeing his wife romantically involved with Vicky he cannot further bear his emotions, he in anger points out her fault for hiding this extramarital affair and breaking his trust. He takes the decision to get the marriage annulled so that Vicky and Rumi can reunite. Robbie takes the blame on himself for the divorce so that Rumi does not have to face the allegations by society. Robbie's decision makes Rumi realize her selfish behaviour and she feels guilty, She then finally breaks all her ties with Vicky and tells him to lead a meaningful life and she even understands that Vicky is doing all this just to prove himself and get Rumi back in his life, she still knows that he is not ready to take the marriage responsibility, she advised him to be responsible she even suggests him to pursue a career in Australia. On the day of signing the divorce paper, Rumi realizes her love for Robbie and she doesn't want to be separated, but she signs on the paper and while on their way back she confesses her love for him, Robbie accepts her and they give a fresh start to their relationship.

Applying Connell's Theory of Masculinity to the Movie Masaan:

"Hegemony, subordination and complicity, as just defined, are relations internal to the gender order. The interplay of gender with other structures such as class and race creates further relationships between masculinities" (Connell 80). The caste system is a deeply rooted cultural institution that is responsible for the creation and reinforcement of social and economic inequality. It is a cognitive factor that determines power and poverty in contemporary Indian society. Through various studies, it is made clear that the lower caste, the former untouchables (Schedule Caste) and Indigenous Tribes (Schedule Tribes) have on average fared worse than those belonging to the upper caste. They have been left lagging in educational and occupational outcomes, wage earnings, ownership. They are also to be expected at receiving ends of crime because of their social status. Religion is the major factor and is a crucial system that is important in forming the identity and collective identity of a community.

Religion shapes attitudes, cultural norms and influences the individual behaviour and group behaviour. Masaan focuses on the life of four characters which are interwoven throughout, yet the movie has no particular closure. Devi Pathak (Richa Chadda) the daughter of Vidyadhar Pathak (Sanjay Mishra) a former Sanskrit Teacher, a Brahmin who earns his living on the ghat of Banaras. The father-daughter duo is leading a simple life in the religious and orthodox city of Banaras. Devi and her boyfriend Piyush Agarwal (Saurabh Chaudhary) a member of the Bania caste, book a room in a hotel so that they can have sex. Unfortunately, they are caught in the police raid and are held accountable for sex trafficking. The police here is a symbol of caste that stands as an obstacle and even reaches into private spaces and moments of individual lives. Caught in an act by the police, Piyush is frightened and panics, he feels powerless and begs the police officer's not to contact his parents. He attempts to protect the caste status quo, He runs into the bathroom to save himself but he was scared and he fears aspersion by society, he commits suicide.

A corrupt Inspector Mishra (Bhagwan Tiwari) records the video of Devi in this vulnerable situation, takes advantage of this situation and threatens to publicly defame her. He blackmails her father and demands a hefty bribe; the police is a new form of Brahmanical apparatus for maintaining the caste rules. Her father is suppressed by the burden of caste and society. Devi's act of liberation has turned into a crime committed against caste. He feels helpless and is ashamed, the fear of being humiliated by society. The police inspector Mishra exhibits a Dominant kind of personality, which is associated with Hegemony. According to Connell, Hegemonic masculinity can be defined by gender practice which incorporates traits that are culturally expected and are dominating in the entire gender order. Inspector Mishra is in an authoritative position and performs power-based domination on Devi's father who apart from being an upper-caste Brahmin is given a marginalized treatment because of the situation he is trapped in due to an unacceptable act committed by his daughter which is considered a taboo in the caste restricted society.

Vidyadhar Pathak is not financially well-off and couldn't afford to pay the hefty bribe demanded by the cop. He begins to arrange money by breaking his fixed deposits; he goes from every pillar to post finding a job for his daughter so that he can pay off the bribe. In the caste-based society Vidyadhar finds it difficult to protest against the corrupt cop, the fear of being defamed and being denounced from his caste stops him from doing so. Mishra is a flag bearer of the patriarchal society; he is a constant reminder and a symbol of how a person with authority and hegemonic traits dominate over the weaker gender. He practices power over Devi's father and demands 3 lakhs to "Protect" the image of his daughter and to save them from the allegations of the society. Religious beliefs are widely accepted in Indian society and they have become a part of the culture and have shaped society.

Vidyadhar Pathak does support the caste hierarchy and its limitations because it is this social category that constitutes a large part of an individual's identity and does follow the rules laid down traditionally, as those rules are associated with the category and are a set of norms and ideals for the manner in which a person belonging to that community should behave. He belongs to the Brahmin community and is a follower of the norms set by the community, his membership in this group has shaped his aspirations. The continuous efforts he takes to hide the deeds of his daughter and agreeing to pay the bribe is his defence mechanism to protect himself and his daughter from the allegations by the caste as well as his way of not letting the image of her daughter stain. He exhibits a complicit form of masculinity, he is the head of his family, he could easily have been a strict and authoritative father, but he is not. Religious belief has been influencing human behaviour and also determines one's actions. He is conflicted because he lives in a society that tries to control women and impose restrictions over them and a system where laws are exploitative for the weaker section. Even though he never tries to control his daughter and gives her freedom. The role of religion and caste here is not static, it is the reality.

Masaan then leaps into another story of Deepak Chaudhary (Vicky Kaushal), who belongs to the Dom/Dalit caste. He is a student of Polytechnic; he studies civil engineering and also helps his father part-time to cremate the dead bodies at the Varanasi ghat. He is a bright student and is focused on his education and is also very conscious of his identity. Through his college friends he meets Shaalu Gupta (Shweta Tripathi) a girl of the Bania caste (upper caste), They both show signs of liking each other. Religion plays a dominating role in one's personality, This system is very crucial to thinking patterns and it is the important information of self-identity. Deepak's personality is entirely framed by the factors that are imposed upon his community through the caste hierarchy; he exhibits a marginalized form of masculinity. For Deepak, a boy from the Dalit caste who has been historically treated as untouchable and kept segregated by the people from the upper caste to which Shaalu belongs too. When his friends first tracked down Shalu on

Facebook they noticed her surname which is the key indication of her caste.

The social media platform Facebook offers a way of connecting the two. They go out on a date to a restaurant where Deepak expresses his attraction towards her by being protective- tell me if anyone bothers you. Later Shaalu bunks her picnic to spend some time with Deepak where they kiss- it is seen as a kind of liberation, given the history of their caste relation in the society. The non-acceptance of inter-caste marriages or relationships by the society is prominent when one of the friends of Deepak say "ladki upper-caste ki hai dost, jyaada sentiyaayie mat " ("Masaan" 00:54:27- 00:54:31) The friend is reminding Deepak that the girl is from the upper caste so he should not go further with the relationship because the rigid caste structure won't approve their relationship and will never allow them to stay together. Deepak fears confessing his caste to his upper caste girlfriend Shaalu, he even hesitates to mention the place where he lives.

Religion is the strongest system of belief that has existed for thousands of years. The Social Stratification construction by the caste places an individual into a hereditary mainly endogamous and to a great extent in an occupation-specific group. It was considered that any type of contact with the people from the lower caste will pollute the upper caste, because of which the lower caste was forced to live in segregated housing and we were denied access to education and we were even restricted to the places of worship which were attended by the elite caste. When Shaalu comes to know about Deepak's caste, she knows that her family would not accept their relationship so she tells him to study hard and find a high paying job; she even says that she will elope with him if the situation demands.

Even after being successful, the lower caste individual may not be viewed on the basis of his merit, but rather is judged by the preconceived notions made due to his stigmatized caste identity. Shaalu leaves for a small pilgrimage trip with her family; she dies in a bus accident along with her other family members. Deepak is asleep and is woken by his brother informing him that there are many corpses and they have a lot of bodies to cremate. Among them is Shaalu's body which Deepak identifies by the ruby ring on her hand, he is devastated, silent and in grief. He is someone who handles dead bodies as a matter of routine but looking at his love he is shattered. The accident, unfortunately, works in favour of the caste norms, according to which Deepak and Shaalu cannot be together or get married; these are the norms of which Deepak was conscious. Yet he was in love and was confident about his ability to provide a promising future to Shalu but this tragedy leave's him shaken. Every day he has witnessed death and has seen the dark grief surrounding it but, Shaalu's presence in his life was like that of rain on barren land, it rejuvenates him. After her death, he feels his pain and suffering are never-ending.

Nevertheless, Deepak tries to move on he has accepted the truth, and the truth is his background that is the caste in which he is born and the social status assigned to his community based on the work of cremating bodies for ages in Varanasi. With his hard work and qualification as an Engineer, he cracks the interview process and gets the job in the Indian railways as an Engineer. As per Connell's views, modern-day technology and education have been one of the reasons for changing the class-based identity she states that "I noted how new information technology became a vehicle for redefining middle-class masculinities at a time when the meaning of labour for working-class men was in contention" (Connell 80). He was the first graduate in his family and also the first one to be employed outside his caste occupation. Deepak's father is a 'Dom Raja' who has experienced discrimination based on his caste which had a major impact on his life. He couldn't escape from this caste-based assigned occupation and couldn't stop his elder son Sikandar to join this occupation. He is anguished about the structural injustice laid by the caste which has also affected the distribution of labour on the Ghats. The young generation is still living in the same old tradition as their culture which is resulting in inequality and exploitation. He does not want Deepak to experience the same, he is too hopeful about his future and he wants him to escape, even though it seems unpleasant that he cannot break out from this marsh.

CONCLUSION

The different type of masculinity portrayed by the men is an important factor in their individual personalities. In traditional Indian Cinema, the depiction of masculinity always emphasizes physical strength, lack of expressing emotions, aggression etc. Whereas in Millennial Cinema, the new man narrative points towards men who are unconventional, more expressive and broad-minded which resonates with changing times. These films have proven to be different from other films based on the distinctive representation of the male characters. The movies before the millennial cinema projected male characters as heterosexual and mostly in the depicted hegemonic form of masculinity; they were often related to the public sphere of work rather than in the private sphere of home and domestic life. The issues and problems related to work were shown in a more significant light than the personal life issues. This type of representation creates pressure on how the men in the real world should be. The movie on the silver screen highly influences and cyclically impacts the audience and society's culture.

Essentially, when distinct types of masculinities are being portrayed the audience perspective broadens and their thoughts are altered. Presently in the Millennial era masculinity portrayed in the movies is perceived as a multidimensional variable and is constructed with the influence of social, cultural and personal factors. The movie's way of narrating various types of masculinity implies that the male audience can identify and find similarities with the male protagonist and can understand what they have in common and the factors that differentiate them. They can link it with different male behaviour in society and will be more inclined to be inspired by them and follow it. Movies create images that help in shaping man's view about types of masculinities, man learns about these various behaviour. My analysis of the films Manmarziyaan and Masaan shows the different types of masculinities represented in the film by discussing their characteristic features and their positionality in the hierarchy of masculinity.

Appreciating Connell's theory of masculinity, provided a lens to analyze and look into the depth of characters' personality and helped to identify the type of masculinity which are inbuilt in them, and also the relationship between the type of masculinity. There are a complex number of factors that play an important role in shaping masculinity; Society, religion, caste, education, upbringing, social status, economic factors to name a few, are basic factors responsible for the social construction of masculinity. Theorizing the power relations among masculinities results in better understanding and is effective in legitimizing the hierarchy of masculinity. This theory helps to identify different types of masculinity portrayed by men, and it can also be the answer to the famous quote that "All men are the same", According to the theory we can conclude that "All men are not the same". Various combinations of studies around masculinity and Bollywood movies are possible, providing a plethora of opportunities for researchers and academicians.

Works Cited

Connell R.W, Masculinities: (2005), 2nd edition.

https://www.routledge.com/Masculinities/Connell/p/book/9781741145199

Manmarziyaan, Directed by Anurag Kashyap, Written by Kanika Dhillon, Performance by

Abhishek Bachchan, Taapsee Pannu, Vicky Kaushal, Eros International, Phantom Film, Colour Yellow

Productions,2018.

https://www.youtube.com/watch?v=arRG_hQT_fc

Masaan, created by Neeraj Ghaywan and Varun Grover, Performance by Vicky Kaushal, Richa

Chadda, Sanjay Mishra, Shweta Tripathi, Drishyam Films, Macassar Production, Phantom Films, Sikhya

Entertainment, Arte France Cinema, Pathe Productions, 2015.

https://www.youtube.com/watch?v=kFxGgoNltkI

BBC, News, Bollywood cinema: 10 lesser-known facts. 5th May 2013.

https://www.bbc.com/news/world-asia-india-22335309
Accessed date 22nd May
2021.

Connell R.W. and James W. Messerschmidth Hegemonic Masculinity: Rethinking the
Concept. Gender and Society. 19.6 (2005): 829-859

Masaan, created by Neeraj Ghaywan and Varun Grover, Performance by Vicky Kaushal,
Richa Chadda, Sanjay Mishra, Shweta Tripathi, Drishyam Films, Macassar Production, Phantom
Films, Sikhya Entertainment, Arte France Cinema, Pathe Productions, 2015.
http://www.scripts.com/script/masaan_13448
Accessed date 17th May 2021.

The Indian Express, With Manmarziyaan, Anurag Kashyap looks at love with fresh lense,
by Anvita Singh. 16th September 2018.
https://indianexpress.com/article/entertainment/opinion-entertainment/manmarziyaan-anurag-kashyap-love-story-abhishek-bachchan-vicky-kaushal-taapsee-pannu-5355990/

Times of India, Masaan Movie Review, by Meena Iyer. 18th December 2015
https://m.timesofindia.com/entertainment/hindi/movie-reviews/masaan/movie-review/48187404.cms
Accessed Date 23rd May 2021.

Bio-Note

Priyal Master is a major in English literature from the University of Mumbai, her areas of interest include Indian English Literature, literary and cultural theory. She is a Cinephile and is fascinated by how literature interacts and intersects with the milieu of identity politics and the emerging question of 'differences'.She wants everyone to take interest in researching and understanding the Behavioral psychology of the fictional characters in literature.

CHAPTER XIX

PSYCHIC PEREGRINATION OF ANITA DESAI'S BYE BYE BLACKBIRD

Ms. Naazish Baig

INTRODUCTION

Anita Desai was born in Mussoorie, a hill station north of Delhi as the Daughter of a Bengal Businessman and A German woman. She began writing in English at the age of seven and published her first story at the age of nine. As a novelist Desai made her Debut in 1963 with ''Cry, The Peacock'' considered as a trend-setter. It deals with the psychic aspects of its characters. It's followed by "Voices in The City" (1965), a story about three siblings, and their three different ways of life. Bye-Bye Blackbird is Anita Desai's third novel. Her next novel "Where shall we go this summer" (1975), presents in detail the tension between the sensitive wife Sita and her rational husband Raman. Another novel of Desai's "In Clear Light of the Day'' [1980] Desai has woven the history of Delhi through the medium of middle-class Hindu families. The novel is Four-dimensional as it's a portrayal of time as a destroyer, as a preserver. And about what the bondage of time does to people. The novel is set in old Delhi, it records the fast changes happening in a Hindu family since 1947.

In ''Custody'' [1984] Desai transcribes the madness of Deven and his search for the safety of his little world. Desai's parental German heritage comes out as the background of ''Baumgartner's Bombay'' [1988]. The novel is a portrayal of loneliness, alienation and an immigrant's existential quagmire. The story is about a malleable Jew, Hugo Baumgartner. Desai narrates the odyssey of Hugo right from his childhood in Germany to his death at the full-fledged old age of seventy in India. ''Fasting Feasting'' [1999] is another novel of Desai that portrays a striking contrast between American and Indian culture and Male and Female roles. This novel is also nominated for Booker's prize in 2000.

Anita Desai dives deep into her characters, their psychological motivations, be it through flashbacks or self-analysis or the rumbling of dialogues. She knows how to project the psychic tension of her characters. Desai is a mute observer perceiving everything minutely and delicately, giving her work the perfect treatment to every minute detail, though her characters are well-aware of the actual reality occurring around them, they carry with them a sense of loneliness, dislocation of normal family, alienation and pessimism. The Theme of exile dominates the majority of her work. Her protagonists are persons for whom alienation is the ultimate reality. They all are fragile introverts longing for their existence. In the view of O.P. Budholia, "The psychological portrayal of characters sometimes links them with feelings of alienation and isolation. The loneliness in the mind of a character gives not only a chance of self-awareness but also self-organization which enables him to search for himself" (18).

Anita Desai's novel under investigation is Bye-Bye Blackbird. It was published in the year 1971. The novel pictures the plight of Indian Immigrants in Landon. The novel Bye-Bye Blackbird is divided into three divisions-Arrival, Discovery Recognition and Departure. This division is related to the content of the novel. Desai uses this division to imply her theme effectively. Dev comes to England for the purpose of pursuing higher studies, stays with Adit and Sarah. He is perturbed and shaken to the core when he finds Indians humiliated in both public and private places. In the second part there comes a vast change in Dev. He begins to feel a charm for the country. In the third part, Adit develops home-sickness for India, but Dev stays back in England.

The Blackbird in the novel is the migratory bird:- the immigrants, The colour of the bird symbolises the colour of the immigrants who lead an insecure life. The motifs of the characters' journeys and departures signify the character's development and their search for identity. The first division tells us about the arrival of Dev one of the blackbirds. The second division is about the plight of the characters in a forlorn land. The last part is about the departure of one of the blackbirds. To portray the alienation and excessive pain of the immigrants Desai has used various symbols, images, styles and techniques throughout the novel. The title of the novel is also very symbolic as it welcomes one and rejects the other. Adit says goodbye to his inferiority complex and his sense of the outside and goes back to his native land. whereas Dev bids goodbye to his earlier apprehensions, and comes out of his Indian Inferiority complex.

The theme of East-West encounter refers to the clashes and reconcilement of two cultures. It is mainly Indian on one hand and American or European on the other hand. It also deals with the personal or rather social levels in terms of love, sex, marriage. The aim of the upcoming chapters is to highlight the encounters faced by the Indians and the Europeans. The problems faced by the immigrants, their fascination for the foreign land. The second chapter deals with the psychological turmoil of the immigrants and the identity crisis amongst the characters. The third chapter talks about the nostalgic feelings of the immigrants their longing for their homeland. The final chapter sums up all the initial chapters and gives a general outlook on the novel as a whole. On the whole, the purpose of this paper is to focus on The Psychic Peregrination of immigrants.

East-West Encounter

A number of writers have written volumes about East-west attractions and repulsions. Anita Desai is an outstanding novelist with marvellous artistic perfection, particularly for the theme of East-West encounter in the present paper. As Anita Desai has herself seen the best of East-West since her childhood. It's very bold on her part to write about East versus West, India versus England. Anita Desai's Bye-Bye Blackbird is an authentic study of human relationships formed-deformed, tormented by cultural encounters.

Bye-Bye Blackbird is similar to Anita Desai's other novels in the sense that it fully embodies her social and political vision. In the present novel, Adit and Dev are the chief leading characters. Both serve as two poles of the thematic burden of attractions and repulsions of England. The characters belonging to the west are more convincing than the protagonist of the east. Anita Desai has extraordinarily worked on the conscious and unconscious level of the protagonist, modification and adaptations in order to reveal the social and political visions in the novel. The two protagonists from India, represent the streams of human perspective.

Love for England is exemplified through Love for the English society, its employment opportunities, economic, social and political freedom. Also love for English literature, history, architecture, museums, churches, art, picture galleries, rivers, valleys and vegetation. Hatred is illustrated by English women and children who are purposely guided against Indians and Asians. Indian hatred is manifested through British colonialism, Exploitation by thc East India Company. The fascination for West is demonstrated through Adit and Dev. The fascination for the East is demonstrated through Sarah and Emma. Because of his love for England Adit marries a European girl, Sarah. Dev comes to England for pursuing higher studies. He does not consider England as the land of opportunities, the way Adit does.

Dev's visit to the National Gallery denotes the fascination theme;' "...all so might, so perfect and immense as to seem to be the handiwork not of human beings but of great, solemn gods..."(58). Dev is so impressed by Da Vinci's St. Anne which made him feel as if the English people possess a genius for preserving the beauty, making it fresh, vivid and miraculously safe from the ravages of time. So that it impresses generation after generation and even outsiders from other corners of the world. British architecture with all its ethereal complexity and grandeur serves to be an object of fascination for Eastern people. Desai has poetically illustrated the architectural perfection of Albert Memorial. " its ballooning grotesquerie, its fantastic black-magic brew of marble....like a piece of architecture having a nightmare following an ample Victorian repast" (83).

The British countryside which is simple, beautiful and glamorous is another object of fascination for Eastern people. Adit longs to see English country dances, thatched cottages, chestnut trees, stout trees and daffodils. He feels, "and here there is no death at all. Everything- animal, vegetable, the mineral is alive rich and green forever"(129). This beauty of the countryside is in striking contrast with Indian culture with its natural calamities like drought, flood, Famine. For Adit things are better in England. A typical romantic admirer of the British and the west. Dev is a pessimist and also a realist about everything as he believes in oriental wisdom. Being a pessimist Dev easily sees the darker side of everything- both of India and England. He has developed sound digestion in provoking war-like reactions in Adit. Dev shudders at the opportunistic approach of Adit and advises him to get out of here, go home and live a peaceful life. Dev advocates for the expansion of Indian culture in England. He goes to the extent of giving a pravachan to Adit like a typical Dharma Guru of India, "Let us abolish the vicarages the rectories and the personages and built Temples and Mosque and Gurudwara. Let us bring across over yogis and gurus" (61).

The passage not only confirms Dev's disrespect towards the culture of England but also reveals the cultural and religious unity of India. The feeling of oppressor and oppressed is very evident when Dev pleads for the abolition of vicarages and rectories. Historically Dev considers England as a country that has practised all kinds of cruel, unjust and dehumanizing practices towards India. Their religion and churches rather than giving spiritual relief give the impression of a sense of tyranny and imperialism. Another habit of English people that Dev finds strange is their habit of keeping doors shut for privacy which gives the impression of silence and emptiness. Meanwhile, he finds it very uneasy to bear people who love making\sex in public places openly, that's a site that can't be seen in India and is a huge taboo in spite of having such a vast population. Also to highlight Dev suffers from joblessness and humiliation as being an Indian with a dark skin complexion,

Dev is enabled to fit in a dignified job. To this state of Dev, Bidhulata Choudhary says, "The unwanted blackbird Dev speaks of the unpleasantness of the English life-the unwillingness of Mrs Roscommon James to accept the oriental faces, lack of suitable place for the black, variation of behaviour in the marketplace places" (72).

Anita Desai's chief concern is to unveil the historical perspectives of human relationships between India and England. Her social vision is wide clear in the matrimonial relation of Adit and Sarah. Sarah a British by birth is detached psychologically from England and is sick of its lifestyle. She terms it 'storms in a tea pot'. Sarah who has married an Indian finds it jittery on an edgy note among white women to marry an Indian. Even her friend Julia Sniff talks about Sarah as "If she's that ashamed of having an Indian husband, why did she go and marry him?"(37) basically there is differences between Sarah and Adit, but this difference sinks in their love. Differences inhabit and ways of life adds-on to the theme of disharmony.

Through the character of Dev Anita Desai has beautifully presented the analysis of both Indian and English temper, when Dev speaks about timing. He says that "orientals we don't really believe in watches. We are romantics who want time to fit in with our moods" (162) The English people are clock-watchers since birth. They coordinate everything with time, which appears monotonous, mechanical and boring to an Indian mind. Sarah is a romantic viewer of India. She develops a sort of strong passionate love for India. The various tiny pictures on stamps give her a glimpse of Indian life, which inspires her to admire India more. Emma is Sarah's co-sharer, both of them love Tagore's poetry. Emma is obsessed with India, its culture and heritage but Sarah views India of her imagination in silence and solitude. The novel contrast the life of imaginative experience with the life lived in reality.

Emma dreams about India which she aspires to realise by forming a 'little Indian club' but what she gets is a distorted, bigoted perception of reality. Meantime Sarah realises that Emma is moving too fast to the dangerous world of fake swamis and phoney sages. Sarah is the true lover of India doesn't want Emma to tarnish the image of a lovely country. Emma shows enormous enthusiasm in the letters coming from India with great wonder, awe and study. Emma appreciates and applauds Tagore's scripts and poetry. She confirms to the Indian spiritualism and the yogic system followed in England, and to the Indian saints and yogis. Both Sarah and Emma are fond of the Himalayan flowers, Bandits of Rajasthan, henna patterns on the palms of ladies, perfumes or attars, food items and music of Bismillah khan and Ravishankar. Anita Desai goes on to describe how British women have read the Indian scientific tools of love: The Kamasutra. The novelist sarcastically details the shallow tourist knowledge of the British women about India.

The whole purpose of Sarah's marriage with Adit is to bridge the social gap between the East and the West. Sarah is a wonderful lady, she instantly and willingly lets go of all claims of her being a European lady. Undertakes responsibility of an ideal wife to Adit, even forgets her own existence, looks at a wider picture and doesn't get stuck in pity issues. "It was her English self that was receding and fading and dying, she knew, it was her English self to which she must say goodbye. That was what hurt not saying goodbye to England because England would remain as it was, only at a greater distance from her" (221).

Sarah in a true sense nurtures and nourishes a vision of reconciliation and association. She says goodbye to England in order to have a wider social consciousness. She fully follows the concept of Indianness as well as the concept of an ideal wife to her Indian husband Adit. Sarah's decision to go to India with her husband is not born out of any illusion. Her people did not encourage her to leave England. Even the Indians talk about the problems she may have to face in India, but she is not bothered or terrified. Her choice is in favour of a happy home. Sarah prefers the real world over an imaginative one, England or Indian she recedes and dies a slow death. Meantime Adit continues to have a biased approach towards European wives. He makes an invidious distinction between the two identities, the Indian and the European. He is pleased to know about Sarah's pregnancy but at the same time shows anxiety for "Sarah's confinement, the expenses the problems of raising a child with an English mother to be an Indian child" (214).

Adit is of the view that the social disparities between the natives and non-natives would persist till he stays in England. Dev's harsh ridiculing against Adit as a British admirer and the improper and immodest treatment of his English Mother-in-law gave place to his homesickness. A stage by which he started developing a sort of black sensation of not belonging to England. The Indo-Pak war is the last straw on the Camel's back. It awakens the National sentiments in Adit, and he makes efforts to raise funds to support the Indian Government. His love for his motherland overpowers him, so he decides emotionally to go back to India. Even though he knew about Sarah's pregnancy and the different climatic conditions that she'll inevitably, have to face, he very plainly says "my son will be born in India"(201). Anita Desai strikes a balance between the East and the West. She attempts to bring out the difference between the colonial past and the democratic present, though it's difficult to determine its genuineness. Anita Desai brings out this concept as and now he was to carry the message of England to the East-not the old message of the colonist... the new message of the free convert, the international citizen, a message of progress and good cheer, advance and goodwill. (226)

Symbolism is at the zenith in the novel, as it plays a major role in bringing out the East-west attractions and repulsions. The focus of the whole novel is on the problems faced by the Indian immigrants who rush to the west and in the process miss their own country. In the words of S. Krishnamoorthy Aithal, "it symbolically represents... the equality of status achieved by India with the countries of the western world with her political independence" (Kajali Sharma, 67). The novel begins with Dev's experiences on his first day in England. He notices the difference between India and England and realises that, unlike India, England is an unsympathetic country. The first thing that he learns is that one must do their own work, as in England people don't work for anyone else other than themselves When Dev opens the window to get some fresh air, To feel the freshness of London. But in the process knocks down "a starving potted plant" (6) which is very symbolic. The potted plant somewhere down the line symbolises Adit, who's starving for his country, and the people of his native land. Adit does not belong to London so he is like a potted plant, struggling to survive in a new place.

Another humorous episode wherein Dev is amused to find Teacups of different colours and designs. Three different types of cups stand for the three members in the house who are different from one another. Adit is an Indian settling in London, his wife Sarah is an English woman, and Devan Indian who wants to go back to India after completing studies. Adit and Sarah are quite different from each other as they belong to different countries with entirely different cultures. They have got their own attitudes towards life which is different on a whole another level. Their different personalities are very symbolically reflected in their dresses. As the novelist draws the Sarah "holding about her a dressing gown of beige wool...she was all in tones of colourlessness that went with the long, straight fall of her pale hair" (9). An adit is a colourful person who loves bold and bright colours. He is an open-minded light-hearted person. While Sarah's dress reveals how dull, lonely and simple she is.

Another very symbolic instance can be seen in the conversation between Dev and Adit, regarding Dev's admission. Dev comments that he came in advance to make all right approaches and please the authorities. Adit in reply tries to make things clear to Dev about education in England. Approaches! Do you think you can get into an English college by sending the principal a basket of mangoes? All you can do is fill in the form and pay the entrance fees, there's no such thing as bribery here you know (8). This remark of Adit is symbolic of the typical Indian attitude towards the

West, The Indians feel that everything in the west is outstanding and the inferior feeling in Indians is that the English people are superior to them. It also reveals the education system in India where corruption is growing rapidly, and manipulated instead of merit. Another symbolic instance that the novelist has focussed on is the hatred of Indian immigrants towards Pakistanis. They feel at ease the moment a Pakistani is insulted at the hands of the English people. Even though the Indians are somewhere too insulted, still they are happy to see the Pakistanis being insulted.

The married life of Adit and Sarah is depicted very symbolically through very ordinary incidents. Adit's lack of interest and sympathy towards Sarah is very clearly visible, as he does not make any effort to involve her in his life among his people or care for her emotions. Although Adit says that he has adopted the European ways but the reality is otherwise. He burst into anger when Sarah's cat puts its nose in the rice pot, about which Sarah is least bothered. This clearly shows that though he looks 'well adjusted' but it's all a façade. His Indian way of thinking still dominates his lifestyle.

On top of that Symbolism can also be seen in nature. The first night of the holiday for Adit, Sarah and Dev at Mrs Roscommon-James house. Adit is very excited to see Sarah's childhood memories. But Sarah does not want to enter the English world which was ones hers which she does not recognise now, and neither wants Adit to see that world of hers. Adit feels offended because he's rejected and thrown out of her private English world. Regarding nature being symbolically used in the novel Kajali Sharma says, "The night becomes an apt symbol of the hidden darkness of mind- the secrets of mind or heart which can be seen in the light of the logical mind symbolised by the moon" (78).

The last part of the novel hints at Adits' departure from London to his native land and the end of his conflict. Mrs Roscommon-James' behaviour towards Adit makes him cognizant of the fact that he is an outsider and will always be so. He realises that he is discarded completely and that no matter what he does the behaviour of the British towards Indians is never going to change.

Adit's confused state of mind ends with the news of war between India-Pakistan. He realises that he belongs to India and leaves England forever. "Dev occupying the same flat as Adit is a strong symbol of the continuation of the fascination of the East towards the West. When he goes to his flat he sings, Makes my bed and lights the light, I'll arrive late tonight. Blackbird bye-bye" (230AD). These lines are highly symbolic as Dev bids farewell to Adit an Indian immigrant. Adit too recited lines quite similar to Dev, "Here I go, singing low, bye-bye Blackbird, Where somebody cares for me, Sugar is sweet and so is she, bye-bye Blackbird" (19AD). These lines suggest that Adit who earlier believed that he belonged to London is now convinced that he is an outsider, and says good-bye to the Indian inferiority complex.

PSYCHO-ANALYSIS OF THE IMMIGRANTS

More than a novel, It is a psychological study of the love-hate relationship the immigrants have towards their country of adoption (Indian express). Bye-Bye Blackbird portrays Indians and Englishmen in England with their problems both physical and psychological. Unlike other artists like R.K Narayan, Mulk Raj Anand and Bhabani Bhattacharya Anita Desai prefer to dwell deep into her characters or scenes rather than beating around the bush. In Bye-Bye Blackbird Desai explores the complexities of the dilemma of Indian immigrants by focussing on their attractions and repulsions towards England. In the novel, Bye-Bye Blackbird Desai deals with the massive topic of adjustment faced by black/coloured immigrants in England. She brings out this topic by portraying the situations of three different characters- Dev, Adit and Sarah by digging into the effect of racial hatred on their sensibility.

The novel presents to us the tales of Bengali youth- Dev and Adit Sen and Adit's English wife named Sarah. Dev is a newcomer to England, carries the feeling of an outsider in the early stage of his stay in London. It's because of the insults catapulted at the black by the arrogant white people. He turns anglophiliac gradually and finds the life of an alien highly enterprising. Adit on the other hand serves as a complete contrast to Dev, married to an English girl, settled in England, has no intention to return to India and is often ridiculed b his friend as a spineless imperialistic lover. He gradually feels disenchanted with London and starts to feel like a stranger and a sense of non-belongingness begin to grasp him. The growing nostalgia torments him. Eventually, he decides to leave for India and live a real and ideal life.

Sarah's situation is more complicated and pathetic than that of Adit. If Anita Desai wouldn't have treated her so realistically then she would have been a great tragic heroine. Sarah unlike the other two is a practical and balanced person she has the guts to face the harsh reality boldly. Married to Adit she feels at times divided unable to know who her real self is. Sarah is an English girl, the Head's secretary in the school of English children or Mrs Sen wife of Mr Adit Sen an Indian. Her mind is engulfed with the thought of whether she has an identity of her own other than these two roles.

Dev the chief character of the novel has some intellectual thoughts has come to study at the London School of economics. He always reacts against the ill-treatment of Indian immigrants in England. They are bluntly insulted, so much that they are not even allowed to use the lavatory meant for the English; "the London docks have three kinds of lavatories-ladies, gents and Asiatics" (17). He vents out his feelings candidly when he tells Adit; "I wouldn't live in a country where I was insulted and unwanted" (17). He finds even a thickly populated place like London, utterly silent and deserted. Dev's alienation and discomfort are objectified in his hellish experience in the London tube.

Dev ventures into the city. "He descends, deeper and deeper, into the white-titled bowls of Clapham tube station...the menacing slither of escalators strikes panic into a speechless Dev as he is swept down with an awful sensation of being taken where he does not want to go" (57). Madhusudan Prasad remarks on Dev; "it creates a terrible sense of claustrophobia in him. It is true but his horror is fright in their journey also reveal his loneliness, sense of insecurity and alienation" (S. Indira 60). what Dev disliked the most was the immigrant's sheepishness and loss of self–respect.

The various instances reveal the dev's emotional insecurities which are more psychic and situational than existential. The situation that starts undergoing a slow change, Dev too starts getting influenced by the charm of England. It all starts with his visit to Sarah's parental house, he is attracted by its scenery and calmness, begins to wonder about London, observing the various attractions, "And so he walks the street and parks of the city, grateful for its daffodil patches of sunshine...he is intoxicated to think that for all the long programmes of music, theatre... he can choose any to go to any day at all...it is a strange summer in which he is a bewildered alien, the charmed observer, the outraged outsider and thrilled sightseer all at once in succession" (84-85).

Dev gives up all his doubts and confusion about his future existence in England. The healing touch of the peaceful countryside makes Dev realise that the scrutiny he is subjected to, is not offending. He begins to see now, he is an alien and that he may seem exotic and strange to the English man. He is no longer an outraged outsider as he accepts everything calmly with his new awareness. Ultimately Dev loses self-control and is caught under England's spell. He changes place with Adit, whom he considered as "boot-licking today" and "spineless imperialist lover". (19) time to time he goes into the zone of schizophrenia that has infected him like a disease, something all Indians abroad are prone to then he announces a final decision to stay there reasoning; "...all I want is, well, yes . a good time. Not to return India, not to marry and breed up." (123) further he clears the real purpose; " I am here, he intoned as an ambassador... I am here to interpret my country to them, to conquer England as they once conquered India" (123).

Dev who earlier rejected Adit's proposal of having a future in England now persuades him not to leave England. Apparently, every character in the novel has double standards of life; a visible one and an invisible one. Anita Desai digs deep into the psychic depths of her characters and reveals their hidden motives to the readers. The peaceful countryside of England surprisingly affects Adit, he feels depressed by it. Another thing very important to remember is the mental state of the protagonist is reflected in response to the outside world. Mrs Roscommon's unconcealed disrespect for Adit and Dev's constant ridicule of his English life tears him from within, suddenly theirs a void, an empty meaningless existence, this terrible inner crisis descends him deep into depression. The depressive mood goes so deep into his consciousness that even his dreams have turned into nightmares. The photographs of England's scenic beauty appear to be "no technic coloured print- but negatives in ghostly black and white" (178).

This dream accentuates the mental sickness that makes him see only stretches of vast darkness. Even the slow, soft notes of Shehnai music which used to fill him once with a sense of peace and sentimental longing are now; "writhing coils of dark blue and purple." (179) Sarah finds him a total contrast to his previous self, she finds black rings forming bcncath his eyes, indicating his intense suffering. Its an undeniable fact that the process of his inner disintegration had already begun long ago, only Adit wasn't aware of it up till now. He is horrified to his sense of belonging turning "fluid" and he finds "his feet sinking in quicksand" (176), drowning all that he cherished and nourished before. Adit's inner conflict is accurately represented through the image of war as it is the war between India and Pakistan that triggers off a strong urge in him to go back to his homeland. "Somewhere at some point that summer, England's green and gold fingers have let Adit go and clutched Dev instead" (228).

Another character that deserves to be acknowledged is Sarah. Although her plight has not been treated properly there are incidents and situations to present her as a solitary, hopeless and helpless person. Sarah is an English woman married to an Indian immigrant, not a vague and unconvincing character, a wise and practical woman who feels that happiness is a question of determination. In Sarah's character, we can see her sense of insecurity and alienation from English society. A fear that she might become a symbol of mockery on the ground of her interracial marriage, makes her wear a mask purposely. A device she adopts to protect her inner being from inner aching. Sarah is a benumbed character with oriental gentleness and submissiveness. Desai aptly brings out the alienated nature of Sarah; "she had become nameless, she had shed her name as she had shed her ancestry and identity...she watched them disappear" (31). Sarah is gripped with fear only when she is in transit from one role to another. As long as she is enclosed in one world, keeping it apart from others, she seems to be cool and contented, sure of herself. Her hypersensitive reactions are clearly visible. Even at home, she feels safe only when the green door of their flat is closed behind her. Sarah can be herself only within the school or within the house. She can be an Indian wife or an English woman but can never be both at the same time. Her conflict of playing two entirely different roles tears her apart.

Sarah feels the two selves in her, uncertain of her identity and feels totally lost. The conflict becomes unbearable at times because she always wanted to be her real self. As Meenakshi Mukherjee points out; Sarah is an unusual character who is displaced in her own country, whose crisis of identity will perhaps never be solved although she believes that going to India will be the final resolution of her ambiguous existence. (S. Indira 58) Sarah begins to play these roles to deceive people and even herself. She would display her letters from India, and discuss her Indian husband, knowing too well that she is parading like; "an imposter, to make claims to a life, an identity that she did, not herself feel to be her own"(37). Sarah's eagerness to know her identity and her disillusionment has been beautifully presented by Anita Desai in her own word; Who was she- Mrs Sen who had been married in a Red and Gold Banares brocade sari one burning, bronzed day in September, or Mrs Sen, the heads secretary...both these elements were fraud, each had a large, shadowed element of charade about it. Where was Sarah? She wondered, whether English or Indian she did not care. (34-35)

Sarah is a realistic picture of a woman under stress who tries hard to escape, to hide and be unnoticed. When Adit decides to go back to India, she agrees to follow him like a typical Hindu wife.

People like Dev and Sarah, born under the spell of rootlessness cannot belong to a single world. It's in their nature and destiny to hang between two worlds Indian and European and be torn by their conflicting loyalties. Sarah represents a typical wife of an immigrant, who have their own personal problem to deal with. Dev is called a wog Sarah is called Mrs scurry and pussy cat. Dev is a stranger a non-belonger in an alien land, whereas Sarah is an exile in her own native land. Dev is an extrovert while Sarah is an introvert. Both are caught between acceptance and rejection. Sarah rejects the antagonistic London and Dev accepts his new home in London. The novel ends on a note of joy just the way it has started. Adit having tasted the luxurious charm of England goes back to India to lead a truthful and peaceful life. Sarah follows him uncomplainingly and hopefully. While Dev stays back to enjoy the marvellous charm of England.

NOSTALGIA IN THE NOVEL

Memory and forgetfulness are as life and death to one another to live are to remember and to remember is to live. (Samuel Butler) Anita Desai espouses a social and psychological treatment of the characters of her novel. The cultural difference, immigrant problems, nostalgia, economic problems, isolation and frustration contributes to the alienation of characters. This alienation leads to an identity crisis which further leads to nostalgia. Anita Desai, who dives deeply into the unconscious and subconscious psyche of the expatriates, reveals their nostalgia and longingness for their native land. Her depiction of characters and situations is not one-sided and her protagonist seems to be sharing a strange love-hate relationship with the land of their adoption. With great precision Adit, the chief protagonist is weighing the merits and demerits of England. but by the end of the novel, he comes up with the conclusion that his English self was fading away and was desperate to achieve his real self, to live a "real life" (204) he must go to India.

Nostalgic feelings of Adit surrounds the whole body of the novel. Adit thinks of his sweet home, where his mother will be cooking for him Hilsa fish wrapped in banana leaves, his sisters dressing Sarah in sarees and gold ornaments, and himself listening to shehnai and sitar till late hours of the night. Despite his love and admiration for England, he feels himself an alien a stranger and at these moments his heart drowns deep into the slumber of nostalgic trance for his native land. On Christmas, he tells Sarah to cook carrot halwa for him as it reminds him of being at home. The roots of this nostalgia are hidden in Adit and it arouses in a form of hatred for England. Adit feels completely out of the world which once he adored. He starts hating the friendly hens, instead, he longs for the vultures of India, heavy-boned birds with their reptilian necks rising out of shoulders. Even the river Tess with its silver-leaved willows makes him think about the rivers of India.

One such instance is when Girl Friday asks about a holiday on the Costa Brava, Adit begins to recall the atmosphere of an Indian railway station. The vision of red-shirted coolies, the tiffin carriers, the unbearable excitements of a small boy, released from school, flashes before his eyes. The ferocity of his growing nostalgia broke down and he felt a sort of illness and an ache within him. He began to explain to Sarah about his hometown, his homeland, his own home. He poetically and emotionally pictures to Sarah each and every corner of his house:- the pillars, the veranda, kitchen, alters, rooftops and the relatives. He longs with pain, to see the fireworks and oil-lamps of Diwali night and join a holy romp of flying coloured water. During their visit to Sarah's village Adit and his friends happen to meet ritual worshippers, which aroused a sort of nostalgia in them, "the sudden, fresh odours released by the plucking and crumbling of mint leaves, and the soft, insistent fragrance of tiny stars of jasmine aroused a thousand different memories in minds always open to the wind of nostalgia" (90).

After returning from Sarah's village he sounds to be a different person. An Indian hunted by the black sensation of non-belongingness. He himself seems to be among the immigrants. Who can never accept their new home and walk through the streets like strangers in an unknown land? The breaking of the India-Pakistan war makes him strongly nostalgic and awakens in him a desire to be in India. The love of his motherland shakes the hidden and dormant sentiments. Everyone was surprised and taken aback at his decision to go back to India. His friend Jasbir makes a comment "I'd like to make sure you actually leave. I cannot believe it otherwise- you the most pukka sahib of all... leaving all the Kala sahibs here" (226). There's wrestling inside his mind whether to leave England or not, in an emotional state he confesses to Sarah, "Sarah you know I've to love England more than you. I've often felt myself half-England, but it was only a pretence, sally, now it has to be a real thing, I must go. You will come" (205).

Sarah who has been throughout feeling the charm and call of India accompanies her husband. She gives up her womanly desires and like a traditional Indian wife accepts her fate. She leaves her motherland for the sake of her husband and motherhood, "she felt it again-this light pinching contraction inside her chest followed by throb and flowering of warmth-when she entered her flat and saw it already stripped of half of its furnishings"(208). Dev who had his reservation in England is thrown totally off at the sight of Battersea power station. He regards it as the massive grey temple of power and asks Adit, "can't you see the puja being conducted in its long chambers, by a priest in saffron robes and vestal maidens in white?"(54).

The national gallery moves Dev to ruptures where the great works of art appeal to him. With all his admiration of things great and fine in England, Dev's patriotic feelings get the upper hand in him when occasion demands. Standing in the middle of petticoat lane, which is a strong reminder for him of the rowdy, libertine atmosphere of an Indian bazaar. Anita Desai like George Eliot leaves her character to grow independently and watches the inner change in them. The novelist has wonderfully diagnosed the inner conflict in Adit and Dev for their respective change towards life. Nostalgia for an Indian way of life and the vastness of landscape arouses a sense of uprootedness in the heart of Adit. Adit feels that India guarantees him love, respect and security which make living worthwhile. England might be heaven but India is the real heaven.

The beauty of London still captivates him, yet at last, he admits the fact that there "everything yells that you're an outsider and not entitled to the country"(162) the symbolic title Bye-Bye Blackbirds seems to come true.

CONCLUSION

Bye-Bye Blackbird is one of Anita Desai's best novels which shows the social and psychological dilemma of the exiles. Desai as a novelist devotes her entire creative energy to the psychological state of the human mind. She makes a study into the innermost region of the human psyche from which the original ideas of the human mind come into operation. She creates certain complicated problems in her characters, that allot them a free choice for their solution. Sometimes they feel isolated and alienated among their self-created problems. As a creative writer, she is interested in complex and eccentric characters rather than in everyday average ones. They enjoy material prosperity but their intellectual aspirations are unfulfilled. As a result, happiness alludes to them and peace never comes to them. They come alive in this dynamic process always evolving and transforming.

In Desai's fiction, the female is not a passive creature. She accepts the traditional role but rebels against the whole system of social relationships, Compelled to make a choice that serves as the thematic development of psychic experience. Sarah is an altogether unique experience in Desai's fiction. For the first time, she creates a career girl and a housewife. The conflict between the two is portrayed convincingly. Another important aspect is that she responds positively to life, "Bye-Bye Blackbird" novel serves the theme of East-West encounter perfectly. Keeping up with the restrictions, the thematic plot pattern is based on Adit and Dev, two Indians living in England. Action in the novel is what they do and the pace is where they move out. The theme of Bye-Bye Blackbird is alienation, man-woman relationship, East-West encounter and lack of adjustment by Indian immigrants in England. According to N. Radhakrishnan, "The theme of adjustment following the return home after staying abroad...many have approached the problem with tragic intensity while in many it has evoked only comic interludes" (136-137).

Desai has a situation for both comedy and tragedy at ones but her range of comedy is limited, essentially Mrs. Desai is not a novelist of social comedy and manners. Her forte is the poetic novel of sensibility and so the tragic aspect appeals to her and gives her some sort of intensity, even then the novel ends up as the psychic peregrination. A textual analysis of her novels makes one perceive the two-fold visionary aspects of her novel, the merging of memories and the present action of the protagonist. Adit being married to an English girl, Sarah, lives peacefully in England. But nostalgia so overpowers him that he wishes to leave England with his wife and the novel takes a problematic twist; the India-Pakistan war and Sarah's pregnancy.

Desai also makes use of various images, myths and symbols to bring out the psychic turmoil of the characters. Desai used the images like windows, pots, cups, doors, houses for making the language more figurative. Bye-Bye Blackbird deals with the dilemma of three expatriates, Adit, Dev and Sarah. Desai in this novel reveals the intense longing of the exiled hero's emotions towards his native land. Like the other novels of Anita Desai, Bye-Bye Blackbird too exhibits the living style of England; it is England that changes Dev's Anglophobia into anglophilia. Adit on the other hand becomes nostalgic about his childhood memories of India. Dev and Sarah also undergo a convulsive change. Dev who hated the ways of English now changes and starts loving England and seeks there his future existence. Sarah is the only character who resigns all her claims of being an English girl and decides to follow the desires of her Indian husband.

Desai does not remain untouched from the central issue of raising the conflict between the traditional social pattern of India and the modern colonization of the west. She deals in depth with the interaction between the native and foreign culture which causes a complete transformation of personality in Dev and Adit. Desai also merges time past with present time in her narrative device.

The merging of these two results in the operation of memories and nostalgia. This technique is also known as stream of consciousness.

WORKS CITED

Desai, Anita Bye-Bye Blackbird . New Delhi: Orient Paperbacks Ltd, 2001.

Budholia, O.P. Anita Desai: Vision and Techniques in her novels. Delhi B.R Publishing Corporation, 2001.

Choudhary, Bidulata. Women and Society in the novels of Anita Desai . New Delhi: Creative Books, 1995.

Indira, S. Anita Desai as an Artist. New Delhi: Creative Publication, 1994.

Joshi, K.N and B. Shyamala Rao. Studies in Anglo-Indian Literature . Bareilly:Prakash Book Depot, 1987

Javcob, Asha Susan. "In their Alien Words:Bye-Bye Blackbird and Baumgartners Bombay" The Fiction of Anita Desai. Vol.1 Bal, Suman D.K New Delhi: Khosla Publishing house, 2002.

Kanwar, Asha The Novels of Virginia Woolf and Anita Desai a comparative study. New Delhi: Prestige Books, 1982

Ram, Atma Essays On Indian Literature. Aurangabad: Perimal Prakashan, 1984.

Sharma, Kajali Symbolism in Anita Desai's novels. New Delhi; Abhinar Publications, 1991.

www.ingramcontent.com/pod-product-compliance
Ingram Content Group UK Ltd.
Pitfield, Milton Keynes, MK11 3LW, UK
UKHW041841190726
13854UKWH00002B/660